Ingolfur Blühdorn (ed.)

In Search of Legitimacy

Policy Making in Europe and the Challenge of Complexity

Barbara Budrich Publishers
Opladen & Farmington Hills, MI 2009

A CIP catalogue record for this book is available from
Die Deutsche Bibliothek (The German Library)

ISBN 978-3-86649- 212-7

Die Deutsche Bibliothek – CIP-Einheitsaufnahme
Ein Titeldatensatz für die Publikation ist bei Der Deutschen Bibliothek erhältlich.

Verlag Barbara Budrich Barbara Budrich Publishers
Stauffenbergstr. 7. D-51379 Leverkusen Opladen, Germany

28347 Ridgebrook. Farmington Hills, MI 48334. USA
www.barbara-budrich.net

Jacket illustration by disegno, Wuppertal, Germany – www.disenjo.de
Typeset by Beate Glaubitz, Leverkusen, Germany
Printed in Europe on acid-free paper by
paper&tinta, Warszaw

Table of Contents

Acknowledgements

This book emerges from research on the transformation of European democracies that has been ongoing for a number of years. At various stages this research has been facilitated by the ANGLO-GERMAN FOUNDATION FOR THE STUDY OF INDUSTRIAL SOCIETY, the BRITISH ACADEMY and the EUROPEAN CONSORTIUM FOR POLITICAL RESEARCH. I would like to take this opportunity to express my gratitude for their respective forms of support. Furthermore, I would like to thank all contributors to this volume for their excellent cooperation, various colleagues at my Department, the Department of European Studies at the University of Bath, for reviewing some of the contributions, and my research assistants for their help in preparing the material for publication. Finally, thanks are due to colleagues at Budrich Publishers for their outstanding dedication and commitment to producing this book to the highest standards.

List of Figures

Introduction
Legitimacy Crises, Efficiency Gaps, Democratic Deficits

Ingolfur Blühdorn

Legitimacy, like democracy, is an essentially contested concept. Sources of legitimacy and patterns of political legitimisation have changed over time and adapted to evolving socio-economic conditions. Since the beginning of the modern era legitimacy has been understood, first and foremost, as *democratic* legitimacy which implies, more than anything, that the people, the *demos*, have given their consent – if not to each and every policy decision, then at least to the selection of representatives who take these decisions, to the rules and procedures through which they are taken, and to the institutions which organise their implementation. In contemporary European polities, the democratic understanding of political legitimacy is hegemonic. However, this does not imply that other forms of political legitimacy and legitimation have become entirely irrelevant, nor does it mean that the evolutionary process in which notions of legitimacy and patterns of legitimisation are constantly recast has come to a halt. Indeed, European societies are currently witnessing a manifest resurgence of concerns about *legitimacy crises*, *efficiency gaps* and *democratic deficits*. These concerns and the responses they have triggered in different countries and different policy areas are the subject matter of this book.

The new debate about legitimacy crises and democratic deficits originates from major developments on both the demand side and the supply side of legitimacy. On the demand side, public expectations for political legitimisation have sharply increased, firstly, because in line with the emancipatory trajectory of modernity claims to individual and collective self-determination continue to grow while the willingness to accept authorities and subordinate personal values or interests to notions of a larger *common good* continue to decline. Secondly, technological innovation and progress have rapidly expanded the range of the technically feasible and thus of decisions to be taken, with the social implications of these decisions becoming ever more wide-ranging, long-lasting and difficult to foresee. Thirdly, the internal differentiation and fragmentation of modern societies, on the one hand, and their integration into increasingly global networks and interdependencies, on the other, have prompted the evolution of new modes of governance which rely on national and transnational institutions that cannot claim democratic legitimacy but still have significant impact on the every-day lives of local communities and individuals.

Complexity is the key concept under which these different developments can be subsumed. Rising levels of complexity have notably increased the demand for political legitimacy and legitimisation. Yet on the supply side there is a marked decline in the ability to generate legitimacy. At the national level, spreading disaffection with political parties, distrust in political elites, and the erosion of civic virtues and capabilities all imply that democratic legitimacy in the traditional sense, i.e. legitimacy that derives directly from the involvement and consent of the *demos*, can no longer be generated to an extent that matches demand. At the transnational level democratic structures and institutions do not yet exist, and even within Europe their construction has proven extremely difficult, not least because a shared European identity integrating European populations into a single *demos* with common values and interests has not yet emerged. Against this background, efficient policy making and a high problem solving capacity of political institutions at national and EU level have been expected to compensate for the weakness of democratic legitimacy in the traditional (input) sense. Yet, the rise of complexity also affects the output side of the policy process, i.e. it impairs the efficiency of policy delivery. Thus the condition of increasing complexity represents a formidable challenge: Whilst it is evident that increasingly complex societies require increasingly complex modes of governance and political legitimation, it is much less evident what such modes might look like. For the time being there is primarily the widening gap between democratic expectations, on the one hand, and the experience of efficiency gaps and democratic deficits on the other. The ways in which European polities are trying to confront this challenge are the topic of this book. It explores the problem of legitimacy generation under conditions of complexity.

Of course, neither legitimation crises nor the problem of complexity are entirely new phenomena. Still, in contemporary European societies the anatomy of these crises and the ways in which these problems are managed are markedly different from earlier phases. When in the 1970s Offe and Habermas, for example, were diagnosing a legitimation crisis, they were, following the post-Marxist tradition, talking about the (in)stability and political (un)sustainability of capitalism (Habermas 1973, 1975; Offe 1972, 1984). Updating classical Marxist analysis for the emerging post-industrial era, they suggested that the order of capitalism will probably not be overthrown by a proletarian revolution but more likely collapse because of its inability to sustain its legitimacy. Capitalist systems, they suggested, are in the long run unable to reconcile the logic of capital accumulation with the bottom-up pressure for political participation and public welfare provision. At the time the *new social movements* seemed to provide powerful empirical evidence for capitalism's mounting legitimation crisis.

In the contemporary context, however, the question is neither what will trigger the collapse of capitalism nor whether the capitalist order can stabilise its basis of legitimacy. Despite the recent meltdown of the financial system and the evident unsustainability of the established socio-economic order in a range of other respects, the continuity of consumer capitalism appears to be beyond doubt. Whilst the free market capitalism of the 1990s now seems to be undergoing a metamorphosis into a more regulated variety, the basic principles of capitalism itself seem to be beyond the need for major justification and legitimation – if only because an alternative is nowhere in sight, indeed barely imaginable, because consumerist aspirations and lifestyles have acquired the status of non-negotiability, and because the social implications of its potential collapse would be of such unimaginable magnitude that it just cannot be allowed to happen. So the question is no longer whether and how the system of capitalism can legitimate itself, but what is now at stake is the very principle and idea of democratic legitimation. In other words, the concept of the legitimation crisis has changed its meaning: whilst in the 1970s it denoted a *crisis of capitalism* emerging from capitalism's inability to stabilise its crumbling basis of legitimacy, it now denotes a *crisis of democratic legitimation*, i.e. the principle of democratic legitimation itself is under review. Whilst in the 1970s there could be no doubt that democratic governance is both normatively desirable and empirically possible, and the diagnosed legitimation crisis was conceptualised as an outstanding opportunity for progressive, emancipatory and authentically democratic politics, this overwhelming confidence has meanwhile grown fainter. It has been superseded by a distinct awareness of the inefficiencies of democratic processes and the limitations of democratic legitimisation. Although at the declaratory level, commitment to democratic empowerment and democratic values remains high – indeed, at this level commitment seems more uncompromising than ever – the discursive celebration of democratic principles is becoming increasingly detached from the empirical reality of governance. Conditions of complexity and the imperatives of their efficient management have given rise to *post-democratic* modes of governance and legitimation. To what extent conditions of complexity may indeed *necessitate* such post-democratic modes is a recurring question throughout this book.

The discussion of problems of complexity management, too, has precursors in the 1970s. In contrast to the intellectuals of the new left, who at the time saw the legitimation crisis of the capitalist system as a chance for progressive potentials, their counterparts on the emerging new right were very concerned about the prospect of an 'overloaded state' presiding over a condition of 'ungovernability' (e.g. Crozier et al. 1975; King 1975). From their perspective, emancipatory movements, societal differentiation and the spread of value pluralism had nurtured over-inflated expectations addressed to the state and led to a fragmentation of power which undermined the state's ability to efficiently fulfil its functions. Reducing citizen expectations, rolling back the state, increasing self-responsibility and reinstating respect for authority and status were the primary remedies proposed. From today's perspective, however, it can safely be said that these remedies were unsuccessful. Effective means for stopping or even reversing the rise of complexity have not been found. The logic of emancipation and differentiation is firmly built into the process of modernity itself and cannot be blamed on supposedly misguided individuals or social movements. Therefore, European democracies are confronted with the inescapable dilemma that the pressure for policy justification and political legitimation continues to increase, whilst the foundations of political legitimation and the capacity for legitimacy generation continue to erode. It is against this background that this book raises the questions:

- How does the increase in societal complexity impact on the efficiency of policy making and on the legitimisation of politics?
- How are political actors and institutions in different European polities and at EU level seeking to *manage* the condition of complexity and generate social acceptance for their policies?
- How do problems of legitimisation materialise in concrete policy areas, and what strategies are being devised for resolving them?
- How does the condition of complexity reconfigure the foundations of democratic politics and transform prevalent conceptions of democratic legitimacy?

Such questions can be approached in a number of different ways. Proceeding from the assumption that there is a set of non-negotiable and unchangeable democratic norms which political institutions and processes ought to comply with, many observers simply demand the fulfilment of the as yet unfulfilled promises of democracy. Others acknowledge that the rise of societal complexity implies significant change and explore how patterns of democratic legitimisation might be adapted. Others again, are less oriented towards advising political institutions but pursue a descriptive-analytical agenda, trying to conceptualise and explain the ongoing transformation of democracy. These observers are more receptive for the changeability of democratic norms, and for them notions like the much-lamented democratic deficit or legitimacy crisis themselves become subject to critical investigation. Empirical research into democracy and legitimacy, finally, explores the ways in which individuals, communities and public discourse factually perceive of democratic institutions and what criteria are constitutive for their respective understandings of legitimacy.

The contributions to this volume do not pursue one uniform approach. Rather than being based on one single theoretical model they explore the problem of legitimacy generation under conditions of complexity from a range of different methodological access points. Some of the chapters offer empirical analyses which give rise to concrete policy recommendations. Others take a primarily theoretical approach and place the emphasis on conceptualising and explaining the ongoing transformation of democracy and reconfiguration of legitimacy in European polities. The first two chapters, in particular, are of a theoretical nature. They do not aim to set out a common theoretical framework for the analyses that follow, but they do provide conceptual foundations on which the later, more policy-oriented contributions build. Chapter 1 has the function of an extended introduction. Whilst in its second half it also develops a very distinct theory of *post-subjective* and *post-democratic* modes of political legitimisation, it first of all offers a detailed analysis of different dimensions of complexity and of the diverse elements constitutive to the generation of democratic legitimacy. Chapter 2 looks more closely at the relationship between democracy and efficiency. Starting out from the observation that especially in conditions of complexity democratic procedures are often not particularly efficient, while efficient procedures are often rather undemocratic, Joachim Blatter distinguishes different understandings of both democracy and efficiency. His analysis is inspired by the notion of *reflexive modernisation* and comes to the conclusion that the alleged tensions between the two objectives can be reconciled if both democracy and efficiency are reconceptualised to reflect the contemporary condition of *second* or *reflexive* modernity.

Chapters 3 and 4 offer empirical analyses of citizens' expectations about the legitimisation of policy making and of government efforts to confront tendencies of political disengagement. Pierre Lefébure takes the case of France to investigate whether citizens are really, as British Prime Minister Gordon Brown once suggested, primarily interested in policy outcomes paying at best secondary attention to how they have been achieved. His focus group analyses produce clear evidence that even in conditions of complexity, citizens value democratic participation and input at least as much as efficient policy delivery and output. Alexandra Kelso, in turn, focuses on the case of Great Britain where the government has committed itself to forging a new relationship with the citizenry that entrusts Parliament and the people with more power. Based on the analysis of various government reports and initiatives, she comes to the conclusion that so far the attempts to overcome the tensions between the stated desire to improve the functioning of democracy and the ambition to retain efficiency in public policy making have not made a significant difference.

The following three contributions then explore different strategies for the governance of complexity. Informal government in the cooperative state, delegation of authority to institutions which are insulated from the political process, and delegation of policy-making to the European Union are all indispensable tools for the management of complexity, yet they are all fraught with problems of legitimation. Uwe Jun investigates informal government in Germany in the Kohl, Schröder and Merkel administrations and suggests that informality does not necessarily imply a lack of transparency and a deficit of legitimacy. Martino Maggetti focuses on independent regulatory agencies and refutes the claims that such bodies produce a better policy output than democratic institutions, that they are more transparent and accountable than the latter, and that they are really insulated from the political process. Timm Beichelt explores the process of EU policy coordination. Again, he takes Germany as his primary case study and demonstrates that even in complex constellations of multi-level governance ways can be found to achieve efficiency in policy making whilst still securing appropriate levels of political legitimacy.

Chapters 8 to 10 deepen the enquiry into the legitimacy of EU policy making. Each of them focuses on one particular policy area. Peter Bursens explores whether the EU's Open Method of Coordination (OMC), itself a prime tool for the management of diversity and complexity in EU policy making, is a suitable mechanism for enhancing the legitimacy of transnational policy making. The European Employment Strategy is his primary case study for assessing the effectiveness of the OMC. Karen Heard-Lauréote investigates to what extent Advisory Committees can enhance the European Commission's legitimacy. She focuses on agricultural policy for evaluating Advisory Committees. Jens Newig and Oliver Fritsch are probing the EU's claim that expanding public participation is an effective means of enhancing the quality and implementability – and thus the legitimacy – of policy decisions. For this purpose they review a large number of empirical cases from environmental policy making. All three chapters are coming to the conclusion that as yet the EU is finding it extremely difficult to supplement its hitherto primarily output-based strategies of policy legitimisation by a dimension of input legitimacy.

The last two contributions, finally, are returning to the level of national policy making and are devoted to the analysis of legitimacy generation in two further crucially important – and contested – policy areas: the governance of technology and health policy. In each case the authors explore how increasing levels of issue complexity and societal differentiation put limits to participatory and consensus-oriented decision-making – and how alternative strategies of generating legitimacy cannot adequately fill the void. Soile Kuitunen and Kaisa Lähteenmäki-Smith assess the attempts of the Finnish government to strengthen the inclusiveness of technology policy, a policy area which has traditionally been characterised by strongly hierarchical and elite-centred structures of decision-making. Claudia Landwehr and Ann-Charlotte Nedlund look at the sensitive issue of the allocation of health goods. Examining the cases of Sweden, Britain and Germany, they argue that in contemporary European societies health policy is increasingly about cutting back entitlements and removing securities. Yet the legitimisation of rationing decisions in health policy is notoriously difficult – and notoriously hard to achieve in democratic arenas.

Overall the analyses collated in this book further pursue a research agenda which had already inspired the earlier publication *Economic Efficiency – Democratic Empowerment* (Blühdorn and Jun 2007). Yet, whilst this earlier book had focused narrowly on the relationship between democracy and efficiency, and had investigated policy making in only two European countries (Britain and Germany), the present book widens the perspective, firstly, by adding complexity and legitimacy as key parameters of analysis and, secondly, by including a much larger sample of European polities, policy areas and policy levels. The evidence presented in the individual chapters is mixed both in terms of the compatibility of efficiency and democracy and as regards the impact of rising levels of complexity on the ability of political institutions to secure legitimacy. Conditions of high complexity clearly increase the pressure for legitimisation and at the same time impair the generation of input as well as output legitimacy. Yet, the rise of complexity also triggers a reconfiguration of democratic norms and patterns of legitimacy generation which necessitate a review of established notions of legitimacy crises, efficiency gaps and democratic deficits. Empirical research and democratic theory are only beginning to get a grip on these ongoing transformations.

References

Blühdorn, I./Jun, U. (eds) (2007): *Economic Efficiency – Democratic Empowerment, Contested Modernization in Britain and Germany*, Lanham, Maryland: Rowman & Littlefield (Lexington).

Crozier, M.J./Huntington, S.P./Watanuki, J. (1975): *The Crisis of Democracy: Report on the Governability of Democracies to the Trilateral Commission*, New York: New York University Press.

Habermas, J. (1973): *Legitimationsprobleme im Spätkapitalismus*, Frankfurt: Suhrkamp.

Habermas, J. (1975): *Legitimation Crisis*, Cambridge, MA: Beacon.

King, A. (1975): 'Overload: Problems of governing in the 1970s', in: *Political Studies* 71/2, pp. 167-76.

Offe, C. (1972): *Strukturprobleme des Kapitalistischen Staates*, Frankfurt: Suhrkamp.

Offe, C. (1984): *Contradictions of the Welfare State*, London: Hutchinson.

Chapter 1
Democracy beyond the Modernist Subject: Complexity and the Late-modern Reconfiguration of Legitimacy

Ingolfur Blühdorn

1. Unsustainable democracy?[1]

The concept of sustainability has originally been understood in a primarily ecological sense and was then appropriated by economic actors committed to sustaining economic growth and competitiveness. Yet, the concept can also productively be applied to political arrangements and especially to liberal democracy. A particular system, practice or social arrangement is deemed unsustainable if it depends on resources – natural or cultural – which are finite, cannot be substituted, and are used up at a faster rate than they can regenerate or be reproduced. In the same sense that the social values, practices, structures and lifestyles which are characteristic of modern society have proven unsustainable ecologically, they may also prove unsustainable politically, i.e. the political order, liberal democracy, to which modernist values have given rise and which currently sustains the capitalist consumer culture may well prove unsustainable.[2] In fact, debates about the crisis and perhaps exhaustion of democracy have been ongoing for some time. In many democratic countries the socio-cultural foundations underpinning democracy seem dangerously eroded and anti-democratic movements are on the rise. At the same time, the label of democracy has been appropriated by political regimes which hardly fulfil even minimal democratic norms, and in the academic debate the notion of *post-democracy* has gained some currency (e.g. Crouch 2004; Buchstein and Nullmeier 2006). Therefore, the question for the sustainability of liberal democracy and, more specifically, how advanced

---

1 I would like to thank Mathew Humphrey, Karsten Fischer, Andrew Dobson, Roger Eatwell and Anna Bull for their valuable comments on an earlier draft of this chapter.

2 In the German speaking debate the suggestion that liberal secular democracy is based on cultural foundations which it cannot itself produce and stabilise is often referred to as the *Böckenförde paradox* (Böckenförde 1964/2004). Daniel Bell has dealt with related issues in *The Cultural Contradictions of Capitalism* (Bell 1976).

modern societies are managing to sustain a political order that increasingly displays signs of unsustainability, is becoming paramount.

This question arises for different reasons and has, accordingly, different dimensions. Firstly, in many advanced liberal democracies declining levels of electoral turnout, receding membership figures for political parties, trade unions and other traditional associations, declining trust in democratic institutions and political authorities, and the erosion of social capital and the capacities of citizenship all seem to suggest that democracy may at some stage simply dry out due to a lack of public participation and capability. Indeed, political disaffection, disengagement, cynicism and apathy no longer seem exclusive to well established and mature democratic systems, but new democracies, for example in eastern Europe, seem to be affected as well. In a way, this kind of concern seems to be the least worrying one, for whilst there is a comprehensive literature that diagnoses and laments a decline of democratic virtues, social capital, civic culture, generalised trust and political engagement in contemporary democracies worldwide (e.g. Bauman 2000; Boggs 2000; Putnam 2000; Macedo et al. 2005; see also Kelso in this volume), there is an at least equally comprehensive literature forcefully arguing that democratic values are enjoying more support today than at any earlier time, that social capital is not declining but only transforming, that citizens have more access to the political process than ever before, and that allegations of political apathy are misleading because the rise of new forms of political engagement is in fact more than compensating for the decline of more traditional forms (e.g. Inglehart 1997; Norris 1999, 2002; Cain et al. 2003; Inglehart and Welzel 2005; Dalton and Klingemann 2007; Dalton 2008). Rather than for the unsustainability of democracy, this literature provides evidence for the 'great flexibility of democracies' (Dalton and Klingemann 2007: 15) and reassures us that ongoing cultural shifts in advanced modern societies actually 'increase the potential for elite-challenging actions' (Inglehart and Welzel 2005: 118) and 'improve the quantity and quality of political participation' (Dalton 2008: 94).[3]

Complementing the worries about the input side of democracy there are, secondly, concerns about the output side, i.e. about the performance of democratic systems. In particular, there is the question whether democratic systems are capable of coping with the increasing diversity of social demands, and whether under conditions of escalating societal complexity democratic structures are still an effective and efficient means of delivering public welfare and wellbeing (e.g. Fuchs 1998; Lijphart 1999; Roller 2005; Fuchs and Roller 2008). Debates about 'democratic overload' and the 'un-

3 For a critical assessment of these optimistic reassurances see, for example, Furedi's discussion of 'Disengagement – and its Denial' (Furedi 2005: 28-48; furthermore: Blühdorn 2006a, 2007a).

governability' of modern societies have been ongoing for a long time (e.g. Crozier et al. 1975; King 1975; Hennis et al. 1977, 1979). They have built on Weberian-Schumpeterian doubts about mass democracy and have recently been reinforced by the internationalisation of politics which tends to further weaken the political effectiveness of – mostly national – democratic institutions (e.g. Beck 1998; Scharpf 1998a; Zürn 1998, 2003; Anderson 2002; Held 2004; Leibfried and Zürn 2006). What is under review here is the problem solving capacity and the political steering capacity of democratic systems in view of increasingly complex and transnational issues such as social justice, environmental problems, security challenges, mass migration or collapsing financial markets. These performance or output related concerns about the sustainability of democracy are a far more serious challenge than the one discussed before. For whilst there is no shortage of academic writing on the strategies which national governments and transnational regimes are devising in order to cope with the complexity of contemporary problem constellations in an efficient and effective manner,[4] only few observers are confident that these strategies comply, or can be made to comply, with democratic norms. Instead, the management of late-modern complexity seems to foster reliance on *post-democratic* forms of governance (Zolo 1992; Rancière 1997; Blühdorn 2004a, 2006b, 2007b; Crouch 2004; Jörke 2005; Buchstein and Nullmeier 2006).

Thirdly, and related to both previous points, there is the question whether and how liberal democracy can adapt to the transformation or even dissolution of the modernist foundations on which it was based. Beyond the notions of the sovereign nation state or the collective identity of the *demos*, these modernist foundations include, in particular, the notion of the *autonomous* and *identical*[5] *subject* (individual and collective) which is the central point of reference of the system of liberal democracy and indeed its very purpose. In contemporary debate, democracy often appears to have the status of an intrinsic value and an essentialist norm, but it is worth calling to mind that modern democracy had emerged as a tool for the political realisation of the modernist idea of the autonomous subject, i.e. for the self-determination and self-realisation of the modernist individual which following the Enlightenment had successfully installed itself as the ultimate value and source of political legitimacy. Modern democracy is based upon the axiom of the autonomous

---

4 Strategies such as the *deparliamentarisation*, *informalisation*, *delegation* and indeed *de-politicisation* of government have been discussed by a wide range of authors (e.g. Benz 1998; Boggs 2000; Burnham 2001; Thatcher and Stone Sweet 2002; Strøm et al. 2003; Braun and Galardi 2005; Fischer 2006; Flinders and Buller 2006; Kettell 2008) and are the focus of several contributions in this volume.

5 The term *identical* here implies: being defined by and claiming a distinct, clearly identifiable, autonomously created, unitary and stable identity. The concept will be discussed in more detail further below.

individual and the belief in the distinguishable and consistent (although always evolving) identity of individuals and social groups. It is 'the institutional reflection of the emancipative forces inherent in human development' (Inglehart and Welzel 2005: 299). In the ongoing process of modernisation, however, this notion of the autonomous subject, this specifically modernist idea of the individual and collective Self, has become outdated. Notions of individuality and identity have changed, and thus the very foundations of democracy are, one might say, rapidly dissolving. Accordingly, democratic systems now have to reconfigure their relationship to the individual citizen and to the *demos* at large. In particular, democratic systems have to adapt the modes in which they generate political legitimacy which is, arguably, the most severe challenge to the sustainability of democracy. Yet whilst a lot has been written about the (im)possibility of democracy beyond the modernist nation state and about changing notions of identity in the late-modern condition, the particular questions whether and how late-modern democracy can cope with the disintegration of its specifically modernist point of reference, and how it can rearrange its relationship to the late-modern Self remain strangely underexplored: 'A massive literature', Inglehart and Welzel suggest, 'has largely overlooked democracy's most fundamental aspect: human emancipation' (Inglehart and Welzel 2005: 300)[6] and, ironically, their own work must largely be subsumed under this verdict.

Thus the question for the sustainability of democracy has normative as well as empirical dimensions. As yet there is no indication that in advanced modern societies *unsustainable* democracy may in fact collapse and be superseded by a different form of political organization. But there is plenty of evidence that in response to increasing levels of societal complexity democratic systems are adapting their modes of governance and that the emerging forms are experienced as failing to comply with established democratic norms. The perceived discrepancies between democratic ideals and experienced political realities are widely conceptualised as *legitimacy crises*, *efficiency gaps* and *democratic deficits* which public discourse and the academic literature are approaching from a variety of different perspectives: Normative democratic theory watches over the fulfilment of established democratic norms and provides guidance on how contemporary politics may generate democratic legitimacy thereby reasserting its moral worthiness of public support and securing factual compliance and cooperation by citizens. Empirical legitimatisation research investigates to what extent and for what reasons individual citizens or social communities consider particular policies, political actors,

6 In Brodocz et al.'s recent volume *Bedrohungen der Demokratie* (Threats to Democracy, 2008), for example, the challenges inherent to changing patterns of identity construction are barely touched upon, even though this volume compiles the expertise of more than twenty leading scholars of democracy.

political institutions and political processes as legitimate, and how the notion of legitimacy is constructed and reconstructed in public discourse. Social and political theorists in the descriptive-analytical tradition try to devise conceptually consistent and empirically plausible descriptions and explanations of how and why democratic norms, empirical democratic practices and societal discourses about democracy are changing.

In the present chapter, it is primarily this third approach which guides the exploration of late-modern democracy. The central questions to be addressed are: How do democratic systems in advanced modern societies respond to the triple sustainability challenge outlined above? How do they address their perceived legitimacy crises, performance gaps and democratic deficits? How do they adapt their modes of generating legitimacy? How do they reconfigure their relationship to the late-modern subject? In a word: How do they manage to sustain a political order that seems increasingly unsustainable?[7] Following Inglehart, the concept of modernisation will be at the centre of the subsequent analysis: Processes of modernisation trigger processes of social value change which in turn affect political culture and trigger democratic change. Yet, the 'emancipative theory of modernisation' which has always informed Inglehart's work (e.g. Inglehart 1977, 1997; Inglehart and Welzel 2005: 299-300) will be extended by an important dimension that Inglehart does not recognise: Beyond the constitution and assertion of the autonomous subject, the process of modernisation and emancipation also entails the reflexive dissolution of exactly this modernist ideal. Honneth describes this second stage of the emancipatory trajectory of modernity as the 'liberation from autonomy' (Honneth 2002).[8] For the currently ongoing transformation of democracy this second order emancipation is, I will argue, of exceptional significance, and to fully explore this significance is the objective of this chapter.

The next section first addresses the two most commonly cited causes of democratic deficits and legitimacy crises: the internationalisation and deparliamentarisation of politics, and then turns to the ongoing process of (reflexive) modernisation which is not only the underlying cause of the latter two phenomena but also a useful access point to the discussion of the most crucial issue in the late-modern transformation of democracy: the reflexive dissolution of modernist notions of the Self. Section three is devoted specifically to the relationship between democracy and complexity, whereby the focus is first on the 'democratic dilemma' (Dahl) that democratic structures tend to be inefficient, whilst efficient structures tend to be undemocratic; then on the

---

7 Indeed, beyond the specific research agenda of this book, the present chapter ought to be read as a further contribution to my ongoing exploration of the *politics of unsustainability* (e.g. Blühdorn 2002, 2004a/b, 2007c/d).

8 Translation of citations from German-language sources here and throughout the chapter by the author.

complexity of late-modern individuals who are embracing *liquid* forms of identity commensurate to *liquid life* in *liquid modernity* (Bauman 2000, 2005); and finally on the structural mismatch between contemporary forms of liquid identity and the institutional order of representative democracy. Section four discusses the strategies developed by advanced modern societies for the generation of legitimacy. It starts out by mapping the key parameters which are constitutive to the generation of legitimacy, then explores a trend towards rationalisation that has transformed legitimacy in late-modern democracies, and concludes by highlighting the shortcomings of the forms of legitimacy generation that have become prevalent. The final section then further explores these shortcomings from a normative as well as empirical point of view. It portrays the simultaneity of, on the one hand, the decentralisation of the individual, the disintegration of the modernist subject and the emergence of objectivist (*post-democratic*) modes of legitimacy generation and, on the other hand, the radicalisation of demands for self-determination, self-realisation and individual-centred legitimisation as the key challenge which advanced modern consumer democracies are having to confront. It suggests that late-modern societies are coping with this challenge by supplementing their expert-based, depoliticised and output-oriented modes of legitimacy generation by something that may be conceptualised as *performative legitimacy*. Under conditions of late-modern complexity performative legitimacy is, arguably, essential for sustaining the democratic order which might otherwise indeed be unsustainable.

2. Reflexive modernisation

Recent debates about legitimacy crises and democratic deficits have been fuelled, in particular, by two factors: firstly, the *internationalisation* of politics, i.e. the increasing extent to which policy is made at the supranational level and shaped by international actors; and secondly, the *deparliamentarisation* of politics, i.e. the increasing extent to which at the national and subnational level policy making has migrated into extra-parliamentary fora and is dominated by actors who do not command a democratic mandate.[9] The first of these developments, i.e. the internationalisation of politics, has a dual impact on national democracies: (a) political power and decision-making competencies in ever more policy areas are moving towards transnational bodies and

9 See, for example: Beck 1998; Greven 1998; Majone 1996, 1998, 1999; Moravcsik 1998, 2002, 2004; Scharpf 1998b, 1999, 2003, 2004; Zürn 1998, 2003, 2004; Thatcher and Stone Sweet 2002; Strøm et al. 2003; Braun and Galardi 2005; Follesdal and Hix 2006; Leibfried and Zürn 2006, and the majority of contributions to this volume.

arenas and therefore away from national democratic institutions; and (b) decisions taken at the supranational level need to be ratified and implemented at the national level, which turns supposedly sovereign national political institutions into executive agencies for policies on the formulation of which they have had at best marginal impact, but for the effects of which – particularly if these are deemed negative – national electorates will hold them fully responsible. Both aspects undermine the effectiveness with which national governments can respond to the priorities and preferences of the *demos*, and they weaken the bond of trust between the latter and their democratic institutions. Indeed, from the perspective of the electorate the internationalisation of politics raises the question why citizens should at all invest commitment into democratic processes, and trust into political institutions, if all major issues are being determined by transnational actors and regimes, with national democratic institutions having very limited scope for autonomous and effective action. At the implementation stage there is the question why citizens should at all accept and comply with policy agendas which, whilst interfering ever more deeply into formerly national policy areas and impacting ever more strongly on their everyday lives, have neither been negotiated nor voted upon in a democratic manner.

The second of the above cited points, i.e. the deparliamentarisation of politics, implies that political issues and decision-making competencies are increasingly delegated to non-majoritarian bodies and agencies. 'The late twentieth century', Moravcsik notes, 'has been a period of the *decline of parliaments* and the rise of courts, public administrations and the *core executive*' (Moravcsik 2002: 613). In many policy areas advanced industrial democracies 'insulate themselves from direct political contestation' (ibid.) with democratic government being superseded by the depoliticised 'regulatory state' (Majone 1996). At the same time, the increasing complexity of policy issues and interest constellations has given rise to patterns of informal government and network governance. Whilst these new policy networks in the 'cooperative state' (Benz 1998) also provide new opportunities for the engagement of interest groups and civil society actors, this 'post-parliamentarian' (ibid.) form of governance once again implies a devaluation of the central arena of democratic deliberation and decision-making, and it raises questions of transparency, accountability and legitimacy (e.g. Fischer 2006: 50).

The internationalisation and the deparliamentarisation of politics disempower national democratic institutions, impair the right to democratic self-determination and disrupt established chains of democratic legitimisation and accountability. They increase the distance between decision makers and decisions takers and thus undermine the democratic ideal of the congruence between the governing and the governed. They trigger complaints about democratic deficits and mobilise protest movements, nationally and internationally. Yet, for an appropriate understanding of the challenges to democracy it is essential to grasp that the trends of internationalisation and deparliamentarisation are not the cause of the perceived crisis of democracy. They are themselves only symptoms of the process of modernisation which is the underlying cause and trigger of the ongoing transformation of democracy.[10] This process of modernisation is driven by its own logic. Its dynamics is difficult to control, probably impossible to reverse, and since its inception rationalisation, individualisation, differentiation and temporalisation have belonged to its constitutive elements.[11]

On the basis of their 'emancipatory theory of modernisation', Inglehart and Welzel have suggested that the 'underlying theme' of modernisation is 'the growth of human choice, giving rise to a new type of humanistic society that has never existed before' (Inglehart and Welzel 2005: 299). They have highlighted how 'rising self-expression values provide a social force that operates in favor of democracy, helping to establish democracy where it does not yet exist, and strengthening democracy where it is already in place, improving the effectiveness of democratic institutions' (ibid.). They assume that the process of modernisation incrementally transforms 'merely formal democracy' into 'genuinely effective democracy' (ibid.). Yet, this rather undialectical account does not recognise that in a number of respects the process of modernisation also represents a severe challenge to democracy:

Firstly, modernisation gives rise to a widening gap between the need for political legitimation on the one side, and the capabilities to produce this legitimacy on the other. As it makes established traditions negotiable and opens up ever new options and opportunities, the progress of modernisation renders both private and social life eminently political. Choices and decisions have to be made at the exclusion of alternative options. Particularly if they impact on the social sphere, such choices need to be publicly justified and politically legitimated. Yet as the process of modernisation is chipping away at all exist-

10 Accordingly, any attempts to renationalise politics or to reverse the process of deparliamentarisation would invariably be doomed to fail. Such neo-national and neo-parliamentary impulses – which predictably surface in political rhetoric from across the ideological spectrum – disregard that societal function systems, individual life worlds, the realm of social interaction and the problems which electorates want to see addressed have irreversibly expanded beyond the boundaries of the nation state, and that the expectations and demands which contemporary electorates regard as non-negotiable cannot be fulfilled by the forms of democratic government which had been designed for conditions of much lower social complexity.

11 Particularly the term *temporalisation* may require further explanation. It aims to capture, firstly, the steady shortening of innovation cycles and, by implication, the declining time span for which any artefacts and social arrangements may be expected to last before becoming subject to a new round of innovation. Secondly, it captures the tightening focus onto the present and the increasing value accredited to the instant servicing of momentary needs, imperatives and desires, which take priority over the values of the past and consideration for the future.

ing normative yardsticks that might be applied for this purpose, the rapidly expanding demand for political legitimisation clashes with the constantly declining ability to deliver on this demand.

Secondly, the process of modernisation also leads into an organizational dilemma. Since their inception, modernity and modernisation have been a process of social differentiation and the build up of societal complexity. The specialisation of knowledge, the diversification of social identities and increasingly multifaceted social relations and patterns of interaction necessitate sophisticated procedures of coordination which can manage the achieved level of diversity and complexity in an efficient and effective manner. Democratic processes, however, are not only cumbersome and resource intensive, but with their ideal of deliberative consensus, their binary logic of yes/no votes and their simplistic dualism of majority and minority they are structurally inadequate for the articulation and management of late-modern complexity (Benz 1998: 203).[12]

Thirdly, the ongoing process of modernisation represents a challenge to democracy in that it implies a transformation of the core value and point of reference of both modernity itself and of the political system of democracy: the autonomous Self. As indicated above, 'modern democracy relies on the axiom of the self-control of individuals' (Beck 1997: 44). 'This principle was postulated and analysed in the political theory and philosophy of the Enlightenment' (ibid.) which has originally created and installed the idea(l) of the autonomous Self as the ultimate bearer of value and subject of rights. The Enlightenment initiated the process of the constitution and emancipation of the modernist subject and its identity, and the process of modernisation has always remained a process that centres on the core value of the subject, steadily extending its rights and nurturing its claims to individuality, self-determination and self-realisation. On the other hand, however, the process of modernisation has continuously increased the complexity of the Self (individual and collective) and its identity, which has affected its internal coherence, consistency and stability. This transformation of the Self and its identity represents a challenge for both normative democratic theory and in an empirical-practical sense. From the perspective of the former, the problem is that contemporary notions of individuality and identity do not provide a solid foundation for any notion of democratic legitimacy. From the empirical-practical perspective it becomes ever more difficult for democratic institutions to integrate and be responsive and accountable to the burgeoning diversity of incompatible, inconsistent and highly volatile demands articulated by late-modern society's 'atomised citizens' (Pattie et al. 2004: 276-80).

Thus, the problems which contemporary democracies are having to confront do not really originate from the much debated internationalisation and de-

12 These points will be elaborated further below.

parliamentarisation of politics but, ultimately, from the dynamics of the modernisation process itself. Trying to capture, firstly, the uncontrollability of this process and, secondly, its tendency to once again dissolve the certainties which modernity itself had once established in its struggle against pre-modern uncertainties, Beck has suggested the term *reflexive modernisation*[13] (Beck et al. 1994; Beck 1997) and notes that 'democracy is becoming reflexive' (Beck 1997: 43): 'Quite independently of whether we like it and approve of it, regardless of whether it is considered progressive or catastrophic' we are witnessing the 'reflexive questioning of the fundamental principles of democracy' (ibid.).[14] Perhaps more succinctly even than Beck's thinking in terms of a *second* or *reflexive modernity*, Luhmann's functionalist theory captures the inadequacy of the modernist ideas underpinning democracy (Luhmann 1995, 2000). Suggesting, as it does, firstly, that the analysis of advanced modern society needs to proceed from the basic category of the autonomous function system rather than the autonomous subject (individual or collective); that, secondly, these function systems are systems of communicated meaning and therefore not tied to national boundaries or delimited and integrated by territorial categories; and that, thirdly, societal interaction and development are not governed by the system of politics[15] but evolve in a largely uncoordinated and uncontrolled manner from the interplay of society's diverse function systems, the systems-theoretical model acknowledges and implies (a) the decentralisation of the autonomous subject (individual and collective), (b) the decentralisation of the nation state, and (c) the decentralisation of the system of politics. It necessitates that democracy be reconceptualised beyond its modernist foundations and modernist categories. In particular it raises the questions:

- *Can there be democracy beyond the autonomous and identical subject?*
- *Can there be democracy beyond the nation state?*
- *Can there be democracy beyond government as the central site of power and societal coordination?*

---

13 The term denotes the automotive and largely unreflected 'self-transformation of industrial society' (Beck 1997: 15) in which 'the foundations of modernization in industrial society are called into question by that very modernization' (Beck 1997: 40).

14 Beck refers, in particular, to the notion of the territorial nation state, the idea of national sovereignty, the belief in the unity of the people (national identity) and in the congruence of the governing and the governed, and to the notion of politics as the centre of power governing all social relations and societal interaction. Yet, like Inglehart, he does not consistently think through the implications of the reflexive modernisation of the most central modernist idea, namely that of the autonomous Self and identical subject which is, ultimately, underpinning all the other beliefs mentioned before.

15 For Luhmann, the system of politics is only one of many societal function systems and in no way superior to, or in control of, the others.

The existing literature on the transformation of democracy addresses primarily the last two of these questions[16], yet the key point is, arguably, the first one. Appropriate conceptualisations of the contemporary challenge to democracy and of the ways in which advanced modern societies are managing this challenge not only need to overcome the *territorial bias* in democratic theory and the social sciences more generally (Beck 1998: 10-19) but also – even more importantly – what by analogy might be called the *subjectivist bias*. They need to rethink democracy beyond the modernist notion of the subject. And whilst transnational or even global political institutions managing the affairs of the transnational or even global community in a democratic manner are, in principle, thoroughly conceivable, democracy without the notion of the autonomous and identical subject seems much less conceivable – indeed inherently contradictory.[17] Therefore, democratic theory needs to pay much more attention to changing notions of subjectivity and new patterns of identity construction which underpin democratic needs and expectations. It needs to take into account that modernisation does not only transform empirical conditions and social relations which are supposed to be ordered in accordance with democratic norms, but also prevalent notions of individuality, identity and subjectivity which are the source and referent of such norms. After all, legitimation crises, efficiency gaps and democratic deficits are *subject-centred* categories: they are *subjectively experienced violations of subject-centred norms*.

Acknowledging the interplay between the modernisation-induced transformation of empirical conditions and the parallel transformation of social norms and expectations, Schneider et al. (2006: 200-202) have distinguished three different types of legitimacy crises:

1. *Crises of democratic institutions*, in which established democratic norms remain uncontested, but political institutions are seen to not comply with them and are therefore deemed to lack legitimacy.

---

16 With the literature on transnational and cosmopolitan democracy (e.g. Held 1995; Albrow 1998; Zürn 1998; Beck 1998, 2006; Beck and Grande 2007) covering the former and the literature on governance, the cooperative state, regulative politics, etc. (e.g. Rosenau and Czempiel 1992; Majone 1996, 1999; Rhodes 1997; Giddens 1998; Czada et al. 2003; Marcussen and Torfing 2006; Sørensen and Torfing 2008) covering the latter.

17 Some post-modernist thinkers (e.g. Lyotard 1984; Laclau and Mouffe 1985; Mouffe 1993) have claimed that the emergence of post-modernist forms of subjectivity and identity provides new opportunities for radical democracy. Neo-modernists such as Beck (1997) or Inglehart (1997) have emphasised that the post-modernisation of society bears major potentials for the further democratisation of democracy. Yet, the implications of the decline of the modernist subject for democratic theory remain underexplored, and in political practice the governance of post-modern complexity seems to have given rise, more than anything, to *post-democratic* forms of governance (Crouch 2004; Jörke 2005; Buchstein and Nullmeier 2006; Blühdorn 2006b, 2007b).

2. *Crises of democracy*, which occur if established democratic norms are no longer upheld, and established democratic institutions are not accepted as legitimate either.
3. *De-democratisation of political legitimacy*, which implies that established and newly emerging political institutions are accepted and perceived as legitimate, but for other than democratic reasons, i.e. not because they comply with democratic norms.

Normative democratic theory in the critical tradition and empirical legitimisation research commonly conceptualise legitimacy crises and democratic deficits in terms of the first of these types, resting assured that 'adherence to the norms and ideals of the democratic process have increased' rather than declined (Dalton 2004: 192). The suggestion here, in contrast, is that the currently ongoing transformation of democracy is, first and foremost, a matter of the third type of crisis, i.e. a reconfiguration of political legitimacy entailing a reconfiguration of democratic norms which, in turn, corresponds to the ongoing reconfiguration of prevalent notions of individuality, subjectivity and identity. While social movements are vociferously demanding the implementation of democratic values, and political institutions from local city councils right up to the OECD are emphasising their commitment to democratic renewal; in other words, whilst declaratory commitment to democratic values has never been as undivided as at present, a silent *de-democratisation of political legitimacy* is, arguably, addressing the dual problem which neo-democratic discourses prefer to discount: the complexity of contemporary social interests and societal relations cannot be processed in an efficient and effective manner by democratic structures, and the complexity of contemporary notions of individuality, subjectivity and identity destroys the very foundations of democratic legitimacy.

3. Complexity and democracy

Complexity is the result of processes of differentiation which, in turn, is the core principle of modernity and modernisation (Luhmann 1995). Ever higher levels of specialisation, diversity and complexity have continuously widened the opportunities for individual and collective self-determination and self-realisation, and increased the problem solving capacities of modern societies. However, rising levels of societal complexity make high demands on the capacities for organization, coordination and administrative efficiency and easily run into conflict with democratic principles. In a seminal article of 1994 Robert Dahl pointed to the 'trade-off' between 'the ability of the citizens to exercise democratic control over the decisions of the polity' and 'the capacity of the system to respond satisfactorily to the collective preferences of its citizens' (Dahl 1994: 28). Citizens are confronted, Dahl suggested, with the 'democratic dilemma' that they have to choose between preserving their ability 'to influence the conduct of their government' (effective participation) and increasing the capacity of the 'political unit to deal more effectively' with the issues that matter most to them (efficient problem solving) (ibid.: 23f.). Using similar language, Arthur Okun was, already in the 1970s, talking of a 'big trade-off' between 'somewhat more equality at the expense of efficiency or somewhat more efficiency at the expense of equality' (Okun 1975: vii). In contemporary societies, much increased levels of complexity have further aggravated these tensions between democratic values (participation, equality, legitimacy), on the one hand, and the need for efficient decision-making and effective policy delivery, on the other. And in the ongoing modernisation of government the drive for efficiency has tended to prevail.[18]

Of course, the politicisation of perceived democratic deficits has reinforced the declaratory commitment to *bringing politics closer to the people* and *closing the gap between policy makers and policy takers* (see Kelso in this volume). Also, some scholars diagnose an 'expansion of citizen participation' (Dalton 2008) and optimistically state 'the new style of citizen participation places more control over political activity in the hands of the citizenry' (Dalton and Klingemann 2007: 15). Yet, most observers note that for the sake of the efficient management of complexity, the role of citizen participation has progressively been reduced. In a process of 'downsizing democracy' citizens are being 'sidelined' (Crenson and Ginsberg 2002). The effort to enhance the efficiency of government and public administration has given rise to practices of depoliticisation and deparliamentarisation and to attempts to limit the number of democratic veto-players and veto-points. Under conditions of high complexity policy making is progressively turning into a matter of scientific experts, professional agencies and independent regulatory bodies which are more or less insulated from the political process (e.g. Heard-Lauréote, Landwehr and Nedlund, and Maggetti in this volume). Contrary to social movement hopes for a 'participatory revolution' (Blühdorn 2009), and despite all reassurances that 'interaction between elites and people' has 'never before in history' been 'shifted so much to the side of the people' (Dalton and Klingemann 2007: 18), there is strong evidence that 'politics and government are increasingly slipping back into the control of

18 In the more recent literature it has also been argued that democracy and efficiency are complementary rather than competing goals (see Newig and Fritsch in this volume). In actual practice, however, efficiency gains are much more commonly pursued by means of tightening than by expanding the scope for democratic engagement and autonomous governance. This is because of the prevalent – narrowly economic – understanding of *efficiency*. For a more detailed discussion of the relationship between democracy and efficiency see Blühdorn 2007c and Blatter in the following chapter.

privileged elites in the manner characteristic of pre-democratic times' (Crouch 2004: 6). 'Citizen participation', Buchstein and Jörke note, has been 'replaced as the basic value of democracy by the *rationality* of the political process' (Buchstein and Jörke 2007: 188). The complexity-induced drive for the 'rationalization of democracy', they argue, leads towards 'a *democracy without democracy*' (ibid.: 189).[19] And this devaluation of participation in empirical politics is mirrored, they suggest, by the 'expulsion of political participation from democratic theory' (ibid.): faced with the problems of escalating societal complexity and the tensions between participation and efficiency, 'current democratic theories opt against political participation' (Buchstein and Jörke 2007: 186).

Buchstein and Jörke are overstating the point: Only a decade ago John Dryzek had announced that the theory of democracy has taken 'a definite deliberative turn' (Dryzek 2000: v), and for the time being there is an abundance of scholars continuing to make legitimacy dependent on inclusive participation and public reason giving (deliberation) (e.g. Smith 2003; Fung and Wright 2003; Gutmann and Thompson 2004; Estlund 2008). Also, the quick critique of *privileged elites* and the *rationalization of democracy* disregards that there have always been very good reasons to insulate government from the changeable moods of the populous and protect democracy against the *tyranny of the majority*. Nevertheless, it is undoubtedly true that in the empirical practice of governance, participatory procedures represent a major risk, because they often contribute more to further inflating demands and amplifying complexity than to reigning them in and making them manageable. The underlying cause for this is that differentiation and complexity are not just a matter of the pluralisation and fragmentation of modern societies into ever more 'atomised citizens' but, beyond that, also affect the internal structure of late-modern identity. The recent literature has considered the issue of identity, first and foremost, with a view to the ongoing emancipation from traditional predetermined and fixed social identities – defined, for example,

19 Benz (1998: 212) speaks of a '*bisected* democracy, whose basis of legitimisation is reduced to the output side' (Benz 1998: 212). To some extent, the emergence of the cooperative state and modern forms of network governance have, of course, also provided new openings for political participation and citizen involvement. Yet, these opportunities tend to be narrowly circumscribed and designed only to enhance the efficiency and effectiveness of the policy process, not to allow for the democratic contestation of underlying structures and principles. Citizens are used as a resource: 'the aim is to gather information for use by other decision makers, not hand over decision-making power' (Parkinson 2004: 385). 'The participatory component of the concept of democracy', Buchstein and Jörke note, has thus turned from an intrinsic value into 'a dependent variable' (Buchstein and Jörke 2007: 187). And this transformation, Parkinson suggests, 'undermines the democratic character of the process by reducing the participants to the status of objects rather than subjects, means to someone else's exercise of autonomy rather than an expression of their own' (Parkinson 2004: 385).

through social class, gender or religious denomination. It has emphasised the rise of freely chosen and consciously adopted identities which have, the argument goes, raised the significance of self-expression and political participation, thus triggering a major democratisation of democracy (e.g. Inglehart 1997; Dalton 2004, 2008; Inglehart and Welzel 2005; Dalton and Klingemann 2007). Much less attention, however, has been paid to the internal structure and quality of the identities which contemporary individuals are constructing and choosing for themselves. Indeed, the complexity of late-modern subjects and identities, i.e. the diversity, incoherence, inconsistence and volatility of the values, demands and commitments of every single individual is, arguably, the most fundamental challenge to democracy.

In the classical modernist sense, identity had been understood as a unitary and stable set of values and qualities. Identity formation was regarded as a long-term, indeed a life-time, project ideally culminating, after a process of maturation, in a *rounded* personality integrating all dimensions of a person and its life, and displaying coherent, consistent and steady (identical) value preferences and forms of behaviour. This modernist notion of identity has, of course, always been an aspirational ideal rather than an empirical reality. In the late-modern condition, however, this ideal has become obsolete. The classical notion of identity that had once guided the emancipation of the autonomous Self and subject has itself turned into a source of restrictions and a burden. In the same sense that societal function systems and contexts of social interaction have grown beyond the container of the modernist nation state, patterns of individual and collective self-construction, self-realisation and self-experience have grown beyond the container of the modernist identical subject.

The reflexive emancipation from the modernist notion of identity and its imperatives of consistency, loyalty, integrity, commitment etc., firstly, promises to release additional potentials for self-realisation. Secondly, contemporary individuals have to adapt flexibly to a societal environment characterised by accelerating innovation and change.[20] Not least to comply with heightened demands for self-responsibility (in the wake of the declining ability of the state to provide welfare and security to its citizens), they need to grasp opportunities and maximise potentials as and when they emerge. Against this background, commitment to a unitary, stable and consistent identity has become counter-productive. 'The virtue proclaimed to serve the individual's interest best', Bauman notes, is 'a readiness to change tactics and style at short notice, to abandon commitments and loyalties without regret' (Bauman 2007: 4). For late-modern individuals 'looseness of attachment and revocability of engagement are the precepts guiding everything in which they engage and to which they are attached' (Bauman 2005: 4). Therefore, the

---

20 Compare Blatter's discussion of the notion of change-value in the following chapter.

modernist ideals of the subject and its *solid* identity have been superseded by late-modern forms of *liquid* identity: 'a permanently impermanent self, completely incomplete, definitely indefinite, authentically inauthentic' (Bauman 2005: 55) and perfectly suited to *liquid life* (Bauman 2005) in *liquid modernity* (Bauman 2000).

This late-modern *liquefaction* – eventually perhaps *liquidation*[21] – of the modernist identical Self not only underlines that the tension between democracy and efficiency is not simply a matter of scale.[22] It also signals a fundamental mismatch between the late-modern individual and the democratic order. From the perspective of the former, democratic institutions and processes are too narrow and restrictive as to allow for the appropriate articulation, representation and realisation of their complex and flexible identity.[23] They are too cumbersome and resource-consuming as to efficiently serve late-modern patterns of self-construction and self-experience which are strongly based on innovation and consumption. From the perspective of democratic institutions, in turn, it is becoming ever more difficult to integrate, accommodate and respond to the diversified and volatile demands of late-modern individuals. These institutions are already weakened by the self-imposing imperatives of the globalising economy and disempowered by the denationalisation of politics. Ever less consistent and predictable, yet more assertive, citizens represent an additional obstacle to efficient policy delivery, and they further complicate the generation of legitimacy.[24]

Thus, in the late-modern condition representative democracy, which had been based on the modernist ideal of the autonomous subject and its solid identity, is becoming increasingly questionable. In the same sense, and to the same degree, that the modernist solid identity has become inappropriate and turned into a burden, this may be said about democracy, too. Whilst post-

---

21 At least for the time being, modernist notions of *solid identity* have not entirely lost their relevance. They exist *alongside* late-modern ideals of *liquid identity*, and exactly this simultaneity of incompatible ideals is, arguably, the key feature and dilemma of late-modern politics (Blühdorn 2007a,b,d).

22 Dahl, for example, had conceptualised the 'trade-off between system effectiveness and citizen effectiveness' (Dahl 1994: 34) primarily in terms of size. In very small political systems, he suggests, 'a citizen may be able to participate extensively' yet the decisions have little impact and 'do not matter much'. Very large systems, in contrast, 'may be able to cope with problems that matter more to a citizen', yet 'the opportunities for the citizen to participate in and greatly influence decisions are vastly reduced' (ibid.: 28).

23 There is consistent empirical evidence that prevalent forms of political engagement are becoming more individualistic, spontaneous, self-controlled, flexible, non-committing, expressive, life-style oriented and at times 'in danger of becoming more of a lifestyle statement than a serious engagement' (Stoker 2006: 88; e.g. Norris 1999; Cain et al. 2003; Dalton 2004, 2008; Inglehart and Welzel 2005; Dalton and Klingemann 2007).

24 Even more than they are 'groaning from the pressure of critical citizens', Stoker notes, democratic systems are 'creaking from the impact of semi-detached but occasional assertive citizens' (Stoker 2006: 87).

modernists had expected the post-modern turn to release major potentials for radical democracy, and others were convinced that the continued rise of self-expression values would render contemporary democracies ever more genuinely democratic (Inglehart and Welzel 2005: 21), the ongoing process of modernisation in fact raises very serious questions about the sustainability of democracy. And as we have seen, these questions do not just arise from Putnam's (2000) *bowling alone thesis* that the erosion of social capital may destabilise civic culture and threaten the viability of democracy, but form the liquefaction of the identical subject. For the post-industrial phase of modernisation in which, as Inglehart and others have rightly argued, the rise of post-materialist value preferences considerably improved the quality of democracy, has meanwhile been superseded by a new phase that, whilst further pursuing the emancipatory trajectory of modernity, is much less conducive to democracy than its predecessor.

In this new phase the liberation from prefixed social roles and ties that gave 'people more room to express themselves *as individuals*' (Inglehart and Welzel 2005: 24; my emphasis) merges into the liberation from that very individuality itself, i.e. from the modernist notions of solid identity and the identical subject.[25] This amounts to a radicalisation of the claim for independence and unrestricted choice. From the perspective of the late-modern individual it raises the questions: *How can the radicalised claim to self-determination be politically implemented? What kind of institutions would be most suited for the kind of participation that late-modern citizens prefer? How can late-modern citizens accept and trust political institutions, and subject themselves to political authorities?* From the perspective of democratic institutions the questions are: *How can democracy uphold the principle of representation if values and demands diversify and transform at a pace that outstretches the capacities of institutions to identify and respond to them? How can it deliver outputs if inputs are contradictory, targets changeable and critical citizens in the way of efficient policy making? How can it generate political legitimacy if both the channel of representation (input) and that of performance (output) are severely obstructed?*

Democratic theory has so far not adequately dealt with these issues.[26] It has refrained from addressing the specifically late-modern dilemma that, on

25 Inglehart and Welzel correctly note that 'rising self-expression values bring an emancipation from authority', yet it is insufficient to conceptualise this emancipation only as the increasing rejection of 'external authority that encroaches on individual rights' with authority becoming 'internalized within people themselves' (Inglehart and Welzel 2005: 26). In a further stage emancipation also entails liberation from this 'internal authority', i.e. from any self-imposed imperatives of identity that might restrict personal choices and opportunities.

26 Just as eco-political theory, for example, keeps focusing on issues such as ecological citizenship, environmental literacy and environmental justice, thereby demonstrating its inability to even address, let alone overcome, what has been referred to above as the *subjec-*

the one hand, democracy remains indispensable because (a) despite the liquefaction of the modernist subject, the claim to self-determination and self-realisation has remained fully in place and in fact been radicalised, and (b) a viable alternative for the legitimation of political power and for securing compliance with political decisions is not available. On the other hand, however, democracy is no longer suitable for the articulation, representation and realisation of late-modern identity, and democratic institutions are increasingly unable to generate the legitimacy that is required. Building on the discussion above of the 'expulsion of political participation' and of the 'rationalization of democratic politics', the analysis will now turn to the question: *How can legitimacy be generated beyond the liquefaction of the modernist subject?* The concluding section will then at least tentatively explore how late-modern democracies manage to reconcile the expulsion of participation and what will be conceptualised as the *de-subjectivation of political legitimacy* with the radicalised claim to self-determination.

4. Political legitimacy beyond the modernist subject

Sources of legitimacy and patterns of political legitimisation have changed over time and adapted to evolving socio-economic conditions. This process has not come to a halt with the transition from traditional, pre-democratic forms of legitimacy to modern democratic legitimacy. Today, the execution of political power is regarded as *democratically* legitimated (as opposed to Weber's forms of traditional, legal-rational and charismatic legitimation) if (a) all citizens have equal rights to participate in the political process and get their interests authentically represented (principle of political participation and equality); (b) political processes are transparent, understandable and accountable (principle of transparency and accountability); and (c) policy decisions effectively address and resolve issues which citizens recognize as relevant for themselves and the community at large (principle of effectiveness). These criteria emphasise, respectively, the input dimension, the procedural dimension and the performance or output dimension of the political process. Whilst classical democratic theory had regarded direct and equal participation of all citizens as the only relevant criterion for democratic legitimacy, the modern understanding is significantly more complex. It recognises that direct and equal participation is one, but by no means the only, way of securing democratic legitimacy. Just as modern democracy is a complex ar-

---

tivist bias in the social sciences, democratic theory, too, has so far largely refrained from thinking through what the liquefaction of the subject implies for democracy and how democracy may be possible beyond the modernist subject.

rangement of diverse political actors and interconnected political arenas, legitimacy and legitimacy generation, too, have become a multi-dimensional and complex matter. For the analysis of its constitutive parameters and the ongoing transformation of their relative significance, it is useful to distinguish between:

1. the norms or values on which democratic legitimacy claims are based (norms of reference);
2. the process in which, or procedures through which, these norms are activated and applied (method of legitimacy generation); and
3. the point or stage in the political process at which the question of norm compliance is raised (point of legitimacy generation).

As regards the first of these, i.e. the norms or values on which legitimacy can be based, it should first of all be reiterated that the basic norm and value on which democratic legitimacy always rests is the modernist idea of the autonomous subject. Following the Kantian tradition, this idea of the autonomous subject – as the only relevant *source norm* – may be said to comprise an individual, a collective and a *pure* or transcendental dimension. Accordingly, the *content norms* on which democratic legitimacy is based can be differentiated into, firstly, the values of liberty, autonomy and individuality, secondly, the values of equality, justice and integration, and thirdly, those of objectivity and impartiality. The first set place the emphasis on the individual subject and the personal good (individual autonomy, self-centred), the second on the collective subject and the common good (collective autonomy, community-centred), and the third on what in the Kantian tradition might be referred to as the transcendental subject and the purely rational and objectively good (absolute autonomy, objectivity-centred).[27]

Similarly, the methods or procedures through which these norms are activated and legitimacy is generated may be differentiated into (a) forms of direct or delegated participation; (b) forms of deliberation, mediation and integration; and (c) forms of professionalization, rationalisation and formalisation. Participation (direct or delegated) aims, in particular, for the articulation and representation of individual interests and rights, i.e. it activates, in particular, individual-centred reference norms. Deliberation, mediation and integration – aiming for majority or ideally consensus formation – are specifi-

27 Note that in his *First Definitive Article of a Perpetual Peace* Immanuel Kant states: 'A republican constitution is founded upon three principles: firstly, the principle of freedom for all members of a society (as men); secondly, the principle of the dependence of everyone upon a single common legislation (as subjects); and thirdly, the principle of legal equality for everyone (as citizens)' (Kant 1991: 99). Whilst Kant was not a democrat, the norms he is specifying here are, clearly, the subject-based norms underpinning democratic legitimacy. With the second principle he is referring to the law of absolute reason which, he assumed, is common to all human beings *qua* rational beings.

cally geared towards the collective subject and mobilise, in particular, the norms of collective autonomy and the collective good. Professionalization, rationalisation and formalisation, finally, are focused, in particular, on the objectively good and rational. Employing strategies of depersonalisation, depoliticisation and scientization, they seek to implement the norms of objectivity and impartiality.

As regards the point in the policy process at which democratic legitimacy is generated it has, furthermore, become common practice to differentiate the three dimensions of *input legitimacy* which is derived from the quality of the input into the political process; *procedural legitimacy* which is based on the quality of the procedural rules governing the political process; and *output legitimacy* which derives from the performance, i.e. from the quality of the output of the political process. Input legitimacy is commonly associated, in particular, with high levels of citizen participation and thus with the representation of individual-centred norms. Similarly, procedural legitimacy seems to have a particular connection to the process of public debate and majority or consensus formation which bring the values of the collective subject to the fore. Output legitimacy, finally, seems especially related to strategies of depoliticisation and scientization which seem particularly conducive to the implementation of the values of objectivity and impartiality. It is important to note that none of these *prima facie* connections withstands closer scrutiny,[28] yet for present purposes it is helpful to organize the parameters which have now been identified as constitutive for the generation and analysis of democratic legitimacy in accordance with the three dimensions of the autonomous subject, i.e. the individual subject, the collective subject and the transcendental subject. Figure 1.1 visualises this systematisation.

---

28 Input legitimacy derives from the *quality* rather than the *quantity* of input. In other words it depends on the authenticity with which the content norms (individual-centred, community-centred, and impersonal, objectivity-centred) are fed into the political process, and this authenticity is not necessarily maximised by mobilising mass participation – which tends to focus rather exclusively on individual-centred norms. Similarly, procedural legitimacy is not really tied to any particular phase of the political process nor to any particular method of activating democratic content norms. Irrespective of the stage of the political process, it derives from the quality of the rules that govern that stage, i.e. from the extent to which these rules implement and realise the democratic content norms (all three categories). Output legitimacy, finally, is neither specifically linked to the norm of objectivity and impartiality nor to the depoliticised and scientised forms of policy making and policy implementation which are said to enhance the efficiency and effectiveness of the policy process. Instead, output legitimacy is a matter of the quality of policy outputs which can be measured by individual-centred, community-centred or objectivity-centred norms.

Figure 1.1: Key parameters in the generation and analysis of democratic legitimacy

	norms of reference	**methods of generation**	**point of generation**
individal subject, citizen	liberty, autonomy, inalienable rights of the individual; self-interest	direct participation or delegated participation (representation)	input stage
collective subject, *demos*	equality, justice, social inclusion; common good, collective interest	majority formation via aggregation or consensus formation via deliberation	process stage
transcendental subject, system	objective truth, absolute rationality; the objectively good and necessary	depoliticisation and objectivation through delegation to science, formal procedures and professional agencies	output stage

On the basis of this illustration, and taking up what has been noted above about the 'expulsion of participation', the process of 'rationalisation' and about 'bisected democracy', the ongoing transformation of democracy can now be conceptualised in terms of a shift of emphasis between different norms of reference for legitimacy, methods of legitimacy generation and places of legitimacy generation. Depending on which of these categories the emphasis is placed upon, the ongoing reconstruction of democratic legitimacy appears as a shift from normative to cognitive modes of legitimacy generation (Jörke 2007: 78-81), a shift from politicisation and participation towards depoliticisation and delegation (Blühdorn 2006b: 75-8; 2007b: 312-19), or as a shift from input legitimacy towards output legitimacy (Scharpf 1999, 2004). In Figure 1.1 this implies an overall shift in relative significance from the top to the bottom which affects the normative point of reference, the method of legitimacy generation as well as the place of legitimacy generation. In all three dimensions there is a noticeable trend of rationalisation and formalisation, in which the relative significance of the individual subject (citizen) is reduced in favour of increasing emphasis on supposedly objective truths, formal rationality and systemic necessities. On the one hand this shift can be understood as the increasing focus on what the Kantian purely rational and thus genuinely autonomous (transcendental) subject would regard as objectively good and rational. In the sense, however, that this shift moves abstract norms of performance,[29] formalised procedures, depoliticised approaches and systemic imperatives into the centre of attention, it may more suitably be conceptualised as a process of *depersonalisation* or *desubjectivization* and thus as a *de-democratisation* of legitimacy. Accordingly, demo-

29 Compare the discussion of the 'metaphysics of efficiency' in Blühdorn 2007c: 75-82.

cratic patterns of legitimacy generation may – in the late-modern condition – be said to be gradually superseded by non- or post-democratic patterns.[30]

This ongoing reconstruction of democratic legitimacy becomes even more graphically visible, if the constitutive elements distinguished in Figure 1.1 are reorganized so as to describe the generation of legitimacy in terms of (a) the relevant norms of reference and (b) the relevant points in the political process (see Figure 1.2). In comparison with Figure 1.1, the advantage of this visualisation is that it captures more clearly that all three norms of reference are relevant at all three points of legitimacy generation in the policy cycle. But in the sense that the modernist era had installed the autonomous individual as the primary norm of reference for democratic legitimacy, and classical democratic theory had regarded the input stage (direct participation) as the central place of legitimacy generation in the political process, the ongoing reconstruction of legitimacy in advanced modern democracies may be portrayed as a shift of emphasis from the top left corner in the diagram towards the bottom right corner. This is a shift towards depersonalised objectivity as the most important norm of reference, and towards the output stage as the most important point in the policy cycle at which legitimacy is supposed to emerge. Whilst the *participatory revolution* of the 1970s and 1980s, as well as the *deliberative turn* which according to Dryzek (2000) occurred in the early 1990s had emphatically reasserted the centrality of the modernist autonomous subject, late-modern democracies are witnessing a desubjectivization of legitimacy and a *post-democratic turn* (Blühdorn 2006b: 75-8; 2007b: 312-19).

30 Using the criteria input-oriented / output-oriented and democratic / non-democratic, Schneider et al. (2006: 211-12) distinguish four different 'patterns of legitimisation': a) democratic and input-oriented, b) democratic and output-oriented, c) non-democratic and input-oriented, and d) non-democratic and output-oriented. Interestingly, their empirical analysis of the ways in which citizens and publics understand legitimacy does not provide evidence of any de-democratisation. Whilst the ways in which advanced modern societies seek to produce democratic legitimacy have factually comprehensively changed, no such changes seem to be noticeable in the standards of legitimacy rehearsed and cultivated in public discourse. A possible explanation for this phenomenon will be offered in the concluding section.

Figure 1.2: From modernist to late-modern legitimisation

place of generation \ reference norm	**Individual** (autonomy, self-determination, self-interest)	**Community** (justice, equality, inclusion, common good)	**Objectivity** (the objectively true, good and rational)
input	direct articulation	representation	expert knowledge
procedure	interest/value aggregation	deliberation, discourse, agreement	depoliticised formal administration
output	utility for individual	utility for collective	formal, abstract, systemic utility

Trying to explain why this late-modern reconstruction of legitimacy is occurring, Scharpf and many others have pointed towards the necessity of 'concepts of legitimisation beyond the nation state' (Scharpf 2004). Moravcsik has emphasised that the trend towards depoliticisation, scientization and objectivization follows 'the logic of commitment' (Moravcsik 2002: 613), i.e. it is precisely the defence of democratic values which necessitates the implementation of seemingly non-democratic strategies (Moravcsik 2004: 346f). From this perspective then, insulation from political contestation or increasing reliance on scientific experts and professional agents are 'not simply an empirical fact' but 'have normative weight' (Moravcsik 2002: 613). From the perspective of sociological theory, however, and in light of the explorations throughout this chapter, a major reason for the late-modern reconfiguration of democratic legitimacy is that in the ongoing process of modernisation the modernist notion of the autonomous and identical subject has become obsolete, and modernist, subject-centred patterns of legitimacy generation therefore have to be replaced by new *post-subjective* (post-democratic) modes.

As outlined above, the late-modern condition of complexity implies, firstly, that society is differentiated into multiple function systems, which are each governed by their own system-centred logic, which confront political decision makers with a perpetual stream of unexpected side effects, and which – by incessantly imposing their systemic imperatives – invalidate modernist assertions that the subject is autonomous, the political sovereign and at the centre of societal development. Secondly, late-modern complexity implies the differentiation, fragmentation and liquefaction of identity (collective and individual), with modernist notions of unitary and steady identity being superseded by fluid contextualised identities and multi-dimensional, ephemeral images. Thus, the increase in complexity is undermining the very foundations of democratic legitimacy. In the late-modern condition legitimacy *can no longer* be generated in the modernist subject-centred mode, and it is, arguably, not least for this reason that a reconfiguration of legitimacy is taking place. In a sense, the 'expulsion of participation' that was outlined above is a *logical consequence* of late-modern complexity – which societal elites can exploit for their own empowerment, carving new political space out of processes of wider cultural change. As the values and demands of late-modern individuals are becoming increasingly inconsistent and changeable, and critical and erratic citizens represent an unmanageable obstacle to efficient policy making, it was perhaps inevitable that the generation of legitimacy had to turn into a matter of science-oriented and supposedly issue-focused professionals applying rule-based procedures in order to optimize policy performance. Accordingly, democracy is now primarily understood and justified in terms of what it delivers (e.g. Fuchs 1998; Roller 2005; Fuchs and Roller 2008), and this quality of delivery provides strong incentives for 'sacrificing the active political participation of its citizens' (Buchstein and Jörke 2007: 189).

A major problem, however, with these post-subjective strategies of legitimisation is that they are not an adequate substitute for modernist subject-centred legitimacy, particularly because, as briefly touched upon above, the process of modernisation has not only differentiated, decentralised and liquefied the supposedly autonomous and identical subject but has, at the same time, constantly nurtured and inflated the individual's claims to self-determination and to being the central point of reference. Late-modern identity may be more differentiated, flexible, volatile and incalculable than ever before, i.e. the notion of the identical subject which provided the foundation for the idea of democracy may be more irrelevant than ever before, yet, the claims to the autonomy and centrality of the individual are more inflated than ever before, and the rhetoric of the *service society*, in which all public and private institutions are portrayed as service providers governed exclusively by the needs of their clients, customers or user groups, continuously reinforces these claims. In democratic theory, this simultaneity of the decentralisation of the individual and the disintegration of the identical subject, on the one side, and the ongoing inflation and emancipation of the individual, on the other, has received surprisingly little attention, even though it presents a major challenge for the generation of legitimacy and for the sustainability of democracy more generally. Therefore, this challenge and the ways in which late-modern societies are confronting it will now, by way of conclusion, be explored in at least some more detail.

5. The paradox of late-modern democracy and performative legitimacy

The post-subjective strategies of legitimisation which have become prevalent in response to conditions of late-modern complexity cannot substitute for modernist subject-centred legitimacy for both normative and empirical reasons. Focusing on the more specific question whether output legitimacy can substitute for input legitimacy, even scholars who – in the name of enhanced policy performance – are making a strong case for insulating policy from political contestation and delegating it to non-majoritarian agencies have conceded that at best *some* policy decisions can be legitimated *by result*. Majone, for example, has distinguished between 'efficiency-oriented policies' (which aim for net gains for all parties involved) and 'redistributive policies' (which bring welfare improvements for some social groups at the expense of others) and suggested that only the former may 'be delegated to institutions independent of the political process', whilst the latter 'can be legitimated only by majoritarian means' (Majone 1998: 28). In a similar vein, Scharpf has argued that 'the reach of exclusively output-oriented arguments [of legitimisation] is restricted to political solutions that fulfil the Pareto-criterion', whereas 'the legitimisation of imposed violations of interests needs to be based, first and foremost, on input-oriented arguments' (Scharpf 2004: 16). But, firstly, the distinction between efficiency-oriented and redistributive policies is difficult to uphold.[31] Secondly, in empirical practice the delegation of policy decisions to non-democratic actors and non-majoritarian processes goes well beyond decisions which are supposedly Pareto-efficient. Thirdly, in conditions of late-modern complexity and liquidity the supposedly objective, depoliticised definition of policy goals and the public good is more impossible than ever, which renders contextualised, political legitimisation more indispensable than ever. And finally, at a more general level, the question whether output legitimacy can substitute for input legitimacy is only one dimension of the much more encompassing question whether late-modern post-subjective modes of legitimacy generation are an adequate replacement for modernist subject-centred legitimisation.

Indeed, more immediately relevant than these theoretical and normative concerns is the empirical point that late-modern citizens do not easily content themselves with the depoliticised and supposedly *responsible* government by technocratic elites. Whilst on the one hand the increase of complexity and

31 This is because distributive questions also arise if there are *net gains for all*, and because efficiency gains are, more often than not, achieved by means of temporarily externalising (invisibilising) certain costs, which at a later stage have to be accounted for (e.g. externalised environmental costs or costs occurring as overly deregulated financial systems or overly privatised welfare systems run into crisis).

uncertainty encourages – as a strategy of complexity reduction – the retreat into the private realm and the focus of attention on individualised life-management,[32] the process of modernisation has also radicalised the demand for self-determination and self-realisation. Also, the condition of complexity entails the proliferation of risks, unexpected side effects and policy crises. And in situations of crisis, in particular, generalised distrust in established elites swiftly translates into vociferous bottom-up demands for more direct citizen involvement, for grassroots empowerment and for effective democratic control. In this sense, late-modern societies can suitably be said to be witnessing 'an increasing subjectivization of legitimacy', i.e. notions of legitimacy 'are increasingly tied to what individuals themselves value and experience' (Sarcinelli 2005: 89). Thus, the marginalisation of the individual, the expulsion of participation, and the objectivation of legitimacy discussed above are going along with a centralisation of the individual, with radicalised demands for empowerment and with the subjectivization of legitimacy.

This paradoxical simultaneity of the *marginalisation* and the *centralisation* of the late-modern individual constitutes a profound dilemma: On the one hand, conditions of complexity and the liquefaction of the modernist subject imply that late-modern society's rising needs for legitimisation must – and can only be – met through post-subjective and output-oriented strategies entailing the expulsion of participation. On the other hand, the demand for legitimisation is only rising because of the ongoing inflation of claims to individual autonomy and self-realisation which implies the subjectivization of legitimacy and triggers calls for more citizen empowerment, for output legitimacy can never be a viable substitute for input legitimacy. As yet, this paradox of the parallel objectivation and subjectivization of legitimacy has remained an insufficiently investigated parameter in the ongoing transformation of democracy. But undoubtedly, what Crouch has described as 'encouraging the maximum level of minimal participation' (Crouch 2004: 112) plays a major role in its management. Citizen consultation exercises, opinion polls, focus groups, election campaigns, community engagement schemes or the mobilisation of *political consumers* may all be interpreted as efforts to achieve this maximum level of minimal participation. Indeed, contrary to the interpretations suggested by those diagnosing a neo-democratic reinvigoration of late-modern democracies, many of these much-celebrated non-traditional forms of political articulation and participation can be subsumed under this category.[33] Such exercises provide citizens with opportunities to

---

32 Bauman notes: '[T]he pursuit of elusive individuality leaves little time for anything else. [...] In the chase for individuality there is no moment of respite' (Bauman 2005: 23).

33 As noted above, there is a broad consensus that these non-traditional forms of political participation tend to be strongly individualistic, expressive, flexible and non-committing. Frank Furedi (2005: 28-48) has been particularly explicit in interpreting them as essentially depoliticised lifestyle statements and a form of post-democratic disengagement (for further

articulate their concerns, experience their identity, and gain a sense of political efficacy, yet they leave the actors and processes of depoliticised technocratic governance essentially undisturbed.[34]

Furthermore, political communication plays a major part in reconciling the inevitable expulsion of participation with the indispensable maintenance of modernist subject-centred legitimacy. It can bring politics closer to the people, relaying to them decisions which they have not been able to influence but which they will have to abide. It can present systemic imperatives and depoliticised policy making as reflecting the will of the people, i.e. it can portray as *representative* or at least *responsive* government what is, in fact, at best *responsible* government (Körösényi 2005). And it can help to discursively sustain the modernist notion of the autonomous identical subject which has lost its role as a relevant ideal of identity construction and as normative yardstick guiding the conduct of private life and social interaction, but which remains indispensable as the foundation of democracy and the ultimate point of reference for all democratic legitimacy.

In other words, the post-subjective modes of legitimacy generation are enhanced by a supplementary mode of legitimisation that compensates for the deficiencies of the former. In contrast to the modernist notion of *subject-centred* legitimacy and the post-subjective notion of *abstract* legitimacy this supplement may be referred to as *performative* legitimacy (Blühdorn 2007b: 324-25). It plays an essential part in managing the paradox of the parallel objectivation and subjectivization of legitimacy. It reconnects post-subjective legitimacy to the notion of the autonomous subject. In all three dimensions of legitimacy it regrounds abstract legitimacy in the modernist notion of the autonomous subject:

1. In the *input dimension* post-subjective legitimacy rests on scientific objectivity and expert knowledge. Yet, its detachment from the modernist subject is counterbalanced by the encouragement of maximum levels of minimal participation (in the sense outlined above) which caters for the

discussion see also Blühdorn 2006a, 2007a). As yet this analytical avenue remains underexplored, although in the particular field of *political consumerism* – widely regarded as one of the most powerful new forms of political articulation and participation – a critical literature is evolving.

34 Democratic theory needs to take care that it does not exhaust itself in exposing and rejecting these forms of 'minimal participation' as fake and as *symbolic politics* arranged by self-interested elites (Blühdorn 2007b, d). The primary objective must be to explore what functions they may fulfil and to what extent they may reflect the specific characteristics and needs of the late-modern condition (Blühdorn 2006a). This exploration has nothing to do with normatively approving or providing a political justification for particular practices, but it is a matter of providing an appropriate conceptualisation and explanation of the specifically late-modern appearance of democracy.

democratic norm that the political process ought to proceed from the articulated will of self-governing *demos*.
2. In the *procedural dimension* abstract legitimacy derives from formalised rationality and codified rules designed to eradicate any scope for subjective judgement. But it is reconnected to the autonomous subject via the notions of transparency and accountability which emphasise the democratic sovereign's power of scrutiny.
3. In the *output dimension* abstract legitimacy is based on the effectiveness with which systemic necessities are executed and on the formal efficiency of the related processes. But the connection to the modernist subject is re-established by insisting that policy makers and public institutions are strictly oriented towards customer needs and firmly dedicated to community service.

Very importantly, however, this supplementary mode of legitimisation only *performs* (simulates) the reconnection to the (deceased) modernist subject – and thus, ultimately, the existence of the autonomous subject itself. In the input dimension, the maximised forms of minimal participation can neither be read as the articulation of identical subjects, nor synthesised into the general will of a sovereign *demos*. In the procedural dimension transparency and accountability can never be a functional equivalent to the democratic bottom-up process, not least because in conditions of late-modern complexity it remains entirely unclear the implementation of what criteria such post-hoc scrutiny is supposed to guarantee. And in the output dimension, the notions of the autonomous customer and the late-modern consumer-citizen are categorically different from the autonomous subject that was at the centre of modern democracy. Therefore, abstract legitimacy which has emancipated itself from the autonomous subject is only seemingly reconnected to this modernist category. In all three dimensions, performative legitimacy is based on narratives which only discursively resurrect and cultivate the modernist subject without aiming to reinstate it as a relevant norm of identity construction or social interaction. It is for this reason that the supplementary mode of legitimisation is adequately conceptualised as *performative* legitimacy.

Further developing what has been said so far about complexity and the transformation of democracy, the late-modern reconfiguration of legitimacy can thus be conceptualised not simply as a shift from subject-centred to post-subjective (abstract) modes of legitimisation, but a distinctive feature of late-modern democracy is the interplay of abstract legitimacy and performative legitimacy. Figure 1.3 illustrates the complementary relationship between the two components and contrasts the late-modern mode of legitimisation with its modernist subject-centred counterpart.

Figure 1.3: Subject-centred, abstract and performative legitimacy

	Conditions of traditional Modernity *subject-centred legitimacy*	**Conditions of late-modern Complexity** *abstract legitimacy*	+	*performative legitimacy*
input dimension	autonomy, equality, justice, inclusion	scientific objectivity, expert knowledge	+	maximum level of minimal participation
procedural dimension	participation, representation deliberation, aggregation	formalised procedures, codified rules	+	transparency, accountability
output dimension	individual and collective utility	system-oriented effectiveness, formal efficiency	+	customer orientation, community service

Performative legitimacy resolves the late-modern dilemma that democratic legitimacy which, as a matter of principle, can only be based upon, and rooted in, the modernist notion of the individual, can after the liquefaction of the identical subject, nevertheless, only be generated in post-subjective modes. It is the solution for the paradoxical attempt to satisfy the rising demand for legitimisation – which is rising only because the ongoing process of modernisation continues to nurture and expand the individual's claim to self-determination and centrality – through the marginalisation of the individual and the objectivation of legitimacy. Performative legitimacy is the remedy for the problematic simultaneity of the objectivation and subjectivization of legitimacy and a constitutive element of the late-modern *politics of simulation* (Blühdorn 2002; 2004b; 2006b; 2007b, d). And the more political reality is reshaped by non-negotiable systemic necessities, by depoliticised and/or transnational institutions which are insulated from democratic processes and, in particular, by the ongoing liquefaction – and perhaps eventually liquidation – of the modernist notion of the autonomous and identical subject, the more does the sustainability of democracy become dependent on the performative regeneration of this vitally important resource.

Just as eco-political analyses of late-modern society continue to be shaped – and distorted – by the (of course commendable) ecological commitments of eco-political theorists, democratic theory, too, has so far remained caught up in normative commitments which from a political point of view are of course most appreciated, but which a descriptive theory of late-modern democracy needs to put aside so as to become able to provide conceptualisations and explanations of the ongoing transformation of democracy that can adequately account for the anti-, non- and post-democratic tendencies which are characteristic of the late-modern condition of complexity. In order to get a grip on the mounting evidence that the process of modernisation may have consumed the very foundations of democracy, and in order to understand how, at least for the time being, late-modern societies nevertheless seem to be able sustain the unsustainable, democratic theory may itself have to undergo a post-democratic turn.

References

Albrow, M. (1998): *Abschied vom Nationalstaat*, Frankfurt: Suhrkamp.
Anderson, J. (2002): *Transnational Democracy. Political Spaces and Border Crossings*, London: Routledge.
Bauman, Z. (1998): *In Search of Politics*, Cambridge: Polity.
Bauman, Z. (2000): *Liquid Modernity*, Cambridge: Polity.
Bauman, Z. (2001): *The Individualized Society*, Cambridge: Polity.
Bauman, Z. (2005): *Liquid Life*, Cambridge: Polity.
Bauman, Z. (2007): *Liquid Times*, Cambridge: Polity.
Beck, U. (1997): *The Reinvention of Politics. Rethinking Modernity in the Global Social Order*, Cambridge: Polity.
Beck, U. (1998): *Politik der Globalisierung*, Frankfurt: Suhrkamp.
Beck, U. (2006): *The Cosmopolitan Vision*, Cambridge: Polity.
Beck, U./Giddens, A./Lash, S. (1994): *Reflexive Modernization. Politics, Tradition and Aesthetics in the Modern Social Order*, Cambridge: Polity.
Beck, U./Grande, E. (2007): *Cosmopolitan Europe*, Cambridge: Polity.
Bell, D. (1976): *The Cultural Contradictions of Capitalism*, New York: Basic Books.
Benz, A. (1998): 'Postparlamentarische Demokratie? Demokratische Legitimation im Kooperativen Staat', in: Greven, Th.M. (ed.) *Demokratie – Eine Kultur des Westens?*, Opladen: Leske + Budrich, pp. 201-22.
Blühdorn, I. (2002): 'Unsustainability as a Frame of Mind – And How We Disguise It. The Silent Counter Revolution and the Politics of Simulation', in: *The Trumpeter* 18/1, pp. 59-69.
Blühdorn, I. (2004a): 'Future Fitness and Reform Gridlock: Towards Social Inequality and Post-Democratic Politics', in: *Debatte* 12/1, pp. 114-36.
Blühdorn, I. (2004b): 'Post-Ecologism and the Politics of Simulation', in: Wissenburg, M./Levy, Y. (eds) *Liberal Democracy and the Environment*, London: Routledge, pp. 35-47.
Blühdorn, I. (2006a): 'Self-Experience in the Theme Park of Radical Action? Social Movements and Political Articulation in the Late-modern Condition', in: *European Journal of Social Theory* 9/1, pp. 23-42.
Blühdorn, I. (2006b): 'Billig will Ich. Post-demokratische Wende und simulative Demokratie', in: *Forschungsjournal Neue Soziale Bewegungen* 19/4, pp. 72-83.
Blühdorn, I. (2007a): 'Self-description, Self-deception, Simulation. A Systems-theoretical Perspective on Contemporary Discourses of Radical Change', in: *Social Movement Studies* 6/1, pp. 1-20.
Blühdorn, I. (2007b): 'The Third Transformation of Democracy: On the Efficient Management of Late-modern Complexity', in: Blühdorn, I./Jun, U. (eds) *Eco-*

nomic Efficiency – Democratic Empowerment, Lanham, Maryland: Rowman & Littlefield (Lexington), pp. 299-331.

Blühdorn, I. (2007c): 'Democracy, Efficiency, Futurity: Contested Objectives of Societal Reform', in: Blühdorn, I./Jun, U. (eds) *Economic Efficiency – Democratic Empowerment*, Lanham, Maryland: Rowman & Littlefield (Lexington), pp. 69-98.

Blühdorn, I. (2007d): 'Sustaining the Unsustainable: Symbolic Politics and the Politics of Simulation', in: *Environmental Politics* 16/2, pp. 251-75.

Blühdorn, I. (2009): 'The Participatory Revolution: New Social Movements and Civil Society', in: Larres, K. (ed) *A Companion to Europe Since 1945,* London: Blackwell, pp. 407-431.

Böckenförde, E.-W. (1964/2004): 'Die Entstehung des Staates als Vorgang der Säkularisierung', in: Böckenförde, E.-W., *Kirche und christlicher Glaube in den Herausforderungen der Zeit*, Münster: Lit-Verlag, 2004, pp. 213-30.

Boggs, C. (2000): *The End of Politics: Corporate Power and the Decline of the Public Sphere*, New York: Guilford.

Braun, D./Galardi, F. (2005): *Delegation in Contemporary Democracies*, London: Routledge.

Brodocz, A./Llanque, M./Schaal, G.S. (eds) (2008): *Bedrohungen der Demokratie*, Wiesbaden: VS Verlag für Sozialwissenschaften.

Buchstein, H./Jörke, D. (2007): 'Redescribing Democracy', in: *Redescriptions* Vol. 11, pp. 178-97.

Buchstein, H./Nullmeier, F. (eds) (2006): Postdemokratie. Ein neuer Diskurs, in: special issue of *Forschungsjournal Neue Soziale Bewegungen 19/4.*

Burnham, P. (2001): 'New Labour and the Politics of Depoliticisation', in: *British Journal of Politics & International Relations* 3/2, pp. 127-49.

Cain, B./Dalton, R./Scarrow, S. (2003): *Democracy Transformed? Expanding Political Opportunities in Advanced Industrial Democracies*, Oxford: Oxford University Press.

Chesters, G./Welsh, I. (2006): *Complexity and Social Movements. Multitudes at the Edge of Chaos*, London/New York: Routledge.

Chryssochoou, D. (2004): 'EU Democracy and the Democratic Deficit', in: Cini, M. (ed.) *European Union Politics*, Oxford: Oxford University Press, pp. 365-82.

Crenson, M./Ginsberg, B. (2002): *Downsizing Democracy: How America sidelined its Citizens and Privatized its Public*, Baltimore: Johns Hopkins University Press.

Crouch, C. (2004): *Post-Democracy*, Cambridge: Polity.

Crozier, M.J./Huntington, S.P./Watanuki, J. (1975): *The Crisis of Democracy: Report on the Governability of Democracies to the Trilateral Commission*, New York: New York University Press.

Czada, R./Lütz, S./Mette, S. (2003): *Regulative Politik. Zähmungen von Markt und Technik*, Opladen: Leske + Budrich.

Dahl, R. (1994): 'A Democratic Dilemma: System Effectiveness versus Citizen Participation', *Political Science Quarterly* 109/1, pp. 23-34.

Dalton, R.J. (2004): *Democratic Challenges – Democratic Choices. The Erosion of Political Support in Advanced Industrial Democracies*, Oxford: Oxford University Press.

Dalton, R.J. (2008): 'Citizenship Norms and the Expansion of Political Participation', in: *Political Studies* 56/1, pp. 76-98.

Dalton, R.J./Klingemann, H.-D. (2007): 'Citizens and Political Behaviour', in: Dalton, R.J./Klingemann, H.-D. *The Oxford Handbook of Political Behaviour*, Oxford: Oxford University Press, pp. 3-26.

Dryzek, J. (2000): *Deliberative Democracy and Beyond*, Oxford: Oxford University Press.

Estlund, D. (2008): *Democratic Authority. A Philosophical Framework*, Princeton, NJ: Princeton University Press.

Fischer, K. (2006): 'Die jüngste Versuchung der Demokratie. Postdemokratie und Politik-Netzwerke', in: *Forschungsjournal Neue Soziale Bewegungen* 19/4, pp. 47-57.

Flinders, M./Buller, J. (2006): 'Depoliticisation: Principles, Tactics and Tools', in: *British Politics* 1/3, pp. 1-26.

Fuchs, D. (1998): 'Kriterien demokratischer Performanz in Liberal Demokratien', in: Greven, M. Th. (ed.) *Demokratie – eine Kultur des Westens?*, Opladen: Leske + Budrich, pp. 152-79.

Fuchs, D./Roller, E. (2008): 'Die Konzeptualisierung der Qualität von Demokratie. Eine Kritische Diskussion aktueller Ansätze', in: Brodocz et al. *Bedrohungen der Demokratie*, Wiesbaden: VS Verlag für Sozialwissenschaften, pp. 77-96.

Fung, A./Wright, E.O. (eds) (2003): *Deepening Democracy*, London: Verso.

Furedi, F. (2005): *The Politics of Fear. Beyond Left and Right*, London: Continuum.

Follesdal, A./Hix, S. (2006): 'Why there is a Democratic Deficit in the EU: A Response to Majone and Moravcsik', in: *Journal of Common Market Studies* 44/3, pp. 533-62.

Giddens, A. (1998): *The Third Way. The Renewal of Social Democracy*, Cambridge: Polity.

Greven, Th. W. (ed.) (1998): *Demokratie – eine Kultur des Westens?*, Opladen: Leske + Budrich.

Gutmann, A./Thompson, D. (2004): *Why Deliberative Democracy?*, Princeton, NJ: Princeton University Press.

Held, D. (1995): *Democracy and the Global Order*, Cambridge: Polity.

Held, D. (2004): *Global Covenant: The Social Democratic Alternative to the Washington Consensus*, Cambridge: Polity.

Hennis, W./Kielmansegg, P.G./Matz, U. (eds) (1977, 1979): *Regierbarkeit. Studien zu ihrer Problematisierung*, 2 vols., Stuttgart: Cotta.

Honneth, A. (ed.) (2002): *Befreiung aus der Mündigkeit. Paradoxien des gegenwärtigen Kapitalismus*, Frankfurt: Campus.

Inglehart, R. (1977): *The Silent Revolution: Changing Values and Political Styles Among Western Publics*, Princeton NJ: Princeton University Press.

Inglehart, R. (1997): *Modernization and Postmodernization*, Princeton NJ: Princeton University Press.

Inglehart, R./Welzel, Ch. (2005): *Modernization, Cultural Change, and Democracy. The Human Development Sequence*, Cambridge: Cambridge University Press.

Jörke, D. (2005): 'Auf dem Weg zur Postdemokratie', in: *Leviathan* 33/4, pp.482-91.

Jörke, Dirk (2007): 'I prefer not to vote – Warum es für immer mehr Bürger gar nicht so dumm ist, nicht zur Wahl zu gehen', in: Brie, M. (ed.) *Schöne neue Demokratie. Elemente totaler Herrschaft*, Berlin: Dietz, pp. 76-87.

Kant, I. (1991): *Political Writings* (ed. by Reiss, H.), Cambridge: Cambridge University Press.

Katz, R. (2001): 'Models of Democracy: Elite Attitudes and the Democratic Deficit in the European Union', in: *European Union Politics* 2/1, pp. 53-79.

Kettell, S. (2008): 'Does Depoliticisation Work? Evidence from Britain's Membership of the Exchange Rate Mechanism, 1990-92', in: *British Journal of Politics and International Relations* 10/4, pp. 630-48.

King, A. (1975): 'Overload: Problems of governing in the 1970s', in: *Political Studies* 71/2, pp. 167-76.

Körösényi, A. (2005): 'Political Representation in Leader Democracy.' *Government & Opposition* 40/3, pp. 358-378.

Laclau, E./Mouffe, C. (1985): *Hegemony and Socialist Strategy: Towards a Radical Democratic Politics*, London: Verso.

Leibfried, S./Zürn, M. (eds) (2006): *Tranformationen des Staates?*, Frankfurt: Suhrkamp.

Lijphart, A. (1999): *Patterns of Democracy: Government Forms and Performance in Thirty-Six Countries*, New Haven, CT: Yale University Press.

Luhmann, N. (1995): *Social Systems*, Stanford: Stanford University Press.

Luhmann, N. (2000): *Die Politik der Gesellschaft*, Frankfurt: Suhrkamp.

Lyotard, J. F. (1984): *The Postmodern Condition*, Manchester: Manchester University Press.

Macedo, S. et al. (2005): *Democracy at Risk: How Political Choices Undermine Citizen Participation, and What We Can Do About It*, Washington DC: Brookings Institution Press.

Majone, G. (1996): *Regulating Europe*, London/New York: Routledge.

Majone, G. (1998): 'Europe's Democratic Deficit: A Question of Standards', in: *European Law Journal* 4/1, pp. 5-28.

Majone, G. (1999): 'The Regulatory State and Its Legitimacy Problems', in: *West European Politics* 22/l, pp. 1-24.

Marcussen, M./Torfing, J. (eds) (2006): *Democratic Network Governance in Europe*, Basingstoke: Palgrave.

Mouffe, C. (1993): *The Return of the Political*, London: Verso.

Moravcsik, A. (1998): 'Europe's Democratic Deficit', in: *European Law Journal* 4/4, pp. 336-63.

Moravcsik, A. (2002): 'In Defense of the Democratic Deficit: Reassessing Legitimacy in the European Union', in: *Journal of Common Market Studies* 40/4, pp. 603-24.

Moravcsik, A. (2004): 'Is there a Democratic Deficit in World Politics? A Framework for Analysis', in: *Government and Opposition* 39/2, pp. 336-63.

Norris, P. (ed.) (1999): *Critical Citizens: Global Support for Democratic Government*, Oxford: Oxford University Press.

Norris, P. (2002): *Democratic Phoenix: Reinventing Political Activism*, Cambridge: Cambridge University Press.

Okun, A. (1975): *Equality and Efficiency: The Big Trade-Off*, Brookings Institution.

Parkinson, J. (2003): 'Legitimacy Problems in Deliberative Democracy', in: *Political Studies* 51/1, pp. 180-96.

Parkinson, J. (2004): 'Why Deliberate? The Encounter Between Deliberation and New Public Managers', in: *Public Administration* 82/4, pp. 377-95.

Pattie, Ch./Seyd, P./Whiteley, P. (2004): *Citizenship in Britain. Values, Participation and Democracy*, Cambridge: Cambridge University Press.

Putnam, R. (2000): *Bowling Alone. The Collapse and Renewal of American Community*, New York: Simon & Schuster.

Rancière, J. (1997): 'Demokratie und Postdemokratie', in: Badiou, A./Rancière, J./Rado, R./Sumic, J. (eds) *Politik der Wahrheit*, Vienna: Turia + Kant, pp. 94-122.

Rhodes, R. (1997): *Understanding Governance: Policy Networks, Governance, Reflexivity and Accountability*, Buckingham: Open University Press.

Roller, Edeltraud (2005): *The Performance of Democracies. Political Institutions and Public Policy*, Oxford/New York: Oxford University Press.

Rosenau, J./Czempiel, E.-O. (eds) (1992): *Governance without Government: Order and Change in World Politics*, Cambridge: Cambridge University Press.

Sarcinelli, Ulrich (2005): *Politische Kommunikation in Deutschland. Zur Politikvermittlung im demokratischen System*, Wiesbaden: VS Verlag.

Scharpf, F. W. (1998a): 'Demokratische Politik in der internationalisierten Ökonomie', in: Greven, M. Th. (ed.) *Demokratie – Eine Kultur des Westens?*, Opladen: Leske + Budrich, pp. 81-103.

Scharpf, F. W. (1998b): 'Interdependence and Democratic Legitimation' *MPIfG Working Paper* 98/2, September 1998.

Scharpf, F. W. (1999): *Governing in Europe: Effective and Democratic?* Oxford: Oxford University Press.

Scharpf, F. W. (2003): 'Problem-Solving Effectiveness and Democratic Accountability in the EU', *MPIfG Working Paper* 03/1, February 2003.

Scharpf, F. W. (2004): 'Legitimationskonzepte jenseits des Nationalstaats', *MPIfG Working Paper* 04/6, November 2004.

Schneider, S./Nullmeier, F./Lhotta, R./Krell-Laluhová, Z./Hurrelman, A. (2006): 'Legitimationskrise nationalstaatlicher Demokratien?', in: Leibfried, S./Zürn, M. (eds) *Tranformationen des Staates?*, Frankfurt: Suhrkamp, pp. 197-229.

Smith, G. (2003): *Deliberative Democracy and the Environment*, London: Routledge.

Sørensen, E./Torfing, J. (eds) (2008): *Theories of Democratic Network Governance*, Basingstoke: Palgrave.

Stoker, Gerry (2006): *Why Politics Matters. Making Democracy Work*, Basingstoke: Palgrave.

Strøm, K./Müller, W./Bergman, T. (eds) (2003): *Delegation and Accountability in Parliamentary Democracies*, Oxford/New York: Oxford University Press.

Thatcher, M./Stone Sweet, A. (2002): 'Theory and Practice of Delegation to Non-Majoritarian Institutions', in: *West European Politics* 25/1, pp. 1-22.

Urry, J. (2003): *Global Complexity*, Cambridge: Polity.

Zolo, D. (1992): *Complexity and Democracy: A Realist Approach*, Cambridge: Polity.

Zürn, M. (1998): *Regieren jenseits des Nationalstaates*, Frankfurt: Suhrkamp.

Zürn, M. (2003): 'Global Governance in der Legitimationskrise', in: Offe, C. (ed.) *Demokratisierung der Demokratie. Diagnosen und Reformvorschläge*, Frankfurt: Campus, pp. 232-56.

Zürn, M. (2004): 'Global Governance and Legitimacy Problems', in: *Government and Opposition* 39/2, pp. 260-87.

Zweifel, T. (2002): 'Who is Without Sin Cast the First Stone: The EU's Democratic Deficit', in: *Journal of European Public Policy* 9/5, pp. 812-40.

Chapter 2
Efficiency and Democracy: Reconstructing the Foundations of a Troubled Relationship

Joachim Blatter

1. Introduction

Advanced modern societies are widely seen to be confronted with fundamental difficulties when it comes to reconciling the two goals of *efficiency* and *democratic self-determination*. As Blühdorn indicates in the previous chapter and has discussed in much more detail elsewhere (Blühdorn 2007a), democratic approaches and principles are in many contexts not particularly efficient, and efficient approaches are oftentimes not particularly democratic. Hence, the two goals of democracy and efficiency may appear to be incompatible with each other, and there seems to be a trade-off between them. Yet, as Blühdorn also points out, both efficiency and democracy have been conceptualised in the literature in many different ways, and hence the claim that the two goals are mutually exclusive is generalising and simplistic. A more nuanced understanding of the democracy-efficiency relationship can, arguably, be achieved if the term efficiency is not understood, following a functionalist logic, as *system* efficiency, but related to core ideas in economic theory on how to create socio-economic welfare. In the present chapter, I will connect the notion of efficiency to the imperatives of socio-economic welfare production, not least because this is in line with the main political debate about the alleged tension between economic imperatives and democratic self-determination.

My main argument is that if we understand democracy in ways which are based on similar conceptual perspectives and ideological orientations that we discover in welfare theory, the main trade-offs are not between democracy and efficiency, per se, but between and within the different perspectives on efficiency and democracy.

In order to systematize different perspectives on efficiency and democracy I start with the assumption that both, the *third transformation of democracy* (Dahl 1989, 1994; Blühdorn 2007b) and the *third industrial revolution* are characterized by what has been called a *second* or *reflexive modernization*. As discussed in the previous chapter, reflexive modernization refers to a

second and much more radical process of disembedding social subjects (individuals, collectives) and objects (goods and meanings) from natural or traditional contexts. It undermines even those elements of society which represented the foundations of first or traditional modernization: especially the autonomous and authentic self and the territorially bounded and sovereign nation state (Beck et al. 2003).

Within welfare theory we can detect two understandings of welfare which represent typically modernist concepts. They will be briefly scrutinized under the headings of *use-value* and *exchange-value*. Furthermore, there are two concepts of welfare which reflect the socio-economic transformations and challenges of reflexive modernity. They can be captured by the notions of *change-value* and *sign-value*. Similarly, two traditionally modern perspectives of democratic self-determination (*input* and *output*) can be separated from two perspectives which focus on the fundamental contingencies of political systems in reflexive modernity: first, the definition and demarcation of the *demos*; and second, the acceptance of politics as problem-solver and identity provider. Both aspects can be expressed in terms of an *in/out* distinction.

The analysis will proceed as follows: First, I will scrutinize the four concepts of welfare. Next, I will lay out four perspectives on democracy. For every perspective on welfare and democracy I will highlight the core assumptions which guide these perspectives and also scrutinize the main ideological disputes. In the final section I will provide evidence for my main argument by showing how each one of the perspectives on welfare is conceptually related – and thus fully compatible with – one particular perspective on democracy.

2. Conceptions of and prescriptions for socio-economic welfare

How do we understand and measure social welfare? And what is necessary for a productive allocation of scarce resources to create and enhance social welfare? Over time, economic thought has produced quite different answers to these basic questions. In the following I will briefly scrutinize four distinct approaches. Two modernist conceptions will be presented under the headings of *use-value* and *exchange-value* since these notions capture very nicely the underlying understandings of socio-economic value on which modern welfare theories are grounded. In contrast, the two conceptions which are closely connected to the current *third industrial revolution* are labelled *change-value* and *sign-value*. In addition to sketching the meaning of each of these, the main ideological cleavage will be indicated for every approach.

Use-value

The concept of use-value is used in Marxist theory to express the assumption that there exists an objective or intrinsic value of a good. This enables it to satisfy a human need or want. Marxists employ the concept of use-value to criticize the destruction of the social nature of society through the commodification of goods. Early non-Marxist welfare theory did not begin with assuming the objective value of products. Instead it focused upon the belief in objective human needs and argued that the satisfaction of these needs could be measured in absolute terms. From such a perspective there is an objective welfare function for a society. A logical consequence is that the overall welfare of a society can be enhanced by the redistribution of goods to those who need it most (Cooper and Rappoport 1984).

Another strand of early welfare theory focused more on the production or supply side of the economic process and generated a set of standard prescriptions for the intervention of a regulatory state. State regulation was necessary to correct market failures because negative and positive externalities would not lead the market to a socially optimal production level or structure (Musgrave 1999; Besley and Coate 1999: 1). A necessary condition for market correcting activities geared towards enhancing the overall welfare of a society is state control over the socio-economic system. A strong central state with enough information and power to control not only the socio-economic system within its boundaries, but also the flows across boundaries was seen as a necessary precondition to effectively enhance social welfare (Scharpf 1999: 27, 35-6).

The central ideological cleavage within this objectivist and functionalist perspective on welfare is whether the state should only reduce (or internalise) externalities in order to make the most effective use of resources in the production process (the ordo-liberal position), or whether the state should also redistribute income in order to effectively satisfy an objective demand (the socialist position). In both cases, the adequate concept to evaluate the quality of a policy or a system is its *effectiveness* (goal-attainment).

Exchange-value

The notion of exchange-value points to the dominant perceptions of values in modern market societies in which a monetary price, reflecting the relationship between supply and demand, is used to express the value of a good. It is not objective needs but subjective preferences that determine the demand for a good. The supply is not reflecting the absolute costs of producing the good, but is based upon the *marginal* calculations of producers (marginal revenue =

marginal costs). In marginal analysis the value of goods is no longer based upon an absolute measure but on an input/output ratio. *Efficiency* rather than effectiveness becomes the corresponding criterion for evaluation.

The central precondition to stimulating efficient provision of goods and services is securing consumer choice through competition on the supply side. Accordingly, the central mechanisms to enhance social welfare are market mechanisms like competition and contracting, which secure an optimal coupling of supply and demand in respect to private and public goods and services. Public institutions should not only fight private cartels but the public sector itself should be differentiated into a polycentric and competitive system. Territorial differentiation (decentralization) allows for *voting with the feet*, while functional differentiation between service production and service provision (out-sourcing) allows collective consumption units like municipalities to choose among different service providers (e.g. Oakerson 1999).

The central ideological cleavage within the exchange-value or efficiency framework of welfare theory is whether competition and contracting really allows people to choose among a variety of goods and services (varying in respect to quality and price) according to their (different) preferences, or whether it primarily leads to reduced costs, and in consequence to reduced quality and reduced investments ('race to the bottom' thesis). The critics argue for policies which restrict the price-oriented competition and favour public investment in production factors (like knowledge of human resources) which increase exchange value. They prefer to enhance efficiency by focussing on higher quality rather than on reduced costs.

Change-value

At the end of the 1990s *innovation* was becoming one of the most central buzz-words in public discourses. This did not happen by accident but reflects the transformational stage of the economy in the contexts of the *third industrial revolution* with enlarged continental and global markets. Within such a transformational period *newness* and *change* has attained value in itself. They indicate the ability of a system (private companies or public entities like nation states or regions) to be at the forefront of the transformation process and to adapt to new challenges. Since many sectors of the new economy are characterized by the logic of *the winner takes it all*, being able to move first is key to securing the competitive advantage.

The new logic of value creation and welfare production can best be captured by the term *change-value*. In the information economy 'the main source of productivity is the capacity to generate and process *new* information' (Castells 1989: 351; emphasis added). As a result of these new challenges we are witnessing a renewed interest in the Austrian School of economic thought, where *entrepreneurship* and the ability to create *new combinations*, together with *creative destruction* (Schumpeter) are becoming more important than equilibrium-oriented neo-classical economic models (Castells 1996).

Welfare enhancement under the conditions of change-value is characterized by new contingencies. New technologies and markets open up new frontiers for production and supply, on the one hand, and for consumption and demand, on the other. For better or worse, it is not the past or current performance of a company or country that determines the calculations and evaluations but the *prospects* and expectations for the future. Not only a strong orientation towards the future (entailing freedom from legacy) but also openness for new forms of organization are seen as prerequisites for innovative businesses and communities.

As a consequence, (un-)learning and risk-taking are important preconditions for enhancing change-value and welfare. Related policy strategies focus on these two preconditions but with quite different priorities. One main dispute is among those who advocate strengthening *social capital*, which allows cooperation and learning on the basis of strong ties and trust. This strategy is embedded in local milieus. In contrast, others argue for the nurturing of *creative capital*. Creative capital is a contrasting strategy because it is based on loose ties, tolerance and global networks (Castells 1996: 36; Florida 2002; Kujath 2005; Straubhaar and Geyer 2005).

Sign-value

The *third industrial revolution* is commonly conceptualised as a transformation from an industry-based to an information-based economy. Within the information-based economy communication and knowledge are taking centre stage in the processes of value creation. The information, communication and advertising industries are already playing major roles in the economies of western countries (Castells 1996). In a socio-economic environment which is characterized by the centrality of communication and an overflow of information, specific signs such as trade-marks or brands are serving as devices for orientation in the market place and beyond.

In critical theory the fusion of culture and capitalism has been primarily interpreted as commodification. It is perceived as the subordination of culture under the logic of capital accumulation. The capital system uses advertising and marketing to manipulate the consciousness of the individual and create a consumer society. In a consumer society, goods do not function anymore as satisfiers of needs and (authentic) wants, but primarily as communicators of meanings. Individuals gain fundamental modes of gratification by consumption. Hence, marketers and advertisers generate systems of meanings, prestige, and identity by attributing certain lifestyles, symbolic values and pleasures to their goods. These meanings are not very strongly connected to the actual goods but much more to the brand or trade-mark of the producer. In semiotic terms this means that value is attached to the signifier (the sign) and not to the signified (the referent, the actual good). This *sign-value* is taking centre stage not only in determining the value of goods but also in influencing the (stock market) valuation of companies.

Lash and Urry (1994) have pointed to the fact that it is not only the cognitive meaning of a sign which is important, but even more its aesthetic dimension. More recently, the emotional aspect of identity creation and activation has received more attention. The body itself has taken centre stage in the attempts to receive attention, to attract others, and to serve as a sign. The notion of a consumer society is therefore not really capturing the central element of a society based on sign-values since it is no longer the process of consuming goods which is the paradigmatic activity. Instead, sign-values are closely connected to the notion of an experience society (*Erlebnisgesellschaft*). This is a society in which individuals are searching for opportunities to express themselves, and where the interactive processes of image creation and social recognition are taking centre stage (Schulze 1992; also compare Blühdorn's discussion of *liquid identity* in the previous chapter). In this context the individual is neither an autonomous Subject nor an externally determined Object, but rather someone who is more or less able to create a recognised image or identity by combining individual strength and current cultural trends.

This leads to two conclusions which go beyond the commodification thesis of traditional critical theory: Sign-values are truly social (cultural/communicative) constructions which cannot be controlled by one (type of) actor. Even large multinational companies cannot rely upon their tremendous marketing machinery to sell their branded products. They use trend-scouts and differentiated strategies to adapt to specific cultural environments and new cultural trends. Furthermore, not only companies need to attach interesting meanings and attractive images to their goods but also individual, collective and corporate actors must invest much more in *face-work* (Goffman) and image creation. The image of city-regions and nations are important assets in the global competition for capital investment and for the creative class (Florida 2002). Not only companies have renamed themselves in order to sound attractive in many languages and to take front places in stock-market listings, but also regions have realized the importance of sign-values. In Germany this has led, for example, to the renaming of the region formerly known as *Mittlerer Neckar* into *Region Stuttgart*. It has also triggered a fierce race to get officially recognized as a *European metropolitan region*.

To sum up, new contingencies which arise from the decoupling of signs (signifiers) and material goods (signified) in late-modern times force all social actors – including political communities – to invest in *performative* actions and to present an image which is able to attract attention from others and to which positive meanings or feelings are attributed. Within this framework public policy can concentrate on the supply side or on the demand side of the economy. In the first case, it focuses on attracting capital investment and creative people mainly through external marketing. In the second case, it tries to activate internal consumption by stimulating a positive public mood or atmosphere through symbolic politics and media campaigns.

The different perspectives on welfare production are summarised in Figure 2.1. In the following section I will demonstrate that understandings of democracy can be differentiated in a manner similar to the distinction of these approaches to socio-economic values and welfare.

Figure 2.1: Perspectives on welfare production

	First Modernity		**Reflexive Modernity**	
Value	Use-Value	Exchange-Value	Change-Value	Sign-Value
Criterion for Evaluation	Effectiveness (Goal-Attainment)	Efficiency (Input-Output-Ratio)	Creativity (Innovation)	Attractiveness (Image-Attribution)
Preconditions	Comprehensive Control	Competitive Contracting	New Combinations	Cultural Constructions
Ideological Cleavages	Regulation *versus* Redistribution	Low Cost *versus* High Quality	Trust *versus* Tolerance	Attract Investors *versus* Activate Inhabitants

3. Concepts of and prescriptions for democracy

Probably the most widely cited definition of democracy is Abraham Lincoln's *government of the people, by the people, and for the people* which he formulated in his Gettysburg address in 1863. It is therefore amazing that this threefold definition has not been used more profoundly as a basis for democratic theory. Those analysts who have used this definition as a starting point for reasoning about democracy have usually focused on only two of its elements, paying very little attention to the first and arguably most fundamental element. One typical example is Fritz Scharpf's distinction between output-oriented legitimisation and input-oriented legitimisation which has been widely used in recent years. By developing this distinction he refers explicitly to Abraham Lincoln's threefold characterization of democracy (Scharpf

1998: 85). Scharpf claims that within national democracies the first element – the *nation* as a pre-constitutional political community – can be regarded as given, so that democratic theory can concentrate on the other two elements (Scharpf 1998: 85). Whereas this might have been correct at that time when he first suggested this distinction (Scharpf 1970), thirty years later narrowing down the debate to two dimensions is certainly no longer adequate.

As indicated in the previous chapter, we are currently witnessing three major transformations which distinguish contemporary societies from those at the height of traditional or first modernity. This poses challenges for democratic self-determination and brings about a situation where neither *input* nor *output* are the central category. Instead, the more fundamental questions of *being in* and *being out* are, arguably, taking centre stage in the search for democratic legitimacy:

First, the end of the Westphalian system of sovereign nation states is characterized by the erosion of a clear-cut locus of political decision-making and governance. Polycentric political systems emerge through the decentralization and unbundling of the state (e.g. regionalization, reliance on independent agencies, quangos; Pollitt and Talbot 2004; Hooghe and Marks 2003; Maggetti in this volume). The monopoly of the state to produce and provide public goods is also evaporating. The boundary between the public and the private is being redrawn and perforated at the same time. At the beginning of the 21st Century we are witnessing a trend towards privatization and deregulation of what has been seen as public service during the 20th Century. This trend is reversing the expansion of the public sector which was characteristic at the turn of the 20th Century. Additionally, and alternatively, public-private-partnerships, calls for *co-production* and the rise of the so-called Third Sector are blurring the boundary between the public and the private sector. At the same time, the boundaries between the main political units of traditional modernity, i.e. the nation states, are getting perforated by international regimes and multi-level systems allowing for more transnational interaction. In sum, the nation state is losing its natural monopoly, and its hierarchical position and structure as a problem-solver and primary identity provider. Instead, in a *polycentric system* of governance various and overlapping (public, private and mixed) institutions of governance compete more or less intensively for recognition, loyalty, compliance and contributions of individual, collective and corporate actors.

Second, it is not only the single locus of decision-making that is evaporating, but the link between the people and government(s) is becoming loftier. In the information society an electronic multi-media system has emerged as the most important transmitter between citizens and government(s). It is pushing more structured and organized channels of interest formation and transportation (parties, interest organizations and associations) to the sidelines and is transforming their structures and processes (e.g. Meyer 2002).

And third, the very basis and starting point of democratic self-determination, the people, is becoming contingent. Naturalness, stability and rather clear-cut and exclusive boundaries of the *demos*, which were taken for granted in the Westphalian container system of nation states, are eroding. Demographics and migration pose serious challenges for the integration, stabilisation and reproduction of social and political communities.

I will argue below that these changes have shifted the first element of Lincoln's definition of democracy, i.e. *government of the people*, into the centre of theoretical and practical controversies about democratic self-determination. Before I scrutinize the corresponding perspectives on democracy I will first briefly describe the core elements of the two traditionally modern perspectives on democracy.

Output (government for *the people)*

For a productive debate about the relationship between democracy and efficiency (understood as welfare enhancement) it is especially important to re-establish the conceptual distinction between an output-oriented concept of democratic self-determination and the concepts of value or welfare generation. In his search for sources of legitimacy for the European Union, Fritz Scharpf (1998, 1999) has mixed up these two aspects. In defining input- and output-oriented strategies for democratic legitimacy he is reinterpreting David Easton's systems theoretical approach about sources of support for political systems. Easton (1965, 1975) distinguished between social demands brought to the political system (input) and the ability of the political system to satisfy these demands (output). Furthermore, he distinguished between the specific support for a political system depending on short-term output and the diffuse support. Diffuse support refers to trust in the long-term capabilities of the system to produce satisfying output, and a fundamental belief in the legitimacy of the political system.

Scharpf, by contrast, does not only fuse output and legitimacy but he also narrows down the understanding of output to enhancing common welfare. '[T]he output perspective emphasizes government *for the people*. Political choices are legitimate if and because they effectively promote the common welfare of the constituency in question' (Scharpf 1999: 6). 'Government *for the people* derives legitimacy from its capacity to solve problems requiring collective solutions because they could not be solved through individual action, through market exchange or through voluntary cooperation in civil society' (Scharpf 1999: 11). Whereas in Easton's concept of output there is no specification of the social demands which should be satisfied by the output of the political system, Scharpf confines the necessary output of a political system to enhancing collective welfare. This not only forecloses other social demands on the political system (e.g. equality) but also accepts only one (a social-democratic/collectivist) approach within the output-framework on democracy. Before discussing the different ideological approaches within the output-framework, the basic element of a general output-oriented understanding of democracy should be restated: it is the capability of a political system to make sure that the will of the people is really fulfilled.

Within such a framework we can distinguish a collectivist and an individualist ideology. They start with quite different understandings of the will of the people and, accordingly, they propose different preconditions for fulfilling the will of the people. Collectivist approaches argue that in order to implement the common will of the people the political system must be able to control the socio-economic system. Ideally, this presupposes a sovereign and centrally integrated government which is able to control socio-economic processes within and beyond its borders. In complex and differentiated societies, where resources are dispersed among private and public collective actors, corporatism and policy networks have been necessary extensions to the central state. They enable better control of the socio-economic processes (Scharpf 1999: 13-21).

When he first introduced his output-oriented perspectives on democratic legitimacy, Fritz Scharpf recognized that quite different concepts of output-oriented theories of democracy exist (Scharpf 1970: 21f). Liberal theorists have argued for a system of checks and balances and for a compound republic exactly because they wanted to reduce the opportunities of the political system (the popular majority) to control society. This was to secure the autonomy or liberty of the individual or of minorities (e.g. Ostrom 1987). In addition constitutionalist approaches to democratic theory focus upon limiting politics in order to secure basic values and individual rights (the will of individual people) (Held 2006: 56-94).

The dualism between collectivist and individualist conceptualisations of democratic self-determination dominated the 19th and the beginning of the 20th Century and resulted in a sharp division between socialist and liberal countries after WWII. After the break-down of the communist bloc, the various compromises between the antagonistic ideologies which had been established in Western democracies came under threat. Social Democrats like Scharpf see the danger in the reduced steering capacity of national governments, and argue that a strengthening of governmental steering capacities (on various levels) is necessary to restore the legitimacy of democratic systems (Scharpf 1999).

Input (government by *the people)*

The ideas and concepts which dominated the public and theoretical discourse on democracy during the second half of the 20th Century within Western countries are all strongly input-oriented (Held 2006: 125-257). The input-oriented perspective on democracy is connected to Lincoln's notion of *government by the people* and focuses on the structures and processes that translate social demand into political decisions. 'Political choices are legitimate if and because they reflect the *will of the people* – that is, if they can be derived from the authentic preferences of community members' (Scharpf 1999: 6). The second transformation of democracy, according to Dahl, changed the dominant mode of transforming the will of the people into political decisions from direct forms to representative forms (Dahl 1989).

As with the output-perspective, the input-perspective does not include just one set of shared prescriptions for gaining democratic legitimacy. The dominant approach in thinking about inputs in representative parliamentarian democracies can be called an *aggregative* concept (Dryzek 2000). Within such an approach, authentic, exogenously determined, and rather stable individual preferences or clear-cut group interests are the sources from which a social demand is formed. The basic concern of this approach is how these preferences and interests should be taken into account in the political process. The advocates of this approach concentrate on formal procedures of interest aggregation and voting and agree on the prescription that competition between different parties, representatives and policy alternatives is crucial (Downs 1957; Dahl 1967).

A first alternative concept within the input-oriented perspective on democracy questioned the individualistic foundations of Anglo-Saxon concepts and revealed other modes of interest aggregation and decision-making. Since Arendt Lijphart's path-breaking study of the political system of the Netherlands (Lijphart 1975), the distinction between majoritarian government and consensus government has become the most influential typology for comparing modern democracies (Lijphart 1999). Whereas majoritarian government seems to adequately describe rather homogeneous societies and corresponds to liberal-universalistic philosophies, the features of consensus government emerged in societies where socio-cultural cleavages are more congruent and not cross-cutting. Furthermore, the principles of consensus government correspond to the philosophy of multi-culturalism.

In recent years, two further alternatives have come to question other assumptions of the formal aggregative model of representative democracy. First, proponents of *deliberative* or *discursive democracy* (Bohman and Rehg 1997; Dryzek 2000) do not assume that there are fixed preferences of individuals or groups. Instead, they postulate that perceptions (of their interests) of people and politicians are shaped by political processes and discourses.

They concentrate on the communicative processes of interest formation and transformation. Their main prescription is a communication system which is open for different voices, perspectives and arguments which in turn allow for individual reflection and learning. Second, advocates of *associative democracy* (Hirst 1994) and *participatory democracy* (Held 2006: 209-216) do not only question the starting points, but also the transmitters and targets of inputs into the process of democratic self-determination. They stress the role of voluntary associations. These are to act as both reflective transmitters of inputs into parliamentarian decision-making, as well as a means for the democratic self-governance of a civil society. In this way the spread of democratic mechanisms goes beyond the modern state organizations.

In sum, while aggregative concepts see the legitimacy of the political system enhanced if the input (a pre-existing demand) is taken into account in the political process, the second group focuses more on constitutive processes like the transformation of inputs into a collectively acceptable demand or on the democratization of institutions (which have formerly only been seen as transmitters of interests towards political loci of decision-making) in order to make them legitimate targets of political decision-making and bearers of democratic self-determination in itself.[1]

Whereas the latter concepts have questioned major cornerstones of modernist thinking about democratic self-determination (individualism and instrumental rationality), they have to be taken one step further in order to capture the fundamental challenges which current Western democracies face. It is not just the amount of political output or the nature of social input in processes of democratic self-determination (the policy dimension) that are challenging modern democracy. Rather the very bases of polities and politics are becoming contingent. This puts the very concepts of democratic self-determination and its institutions at the forefront of political controversies.

In/Out I (government of the people*)*

The first in/out-oriented perspective on democracy focuses on the increasingly salient issue of inclusion and exclusion. The central point of reference in Lincoln's definition of democracy, *the people* itself, or the *boundaries of the demos* take centre-stage in this perspective.

One of the most important aspects of the second transformation of democracy is the fact that the transformation from direct democracy towards

1 Proposals for a stronger role of direct or semi-direct democratic procedures (e.g. referenda and initiatives) are going beyond the representative parliamentarian character of modern democracies but they stay firmly within the input-oriented perspective. These (semi-)direct procedures are either believed to guarantee a more 'correct' aggregation of the will of the people or they are supposed to trigger a broader deliberation about political issues.

representative democracy has been accompanied by a – fiercely contested – expansion of the demos to include all adults who live within the territory of the nation state (Held 2006: 94). For a while, the struggles about the formal inclusion of people into the demos seemed to be settled and the controversies focused on how to reach a full and fair representation of the will of the included people in the decision-making process (the input-perspective). Currently, this is changing again because the *naturalness* of the people is being questioned again. The modern solutions to the boundary problem – the demos is conceptually equalised with the nation and political membership is provided to all adult humans on the territory of the nation state – no longer holds. Two challenges in particular should be given attention.

Migration is undermining the naturalness and the stability of individual membership in a political community (citizenship). In contrast to earlier migration flows, the processes of emigration and immigration are not characterised by a clear-cut transplantation from one place to another. Instead of individual assimilation into the existing community, the situation (especially in metropolitan areas) is characterised by growing trans-national communities with ties to their current host country/city and ties to the place they come from (Smith 2005). Especially the (non-)acceptance of dual citizenship is a fundamental issue within this perspective on democratic self-determination because it undermines the exclusivity and integrity of *a people* (Faist 2004). The empirical salience of this aspect has already become very obvious. In Germany, the mobilisation of Christian Democrats against a government proposal for dual citizenship led in 1999 to a power shift in the second chamber, the *Bundesrat*. This meant *de facto* the end of the red-green project because the room for manoeuvre available to the red-green coalition was drastically reduced (Hell 2005). In the Netherlands, quarrels about incorrect information provided in the naturalisation procedure of a famous immigrant politician, Aryaan Hirsi Ali, resulted in 2006 in the collapse of the governing coalition. In the United States, the issue of immigrant rights also led in the spring of 2006 to the largest demonstrations the country had witnessed in 30 years.

Demographic changes and imbalances in the generational structure of the population have led to new challenges regarding the 'reproduction' the people in many developed countries. The demographic changes are leading to new political cleavages between generations since older people more and more dominate the aggregative processes of political decision-making. Younger people, in particular, see this as a threat which endangers the opportunities of the political system to produce future-oriented policies. This in turn might reduce the reproduction of the population even more. As a response, we are witnessing political initiatives to expand citizen rights to young people and children (represented by their parents). In sum, also with regard to age the modern boundaries of the demos are no longer sacrosanct.

Two ideological approaches provide different solutions to the challenges which are accompanying the renewed contingency of the boundaries of the demos. A conservative approach would focus on rules and policies which secure the reproduction of the native people. Accordingly, controlling the inflow of foreigners in order to defend a coherent culture is an important means to provide a feeling of security and for social integration (Huntington 2004; Renshon 2004). Such a feeling of security in turn seems to be necessary to enhance the confidence of the people into the future which has a major influence on the birth rate. Progressives and liberals would not only balance the goal of reproduction of the people with individual rights (of migrants) but also accept and even advocate cultural transformation and differentiation. It is not cultural coherence, internal integration and security, but creative combinations (creolization) and connectivity (integration into the external world) that are seen as necessary means for a successful reproduction of the people (Turner 2000; Carens 2001; Benhabib 2004; Bauböck 2005).

*In/Out II (*government of *the people)*

The second in/output-oriented perspective on democracy puts a question mark on the most fundamental aspect of Lincoln's characterization of democracy as '*government of* the people'. Its assumptions – that there exists one single point of political decision-making and problem-solving as well as rather stable links between the people and the (single) government – are becoming contingent because of the transformations towards a polycentric system of governance and towards a mediatised society which have been scrutinized above.

The strong poly-centricity of the political system is taking competitive elements to a more fundamental level. It is no longer only the competition between politicians, parties and interest groups which secures the representation of particular interests at the (single) locus of decision-making. Instead various forms/organizations of governance are competing with each other for being an important locus of decision-making. And not only the various levels and functional segments of the political-administrative system have to fight for competences and recognition, but the political-administrative system as a whole is challenged (by other sub-systems such as the economic and cultural systems) in its role as problem-solver and identity provider. Many issues which during the 20th Century were accepted without question as public tasks are now up for debate again (especially network services like transportation and telecommunication but also issues as central as security). They are being handed over to private companies or technocratic regulatory agencies. This has been described as a process of depoliticisation (e.g. Boggs 2000; Burnham 2001; Buller and Flinders 2005; Blühdorn 2007b), but this kind of criticism can be traced back to the Frankfurt School (e.g. Marcuse 1964). If we take seriously the notion that 'politicisation is the realisation that established social norms, practices and relations are contingent rather than sacrosanct' (Blühdorn 2007b: 313) – in contrast to the view that politicisation means that the political system is responsible for the solution of social problems/for the delivery of services – then we have to acknowledge that today we are witnessing an unprecedented extent of politicisation (Greven 1999). The In/Out-perspective on democracy highlights the paradoxical situation that political self-determination currently means that the people can choose whether or not they want politics/the public sector to be the method of collective decision-making and implementation. This 'choice' is, however, strongly influenced by a second transformation which makes the link between the people and the government(s) even more contingent. In order to fully grasp the meaning of this first in/out-perspective on democracy we have to turn to the role of the electronic media.

The electronic media radicalises and, at the same time, makes more obvious that intermediate organizations do not function as *neutral transmitters* of individual preferences into the political system, but shape political demands (preferences) and political supply (programs, public products) themselves. Whereas this has been the case with parties, interest organizations and formal rules of aggregation as well, the speed of information processing and the overflow of information which are characteristic for an electronic multimedia society make preferences and political agendas much more unstable. Traditional patterns for political orientation (especially the ideological continuum between left-right) are eroding. Instead, the electronic media system has its own selection criteria for filtering the flow of information between governments and people, and its own logic of orientation. Both elements (selection and orientation) are shaped primarily by an *economy of attention* which characterises the internal functioning of the electronic multimedia system (Meyer 2003; Nolte 2005). Since this economy of attention favours personalities in comparison to programs, form (staging) in contrast to content (solutions to social problems), the increasing influence of the electronic media system on the political system can also be seen as a process of depoliticisation or as the emergence of *pseudo-politics* (Falter 2002; Meyer 2002; Elchardus 2002). Nevertheless, it can also be described as a process that reveals new and more fundamental contingencies and has to be interpreted as extended politicisation. Political struggles are no longer only about the right responses to a social demand, but the logically prior decision whether a social demand is being recognized as relevant or not is taking centre stage. Seen from this perspective, the rise of the media society makes us more aware that democratic politics is not only about the *right response* and the *correct reflection* of a social demand (output- and input-perspective). It is also, and more fundamentally, about the *recognition of relevance* – and not only of social *demands* but also of (public, private or mixed) *supply*.

In a society where public discourse is shaped by the logic of the mass media and where a plurality of modes and institutions of governance exists, each individual government has to strive to be present and prominent in public awareness ('in'). Furthermore, they need to avoid blame ('out') in order to be recognised and respected as an important focal point for decision-making, problem-solving and identity provision. Figure 2.2 summarises the different perspectives on democratic legitimacy.

Figure 2.2: Perspectives on democratic legitimacy

	First Modernity		**Reflexive Modernity**	
Legitimacy Government ..	**Output** ..*for* the people	**Input** ..*by* the people	**In/Out I** ..of *the people*	**In/Out II** ..*of* the people
Criterion for Evaluation	Fulfilment of the will of the people	Full/fair reflection of the will of the people	Future existence/ consistence of the people	Recognition of relevance by the people
Preconditions	Political Control/ Control of Politics	Competition/ Deliberation	Connected Populations	Productivity/ Prominence
Ideological Cleavages	Collective *versus* Individual Self-Determination	Aggregative *versus* Associative Procedures	Coherent *versus* Creative Cultures/Identities	Actual *versus* Cultural Performance

Realising the empirical relevance of such an in/out-perspective on democracy is just a first step. As in all other perspectives, different normative approaches exist regarding how to enhance democratic self-determination and legitimacy under these conditions. Rationalist approaches concentrate on the regulation of the media industry. They aim to make sure that the electronic media system functions as an open and fair provider of information about the actual problem-solving and preference-satisfying *performance* of various forms of governance. This enables people to compare and make informed choices. Cultural approaches, in contrast, are much more concerned with the public recognition of the relevance of politics and of the political system. They concentrate on the capabilities of politics to stage successful *symbolic performances* in order to compete with other social systems for the attention of the people and for being a relevant point of reference for the identity formation of the people. Furthermore, a major issue of cultural approaches is the coupling between symbolic performances and actual socio-economic problems or objective social demands (e.g. Meyer et al. 2000; Siller and Pitz 2000).

4. Conclusion: Efficiency and democracy – corresponding transformations rather than trade-offs

The previous sections have made clear that there is not one single perspective on efficiency (understood as welfare provision) or on democracy. If there appears to be a trade-off between these two political goals, this is most commonly because understandings of democracy and efficiency are being related to each other which are not based on the same conceptual perspective and/or ideological approach. For example, we can follow the social-democratic assumption that in order to enhance efficiency (welfare) we need to have strongly integrated and capable government institutions. If we relate this perspective on efficiency not with a similar output-oriented concept of democracy (where democratic self-determination is translated into the capacity of the political system to control the socio-economic system) but, instead, with input-oriented concepts where the aggregation and/or constitution of particular interests through various modes of participation and discussion takes centre stage, it cannot come as a surprise that we discover trade-offs.

But if we systematically distinguish the different approaches to welfare production and those to democratic self-determination, we discover not only striking similarities between the corresponding modernist concepts, but also similar transformations towards reflexive modernity.

Both, the *use-value* concept of welfare and the *output-oriented* perspective on democracy are based on an objectivist-functionalist ontology. They assume that an objective welfare function or an objective political will of individuals and collectives exists. Control is a precondition for enhancing welfare either through redistribution or through the regulation of externalities. Different forms of control are also necessary for democratic self-determination since only political control of the socio-economic system makes sure that the political will of a collective entity can really be fulfilled and institutionalized control of the government secures individual autonomy.

The concept of *exchange-value* and the *input-oriented* perspective on democracy, in turn, add and focus on the input-side of welfare production and democratic legitimisation. The inputs are either production factors or political preferences. There are different normative assumptions about how much these inputs are stable or constructed within a social process. Those who assume exogenously derived and rather stable inputs see competition as the central means for efficient allocation of scarce resources or as means for efficient aggregation of preferences. Those who assume endogenously created and rather flexible inputs argue for investments and/or institutions which enhance the quality of the inputs through education or deliberation.

Both, the concept of *change-value* and the *first in/out*-oriented perspective on democracy (in which the definition and the demarcation of the demos are taking centre-stage) are not concerned any more with the processes and effects within a system but with the boundaries and the temporal stability of the system in general. An orientation towards the future and openness towards the external world are seen as necessary preconditions for business organizations as well as for economic and political communities. Nevertheless, there are strong disputes about the extent to which a break with the past and openness for external ideas, investment and individuals are necessary for stimulating innovation and for connecting and integrating people.

Finally, the concept of *sign-value* and the *second in/out*-perspective on democracy (which highlights the need of governments to get recognized in a poly-centric and mediatised society) are both starting from the assumption that there are no natural or unquestionable starting points and no stable and unidirectional links any more: neither between the signifiers (meanings) and the signified (objects), the authentic needs/wants and the articulated demands, the material production factors and the supply; nor between the principals (the people) and the agents (the government or the political system), the factual performance of actors or systems as problem-solvers and the perceived performance measured in their popularity. All these links are not only getting multi-directional, they are getting contingent. In a world of information-overload and fundamental insecurity, gaining attention and recognition as well as creating attractive images and atmospheres is not only important for stimulating economic growth and social welfare but also for maintaining democratic legitimacy. Whether actual or symbolic performances are more important for these purposes is a matter for further discussion.

We should be aware that neither socio-economic welfare nor democratic self-determination can be enhanced if we do not recognise the new frontiers and focal-points in both fields. The contingencies of a de-materialised economy and a de-bordered polity produce new contingencies and new challenges for politics to gain and maintain public support and legitimacy. Hence, contrary to much academic writing about the relationship between efficiency and democracy, the main problem is not a fundamental trade-off between democracy and efficiency. Instead, the problem is that the debate about the *third transformation of democracy* is *lagging much behind* our understanding of the *third industrial revolution*. As long as we evaluate the current forms of governance and the current political processes with criteria based on outdated understandings of democracy we are not only undermining the legitimacy of politics and the political system. It might well be that democracy in itself is devalued if we are not able to adjust our understandings and normative prescriptions in a similar way as economic theory has been able to do with welfare theory.

References

Bauböck, R. (2005): 'Citizenship Policies: International, State, Migrant and Democratic Perspectives', in: *Global Migration Perspectives* 19, Geneva: Global Commission on International Migration. Online. UNHCR Refworld, available at: http://www.unhcr.org/refworld/docid/42ce4dd54.html [accessed 8 Dec. 2008].

Beck, U./Bonss, W./Lau, C. (2003): 'The Theory of Reflexive Modernization. Problematic, Hypotheses and Research Programme', in: *Theory, Culture & Society* 20/2, pp. 1-33.

Benhabib, S. (2004): *The Rights of Others: Aliens, Residents and Citizens*, Cambridge: Cambridge University Press.

Besley, T./Coate, S. (1999): 'The Public Choice Critique of Welfare Economics: An Exploration', National Bureau of Economic Research, Working Paper 7083, Cambridge, Mass., at: http://www.nber.org/papers/w7083.

Blühdorn, I. (2007a): 'Democracy, Efficiency, Futurity: Contested Objectives of Societal Reform', in: Blühdorn, I./Jun, U. (eds) *Economic Efficiency – Democratic Empowerment. Contested Modernization in Britain and Germany*, Lanham, Maryland: Rowman & Littlefield (Lexington), pp. 69-98.

Blühdorn, I. (2007b): 'The Third Transformation of Democracy: On the Efficient Management of Late-modern Complexity', in: Blühdorn, I./Jun, U. (eds) *Economic Efficiency – Democratic Empowerment. Contested Modernization in Britain and Germany*, Lanham, Maryland: Rowman & Littlefield (Lexington), pp. 299-331.

Boggs, C. (2000): *The End of Politics. Corporate Power and the Decline of the Public Sphere*, New York/London: Guilford Press.

Bohman, J./Rehg, W. (1997): *Deliberative Democracy: Essays on Reason and Politics*, Cambridge, Mass.: MIT-Press.

Buller, J./Flinders, M. (2005): 'The Domestic Origins of Depoliticisation in the Area of British Economic Policy', in: *British Journal of Politics and International Relations* 7/4, pp. 526-43.

Burnham, P. (2001): 'New Labour and the Politics of Depoliticisation', in: *British Journal of Politics and International Relations* 3/2, pp. 127-49.

Carens, J.H. (2001): 'The Rights of Residents', in: Hanson, R./Weil, P. (eds) *Reinventing Citizenship: Dual Citizenship, Social Rights and Federal Citizenship in Europe and the U.S.*, Oxford: Berghahn Books, pp. 100-120.

Castells, M. (1989): *The Informational City. Information Technology, Economic Restructuring, and the Urban-Regional Process*, Oxford, Cambridge, Mass.: Blackwell.

Castells, M. (1996): *The Information Age: Economy, Society and Culture, Vol. I, The Rise of the Network Society*, Oxford: Blackwell.

Cooper, R./Rappoport, P. (1984): 'Were the Ordinalists Wrong About Welfare Economics?', in: *Journal of Economic Literature* 22, pp. 507-30.

Dahl, R.A. (1967): *Pluralist Democracy in the United States: Conflict and Consent*, Chicago: Rand McNally.

Dahl, R.A. (1989): *Democracy and its Critics*, New Haven: Yale University Press.

Dahl, R.A. (1994): 'A Democratic Dilemma: System Effectiveness versus Citizen Participation', in: *Political Science Quarterly* 109/1, pp. 23-34.

Downs, A. (1957): *An Economic Theory of Democracy*, New York: Harper.
Dryzek, J.S. (2000): *Deliberative Democracy and Beyond. Liberals, Critics*, Contestations, Oxford: Oxford University Press.
Easton, D. (1965): *A System Analysis of Political Life*, New York: John Wiley & Sons.
Easton, D. (1975): 'A Re-assessment of the Concept of Political Support', in: *British Journal of Political Science* 5/1, pp. 435-57.
Elchardus, M. (2002): *De Dramademocratie*, Tielt: Lannoo.
Faist, T. (2004): 'Dual Citizenship as Overlapping Membership', in: Joly, D. (ed.) *International Migration in the New Millenium. Global Movement and Settlement*, Aldershot: Ashgate, pp. 210-32.
Falter, J. (2002): 'Politik im medialen Wanderzirkus. Wie Inszenierung die Politikverdrossenheit befördert', in: *Vorgänge* 2, pp. 5-9.
Florida, R. (2002): *The Rise of Creative Class*, New York: Basic Books.
Greven, M. (1999): *Die politische Gesellschaft*, Opladen: Westdeutscher Verlag.
Held, D. (2006): *Models of Democracy* (3rd ed.), Cambridge: Polity Press.
Hell, M. (2005): *Einwanderungsland Deutschland?*, Wiesbaden: VS Verlag.
Hirst, P.Q. (1994): *Associative Democracy: New Forms of Economic and Social Governance*, Cambridge: Polity Press.
Hooghe, L./Marks, G. (2003): 'Unravelling the Central State, but How? Types of Multi-Level Governance', in: *American Political Science Review* 97/2, pp. 233-45.
Huntington, S.P. (2004): *Who Are We? The Challenges to America's National Identity*, New York: Simon & Schuster.
Kujath, H.J. (ed.) (2005): *Knoten im Netz. Zur neuen Rolle der Metropolregionen in der Dienstleistungswirtschaft und Wissensökonomie*, Münster: LIT Verlag Münster.
Lash, S./Urry, J. (1994): *Economies of Signs and Space*, London: Sage.
Lijphart, A. (1975 [1968]): *The Politics of Accommodation: pluralism and democracy in the Netherlands*, Berkeley, Los Angeles, London: University of California Press.
Lijphart, A. (1999): *Patterns of Democracy: Government Forms and Performance in Thirty-six Countries*, New Haven: Yale University Press.
Marcuse, H. (1964): *One-dimensional Man*, Boston: Beacon Press.
Meyer, T. (with Lew Hinchman) (2002): *Media Democracy. How the Media Colonize Politics*, Cambridge: Polity Press.
Meyer, T. (2003): 'Die Theatralität der Politik in der Mediendemokratie', in: *Aus Politik und Zeitgeschichte* 53, pp. 12-19.
Meyer, T./Ontrup, R./Schicha, C. (eds) (2000): *Die Inszenierung des Politischen: zur Theatralität von Mediendiskursen*, Wiesbaden: Westdeutscher Verlag.
Musgrave, R.A. (1999): 'Fiscal Federalism' in: Buchanan, J.M./Musgrave, R.A. (eds) *Public Finance and Public Choice. Two Contrasting Visions of the State*, Cambridge, Mass., London: MIT Press, pp. 155-76.
Nolte, K. (2005): *Der Kampf um Aufmerksamkeit: Wie Medien, Wirtschaft und Politik um eine knappe Ressource ringen*, Frankfurt am Main, New York: Campus.
Oakerson, R.J. (1999): *Governing Local Public Economies*, Oakland: ICS Press.
Ostrom, V. (1987): *The Political Theory of a Compound Republic: Designing the American Experiment, Lincoln*: University of Nebraska Press.

Pollitt, C./Talbot, C. (eds) (2004): *Unbundled Government. A Critical Analysis of the Global Trend to Agencies, Quangos and Contractualisation*, London: Routledge.

Renshon, S.A. (2004): 'Dual Citizenship and American Democracy: Patriotism, National Attachment, and National Identity', in: *Social Philosophy & Policy Foundation* 21/1, pp. 100-20.

Scharpf, F.W. (1970): *Demokratietheorie zwischen Utopie und Anpassung*, Konstanz: Universitätsverlag.

Scharpf, F.W. (1998): 'Demokratische Politik in der internationalisierten Ökonomie' in: Greven, M. Th. (ed.) *Demokratie – eine Kultur des Westens? 20. Wissenschaftlicher Kongress der Deutschen Vereinigung für Politische Wissenschaft*, Opladen: Leske + Budrich, pp. 81-103.

Scharpf, F.W. (1999): *Governing in Europe: Effective and Democratic?*, Oxford, New York: Oxford University Press.

Schulze, G. (1992): *Die Erlebnisgesellschaft. Kultursoziologie der Gegenwart*, Frankfurt am Main: Campus.

Siller, P./Pitz, G. (eds) (2000): *Politik als Inszenierung: zur Ästhetik des Politischen im Medienzeitalter*, Heinrich-Böll-Stiftung Baden-Württemberg, Baden-Baden: Nomos.

Smith, R.C. (2005): *Mexican New York. Transnational Lives of New Immigrants*, California: University of California Press.

Straubhaar, T./Geyer, G. (2005): 'Welten des Kapitalismus II: Globalisierung und Loyalität: Wer sind „Wir"?', in: *Beilage HWW* 04, pp. 1-2.

Turner, B.S. (2000): 'Liberal Citizenship and Cosmopolitan Virtue' in: Vandenberg, A. (ed.) *Citizenship and Democracy in a Global Era*, Houndsmill: MacMillan Press, pp. 18-32.

Chapter 3
Citizens' Expectations: Is *What Matters* only *What Works*?

Pierre Lefébure

1. Legitimacy, Efficiency and Representation

Whilst it would be inappropriate to claim that back in the 18th and 19th Centuries representative government was established in Western countries against a well defined and strongly supported democratic project, it is certainly true that it has been installed in order to restrain more radical demands for democratic self-rule. One of the most debated points at the time was the issue of suffrage: Who should be given the right to vote, and what criteria of selection would be applicable? Most contributors to the debate then emphasized that voters would need to exercise social responsibility, in particular with a view to the economy, which could be expected only from people with property or an income (Romanelli 1998). This 'bourgeois' relationship with institutional power was based on the assumption that if poor people are given access to government, government tends to be mainly concerned with redistributing goods and wealth generated by businesses, thereby weakening the economy and in the end undermining the common good (Pitkin 1967; Manin 1997). Thus, the main argument supporting representative government centred not so much on notions of legitimacy but, first and foremost, on concerns about efficiency as defined by the interests of the growing bourgeoisie. Representation itself was considered a sufficient criterion for fair government, irrespective of how exactly it would work in practice. Very importantly, it was assumed that elected representatives are not necessarily required to abide by the will of their voters (*delegate* theory), but would base their decisions primarily on their own wise reasoning (*trustee* theory). This independence was the safeguard that the system of representation would, whilst honouring the relationship of trust between the representative and the represented, still function as an institutional mechanism for the pursuit of efficiency.

This understanding of representation was shared not only by elites but also by most of the middle-class (Daumard 1987; Gay 1993: 257ff). It was deeply rooted in a cultural frame of the bourgeoisie: the political ethics of property. Hence, it does not come as a surprise that these views are reflected even in the writings of novelists such as Choderlos de Laclos (*Dangerous Li-*

aisons, 1782) or James Fenimore Cooper (*The Last of the Mohicans*, 1826). The former was vigorously opposed to any participation of the poor, the latter, whilst being slightly more open-minded, still warned that 'universal suffrage is capricious and uncertain in its minor consequences, often producing results directly contrary to those which were expected' (*The American Democrat*, 1838). This specific political culture of the Western bourgeoisie is well summarized by Guizot, the prominent minister of the 1830 French constitutional monarchy (where the voting system was based on tax qualification): 'Get richer through work and savings [...] and you will become entitled to vote'.

Today, universal suffrage is the rule in all Western countries, an uncontested political norm referred to in any speech about democracy and democratization. Whilst representation was once a mechanism designed to defend the interests of the bourgeois elite vis-à-vis the democratic demands of the lower social strata, representation and democracy are now regarded as closely interconnected thus signalling that the cultural framework underpinning and supporting politics has comprehensively changed. But does this mean that democratic legitimacy has overtaken the desire for efficiency as the primary criterion against which government is being measured? Whilst the issue of legitimacy is most commonly addressed from a top-down (institutional or theoretical) perspective, it is also relevant, and perhaps even more so, from a bottom-up perspective, i.e. from the perspective of common citizens. What do citizens expect most from a political system that claims to be guided by the ideal of democracy and relies on representation as an institutional mechanism? Gordon Brown, Chancellor of the Exchequer of Tony Blair's New Labour governments in Britain, famously claimed that *what matters is what works*, thereby suggesting that efficiency and outcomes are valued more highly than democratic legitimacy and inputs. But is there evidence to support this claim? And are there differences between different European countries?

Obviously since the rise of modern representative government, societal complexity has much increased. The ever increasing division of labour, the growth of the tertiary sector, the fragmentation of cultural identities, the increase of immigration, secularization and changes in party systems and party discourses have diminished the significance of class conflict as a central political category. For much of the 20th Century political scientists focused attention, on the one hand, on party competition within democratic systems and, on the other hand, on the competition between liberal democracy and authoritarian systems. In comparison, not much emphasis was placed on investigating citizens' attitudes towards the democratic systems they were living in. From the 1970s onwards, the new social movements, the hypothesis of value change and mounting survey evidence of citizens' dissatisfaction with the practical functioning of democracy then refocused attention on the question how people perceive their democratic institutions. In view of societal complexity and widespread political disaffection, in particular, the question for the relative value attributed to legitimacy and efficiency is no longer narrowly focused on voting rights, but has evolved into the more encompassing question why citizens are in favour of democracy. As the democratic system is no longer underpinned by the bourgeois political ethics of property, what might have become the new cultural foundation supporting democratic systems? Or as Dahl has put it:

> If people in democratic countries continue to express their support for democracy, what is it, exactly, that they wish to support? What do they value about a democratic system? How can people who seem to have little regard for actual democratic institutions and leaders nonetheless strongly approve of democracy as the best system of government? (Dahl 1999: 8)

These questions are indeed challenging, in particular, because they point beyond the well trodden paths of behavioural, institutional and theoretical research towards the much less investigated field of interpretive sociology. Dahl continues:

> It is ironical, if not downright shocking, that amidst the enormous amount of survey data about democratic institutions, political participation, attitudes, ideologies, beliefs, and what-not, we have astoundingly little evidence in answer to a seemingly simple question: When people say they support democracy, what is it that they wish to support? (Dahl 1999: 8)

Existing research provides us with few pointers. Writing about the case of Switzerland, the only modern country still closely in line with classical democratic theory, Kriesi (1995: 80-125) notes that the strong belief of Swiss citizens in, and their regular use of, their set of direct democracy institutions does not protect the system from being criticized for the huge discrepancy between democratic inputs in terms of articulated political demands and political outputs in terms of government decisions. Nevertheless, it seems that the cultural belief in democracy is strong enough to outbalance this weak responsiveness because, as Kriesi points out (relying on Schmid 1981), political socialization at school age deeply roots an abstract idea of what the state should be. Thus the Swiss political system seems to rely on cultural frames enhancing democracy. But more detailed research into what citizens expect most from their democratic institutions, what makes them support their liberal democracy institutions and what makes them consent to being governed the way that they are is urgently required (Hibbing and Theiss-Morse 2002; Farnsworth 2003). In order to obtain empirical evidence, we need to investigate concrete cases with qualitative methods which may help to reveal the cultural background and foundation – which may well vary from one country to another.

This chapter investigates the case of France which is particularly interesting, firstly, because of the long-going debate in France about proportional representation (which is supposed to give voters a stronger democratic voice than the first-past-the-post rule) and, secondly, because of the growing demand in France for a more participative system (involving referenda, citizens' juries, city district consultative committees). The next two sections will introduce the conceptual framework and the research design for investigating why citizens support the democratic system and what they value most about it. The following two sections then focus specifically on the issue of referenda (section 4) and the relationships between citizens and their representatives (section 5). These two issues have been selected for closer discussion because they are particularly well suited for investigating whether citizens hold more legitimacy-oriented (input-oriented) or more efficiency-oriented (output-oriented) views about how political institutions and the democratic system should work.

2. Four sources of democratic approval

In order to identify the preferences of citizens regarding the values of legitimacy and efficiency, it is useful to establish their attitudes to the main mechanisms which are used to generate legitimacy in representative democracies between two national elections. These are, firstly, a set of mechanisms through which incumbents come under citizens' scrutiny, i.e. the mechanisms of *accountability*. Secondly, there is a set of mechanisms designed to negotiate policy agendas and decisions, which might be referred to as the mechanisms of *deliberation*. Thus the question is whether the mechanisms of accountability or those of deliberation, or indeed which combination of the two, contribute most to sustaining a high degree of approval of the democratic system, based on its perceived legitimacy, even when public satisfaction with the government's performance, i.e. with the system's efficiency, reaches a long-time low.

As regards their capacity to generate democratic approval, both the mechanisms of accountability and those of deliberation can be related not only to the value of citizens' input and participation (legitimacy), but also to the category of government performance or political output (efficiency). Yet, it seems that the mechanisms of accountability can enhance democratic approval in only one of two ways: either by boosting the system's legitimacy or its efficiency. Either democratic approval is based on the *commitment* of decision-makers to the promises they made at the time of election, or it is based on their *pragmatic* pursuit of outcomes which voters will judge at the time of the following election. Similarly, mechanisms of deliberation can be used either to boost legitimacy, in which case they put the emphasis on the *fair* representation of all citizen interests, or to boost efficiency, in which case they place the emphasis on *rationality* and functionality with regard to the desired outcome. Yet it seems difficult for policy makers to pursue fairness and rationality at the same time. Thus, approval for democratic systems seems to emerge from four different sources, tentatively conceptualised in Figure 3.1 as commitment, fairness, pragmatism and rationality. The first two of them are input-related and emphasise the legitimacy of the system, the latter are two output-related emphasising the efficiency of the system. All four sources of democratic approval require some further explanation.

Figure 3.1: The legitimacy-efficiency dilemma[1]

		normative preference (ends)	
		legitimacy	efficiency
institutional mechanism (means)	accountability	COMMITMENT	PRAGMATISM
	deliberation	FAIRNESS	RATIONALITY

COMMITMENT: Democratic approval deriving from this source is based on the assumption that the government ought to put into practice what it promised during the election campaign. Accountability is therefore, in this case, *retrospective* accountability, and commitment is retrospective in that it refers to an earlier process (the election) when trust has been requested and formally granted. The relationship of trust between government and citizens is the pivotal element of this source of approval. Citizens (voters) invest trust in

1 Note that legitimacy and efficiency are conceptualised here (as throughout this chapter) as competing values or goals. In the more recent literature, Scharpf's distinction between input-legitimacy and output-legitimacy (Scharpf 1999; also see the earlier chapters in this volume), in particular, has reconceptualised this relationship, but in classical democratic theory legitimacy derives from the input dimension alone. Also, what is now commonly referred to as output-legitimacy can, arguably, not adequately substitute for political legitimacy derived from bottom-up democratic input (on this point also see Blühdorn in Chapter 1 of this volume).

their representatives, and politicians are expected to be committed to fulfilling their promises.

PRAGMATISM: Democratic approval deriving from this source is based on the belief that the government ought to take decisions which secure that it is not defeated in the next elections. Accountability in this case is *prospective*, in that government performance is measured by citizen's preferences and demands at the time of the next elections. In anticipating how voters may respond to government performance, pragmatic politicians may either focus on producing policy outputs which factually improve the wellbeing of citizens, or they may rely on strategies of political marketing which emphasise presentation, image and symbolic action (see Blatter's discussion of *sign-value* in the previous chapter).

FAIRNESS: In this case democratic approval derives from *input-maximising* deliberation, and it is based on the view that whatever the policy outcomes, policy measures have been fairly negotiated and decided giving each point of view an equal opportunity to be considered. Legitimacy is based here on agreed and transparent procedures of pluralism and the main expectation is that government abides by the codified institutional rules.

RATIONALITY: Here democratic approval derives from what might be called *output-optimizing* deliberation, and it is based on the view that government ought to pursue policy solutions informed by best available knowledge. Deliberation here is used as a means to improve the quality of decision-making (compare Fritsch and Newig in this volume) and to identify, through reasoned argument, the objectively best solution to the problem at stake.

As the table shows, legitimacy-oriented sources of democratic approval are related to the inputs into the political system, whereas efficiency-oriented sources are related to its outputs. So with regard to the issue what citizens value more, the question is: Are their attitudes towards their political system mainly structured by the inputs (legitimacy) or the outputs (efficiency)? If their appreciation of the input side is so strong that it makes up for a high level of discontent with the outputs, this would signal strong commitment to democratic principles in the classical sense. That is to say, answering Dahl's question what it is about democracy that people value and support, that citizens would primarily be concerned with *how the system is run* and not so much with *what the system delivers*. It would disprove the claim that what matters is only what works. It would confirm that in public perception democracy is, like in classical theory of democracy, substantially defined and legitimized through the input-side and not, as Scharpf (1999) and others have more recently suggested, through the output-side and a new kind of output-legitimacy making up for diminishing levels of input-legitimacy. The increasing level of societal complexity, however, has a strong impact on both the potential for enhancing inputs as well as the potential for enhancing outputs. Therefore, it is necessary to also assess how the rise in societal complexity affects citizens' preferences.

3. A qualitative and interpretive research design

In order to investigate how ordinary citizens deal both with democracy as a positive principle and representative government as its present institutional form a qualitative approach based on focus groups has been implemented. The research design is intended to provide data allowing an analysis of uncertainty and speculation which are expected to characterize the way ordinary citizens discuss democracy and representation.

The objective here is not to provide further evidence for the growing dissatisfaction of citizens with their political system (Klingemann and Fuchs 1995; Nye et. al. 1997; Norris 1999) such as the declining voter turnout, declining party membership or negative attitudes towards parliaments. The results of the existing studies on these issues support the *crisis of representative government* thesis which can indeed hardly be questioned. However, I start out from the assumption that this more or less acknowledged crisis of trust towards representatives does not equal a crisis of representative democracy as a principle. Certainly, legitimacy and efficiency can be seen as two combined components as one could expect feedback effects from the dissatisfaction with government towards the beliefs in the democratic principle itself. Nevertheless, as mentioned by many authors (Kavanagh 1997; Montero et. al. 1997; Dennis and Owen 2001), perception of democratic legitimacy and satisfaction with government must be distinguished. These two components of the political system's assessment indeed do not deal with the same levels of the system nor imply the same kind of reasoning. It seems that many authors who suggest that dissatisfaction with policies weakens both confidence in politicians and support for the regime neglect this perspective though it has been fruitfully put forward by Easton (1965) some decades ago.

Thus, one should start from the idea that assessments in terms of positive belief in a principle and those in terms of discontent with the actual functioning of the institutional system relate to different kinds of reasoning. Close to that point are the findings about the autonomy of the political sphere regarding mass belief in democratic legitimacy and the fact that support for democracy is not strongly correlated with a perception of its system efficacy, or with satisfaction with its near-term performance in the case of developing countries (Diamond 1998). Such results are valuable as they promote approaches in terms of political cultures. One should therefore carefully take them into account. Yet, they still rely on sets of quantitative data which does not allow us to analyze meanings and reasoning. Research should therefore also explore qualitative data.

Qualitative research involving focus groups can be conducted in different ways, from the most supervised sessions to the most open and interpretive approach. But there is no doubt that it has proved to be methodologically relevant from two points of view in social sciences. First for providing discourse data whose analysis produces results consistent with what quantitative data can tell about the investigated topic and also original results regarding specific insights such as devices used by the groups' members to strengthen, revise or even change their mind. These mechanisms are connected with the dynamic use of talks and arguments showing that opinion is a view open to orientation and intensity reshaping processes through interactions with other people (Billig 1989, 1998). Secondly, focus groups are methodologically relevant for providing discourse data about mixed matters because the focus group approach is flexible enough to let people express their views on various topics which are more or less closely related to each other. As such it has proved to have twofold relevance for a wide range of subjects.

For instance it proved useful to explore the conceptual constructs used by citizens in a democratizing African country to frame political topics (Bratton and Liatto-Katundu 1994). In another research aiming at understanding what kind of moral categories of thinking could enhance the consumption of, and talk about, popular television narratives, it allowed to explore contradictory and fragmented moral identities and the distribution of moral responsibility (Barker 1998). The study conducted by William Gamson (1992) on the effects of media discourse on the disposition towards collective action in the US also helped and inspired the growth of media studies using focus groups to investigate social and political issues (e.g. Lunt and Livingstone 1996; Hunt 1997). Gamson's work also inspired the research presented in this chapter in that the latter has been designed to combine media studies and the study of citizens' attitudes towards democracy. The members of the focus groups were shown excerpts from various political TV programs involving both politicians and ordinary citizens and then they were encouraged to comment on them and talk about politics more generally.

The method used was guided by two empirical criteria. First it seeks to be as close as possible to everyday life interactions. This is why the groups comprised people who knew each other well and were used to talking to each other: relatives, friends, colleagues. Thus they could be described as friendly and even cooperative groups. This cooperative disposition is all the more important for this research as it aims to observe people in a context of casual conversation rather than argumentative discourse. The objective is to reveal and explore their attitudes towards the political system including all their potential inconsistencies. Of course there may still be elements of rational argumentation, but it is expected that the situation of casual conversation will facilitate that people, first and foremost, speak their minds. Thus, if focus group members have a consistent attitude towards democracy (which is precisely what the research seeks to explore), this should appear through the speaking process of cooperative interaction.

Secondly, group meetings have been held at one member's home in order to let participants feel comfortable speaking about a theme that might trigger shyness and restrain, if discussed in an explicitly experimental location such as an academic building. The mediator takes part in the interaction only to keep the conversation close enough to the investigated issue, but he does not actually get involved in the conversation and makes every effort not to disturb the atmosphere of casual conversation. Of course, it is imaginable that some people do not have any attitude at all towards democracy. But there was no evidence of this in the nine groups of our sample which included a total of 34 individuals selected, as summarised in Figure 3.2, to ensure sociological and political diversity. Out of all the themes addressed by them two major topics related to representative democracy were discussed in a very similar way: the referendum and the relationship between citizens and their representatives.

Figure 3.2: Focus groups held in the Paris area between 1999 and 2004

Groups	Members	Age	Average ipol
Group 1	2 married Socialist Party activists	58 and 61	3,5
Group 2	4 students (Business Studies)	22-24	2,25
Group 3	4 conservative party (RPR) activists	25-32	3,75
Group 4	4 non-manual workers (2 married couples)	46-51	2,25
Group 5	3 high school teachers	29-30	3
Group 6	4 conservative party (UMP) activists	29-73	4
Group 7	3 black workers	36-37	3
Group 8	5 young workers living in a workers' hostel	19-22	2
Group 9	5 Communist Party activists	33-56	3,75
		Total average ipol:	3,05

ipol = interested in politics (very = 4; rather = 3; a little = 2; not at all = 1)

4. Citizens' views on referenda

As regards the extended scope and use of referenda as a way of improving democracy, opinion polls usually give a very positive answer. From 1999 to

2003 (the period of time when our focus groups were held) figures registered in seven available surveys in answer to the basic and binary question of (dis)approval were unambiguously positive. The lowest level of support was 79 per cent in an exit poll on the day of the vote on the shortening of the presidential term from seven to five years (CSA-Le Parisien, 24/09/00). All the other six results were above 80 per cent going as high as 88 per cent approving that 'a referendum should be held if a high number of people are asking for it' (Sofres-CEVIPOF/Stanford University survey, 4 May to 27 June 2000). Thus it seems that citizens want representative democracy to become more participative.

However some further insights from opinion polls suggest that this issue is more complex. If the binary choice of approval or rejection is supplemented by reasoned arguments for and against, the support significantly decreases – as illustrated in Figure 3.3 – from more than 80 per cent to about two thirds of the sample.

Figure 3.3: Support for more referenda in France

In general, do you think that having more referenda in France...	
...would be a good thing since citizens could then tell their mind directly on different issues	67%
...would not be a good thing because it may prompt more demagogy in the political debate	28%
do not know	5%

Source: *Sofres-Le Pèlerin Magazine*, 23/24 January 1998

Some propose to hold more referenda on important political issues. Do you think it would be...	
...good to hold more referenda so that people can decide on important political issues	67%
...bad because referenda would always be held about issues regarding particular groups	27%
do not know	6%

Source: *Sofres-Le Figaro*, 20-22 September 2000

As no variations among class, age or education categories are to be found in these survey results, one should conclude that providing arguments about possible consequences induces a cross-sectional effect moderating the pro-referendum attitude. This is not to say that support for referenda suddenly disappears, but it suggests that further research into the dynamics of political reasoning about referenda is required. This seems all the more appropriate as even lower levels of support are registered once the wording and scales of items are more complex and open in survey questions. For instance, when asked what kind of issues they would like to decide through referenda, almost half of the interviewees were not able to mention a single relevant potential topic, not even one in which they would have been personally interested

(Sofres, September 2000). Besides, when asked which institutional reform they wish to see implemented (choose among a list of eight or nine items with multiple answers allowed), less than one interviewee out of five (18 per cent) select 'the opportunity to hold more referenda' (Sofres-Le Figaro Magazine, 23-25 August 2000) or 'to establish the popular initiative referendum' (16 per cent, Ipsos-Challenge, 20-23 January 1995). Thus what first seems to be overwhelming support does not necessarily signal a real preference for getting involved in a more participative way. The attitude towards referenda should therefore be questioned in order to assess if it is actually very consistent. Yet such an analysis goes beyond what standard survey research allows us to investigate. Qualitative research based on the analysis our focus groups' discourse is a more promising tool.

The group members encounter the issue of referenda as they watch an excerpt from a TV debate about the 1992 European Union Maastricht treaty dis/approval campaign. In this excerpt taken from a special political program of the first French TV channel former President Mitterrand answers the questions asked by selected citizens. European integration rather than the referendum itself appears to be the issue at stake but comments expressed within the groups finally turn to direct democracy. Among those members who were old enough to vote in 1992 (7 groups out of the 9), memories of the Maastricht Treaty as an issue which was very difficult to understand help to say that the referendum as a principle does not mean anything really relevant: what counts is the issue at stake and the wording of the question on which voters have to make up their mind and choose between the binary options yes/no. At this point none of the groups developed further remarks and they all just kept commenting on the 1992 event. However, the issue of referenda itself has always been discussed later in the course of the session. Most of the time the group members start from a rather abstract and positive approach related to previous opinions on democracy and finally elaborate on some practical reservations. So say the members of group 4 (married couples of non-manual workers):

HUSBAND 2 – oh yes, I wish there were more referenda, on more issues!
WIFE 1 – I feel the same… but be careful, not doing it in every case, not on all issues… because, you know…
W 2 – Well, it depends on the campaign, if it's clear, understandable, with everything explained. Because you have to make an informed decision.
H 2 – Sure, sure, it's not to say that a referendum is a good thing just because you let people vote.
W 1 – And even more than that! You can't go and vote just like that on this or that. Nor too often… because it's impossible to be interested again and again.
MODERATOR – And you, … would you like to have more referenda?
H 1 – Well, yes, of course, because people can speak their mind that way. But, you know, I don't think there should be too many referenda. Because some…

Well it shouldn't be about making us think that we have to decide about all and everything. Or, worse, about making us decide that way because those in office failed to pass their bill in a different way. It must be democratic, I mean…

W 2 – Right, I'm OK for the referenda but not to switch from the other ways. The referendum, you know, it's special and it's not good… well, it's my mind, but you can't say that you want to have your referendum and you just get it and it's done. It's more than that, it's special.

H 2 – Oh, yes, but I didn't mean that… it's seldom as simple as what you say. I just said that we don't have that many referenda and so… we could have some more.

H 1 – OK, we could have some more. But not too many…

Just as in the surveys' series of binary questions intended to test (dis)approval of an extended use of referenda, 'husband 2' asserts a basic general support. This is clearly a 'top of the head' answer (Zaller and Feldman 1992) stimulated by the question of the moderator. This kind of answer is not unreasoned but it does not reflect a structured attitude as it is mainly determined by the context (e.g. the question wording and the state of mind deriving from previous conversation). In our group discussion this effect of circumstances is revealed by the contradictory statements provided by wives 1 and 2 which then make husband 2 come closer to their view. This process of discursive interaction shows how socially structured and adjusted opinions and preferences are. It operates as the fulcrum on which talk turns to be a cooperative behaviour allowing social actors to set and use normative criteria for assessing various objects such as political institutions. At this point of their discussion, the group members establish that the referendum is not appropriate on the basis of a principle but rather on a practical basis renewed from one case to another.

The same kind of doubt and uncertainty about the use and frequency of referenda was expressed by most of the other groups (students in business, conservative activists, high school teachers, black workers, young workers, Communist party activists). Such rationales as the risk for minorities to metaphorically get run over by a sudden and overwhelming majority, the risk to be manipulated by a media bias in the short period of time of the referendum campaign or the risk to let politicians make people seemingly decide and be accountable for what has actually been so tightly squared by the question are the main concerns casting doubt on referenda as a genuine democratic tool. A rather sophisticated kind of reservation is stated by the Socialist party activists (Group 1) as they point out that the referendum is a 'one-shot' tool and could thus be appropriate for deciding on general issues such as those about values but would not be suitable for policies about most current issues which often require feedback and reworking. The abstract theoretical desirability of referenda is thus strongly counterweighted by different kinds of practical reasons preventing our groups' members from promoting the extended use of referenda.

Does this dilemma about referenda reflect the more general dilemma about inputs (legitimacy) and outputs (efficiency) as it has been laid out in Figure 3.1? A first observation is that the referendum is an alternative to regular representative government, thus making the mechanism of accountability not that relevant any more. Out of the two mechanisms the only one still relevant is deliberation. In that respect, the practical reservations stated by the groups towards the referendum are not connecting the claim for deliberation with efficiency. It is actually not a question of making the best choice through a referendum and no statement presents it as a tool for improving policies. As a matter of fact, most of the reservations of all the groups are connecting deliberation with legitimacy: the criterion is that the conditions under which citizens are called to the polls should make sure that, whatever their choice may finally be, they are asked a fair 'yes' or 'no'. In this perspective, the way our sample tends to promote deliberation is as a means to sustain a high level of democratic legitimacy through an institutional process – the referendum – that entails the risk of distorting democracy into a populist acclamation rite with no regard either to direct consequences or the long-term relationship between citizens and institutions[2]. Thus, compared to the results of quantitative surveys which tend to show a high level of approval for referenda, our qualitative analysis reveals a rather cautious approach connected with the will to sustain procedural fairness implying deliberation as a control-input for a legitimate use of referenda. Relating the referendum to such rationales clearly puts the emphasis on legitimacy through 'Fairness' as in the bottom left corner of Figure 3.1.

5. Citizens and their representatives

Activists involved in parties (Groups 1, 3, 6 and 9) seem to share with ordinary citizens a weak disposition towards a political career and do not identify with political elites. Speaking about themselves compared to the leaders of their parties, they often use the same rhetoric distinguishing the mass of people from the few deciders. They even feel a stronger frustration about the democratic ideal of connecting the base with the top in so far as their relationship with their party leaders is biased by electoral strategies and political marketing. They often complain about the compromises they accept for the 'common good' of their organization instead of sticking with what they basically expect from their ideological involvement. This is particularly clear with regard to their interest in debates which they consider as a significant democratic practice within parties (Groups 3 and 1):

2 Similar results in Hibbing and Theiss-Morse 2002: 47-53, 89-94.

CONSERVATIVE A2 – Well, as party members we are rather conditioned to campaign for the leader even if we don't really support him as a person. I don't like Séguin at all but I supported him because the game has to be played that way. We have to stand as a group… and we shut up.
C A3 – Oh, it's not impossible to debate in the party.
C A1 – Hmm, so you think? It's difficult, anyway. And there are not so many things we can debate about.
C A4 – I really do think that the party member is an endangered species and I really think this is someone that should be cared about. I don't know… He deserves some respect! Because it's something serious for people to be a party member. […] Remember the consultative round of members by Séguin. Nice but… You know, just when one of his closest advisors came in at that debate planned for designing the manifesto then he left after 10 minutes, saying "sorry, I have to go, I'm so busy with writing this manifesto". Well, he's just one of these top technocrats and he's gonna piss one more technocrat's report!

SOCIALIST 2 – You remember that meeting, when the section-chief got angry about the two people. He told them 'don't be against this, don't be against that…'. And he gave them hell. I told him 'if you start talking like that to your members, don't be surprised that you don't have so many of them here'. And you know what? He turned against me. 'Oh, shit' I said, and I left.
S 1 – It's crazy! To give hell to a woman like that at a time when we are trying to make women better involved. He got angry against women only… I don't remember if I thought he was right or wrong about what we debated but the fact is that it was impossible to debate.

Thus, contrary to what could be first hypothesized, activists do not tend to surrender their democratic principles because of party discipline, and this generates a high level of frustration. Party activists experience the status of being a neglected 'citizen' of their organization and most often relate it to a perverted vertical relationship, just as ordinary citizens also talk of politics in general. Hence one of the activists said:

> All of those chiefs and executives who don't let us debate, they are liars. And they know they're liars but they don't give a shit about that. They're not interested in debating but in deciding and we should just be OK. It's a big cheat! It falls on us, the grassroots, and we are supposed to obey. You know, some are above the others or they think they are though, in theory, we, the grassroots, we are the party.

The most frequent criticism ordinary citizens not involved in parties voice about how the political system is run by representatives is echoed by party activists complaining about the hierarchical tendency of party elites. The gap between citizens and their representatives is not perceived as horizontally widening because of practical reasons of time and space but as vertically structured because politicians are not able or don't want to fulfil citizens' expectations. In group discussions this view is supported by concrete examples taken either from the participants' own experience or from media reports which suggest that representatives tend to avoid citizens, thus weakening representation as a linkage.

One reason for this neglect is that, whatever their skills, politicians tend to lack understanding for, and appeal to, citizens' everyday life: language, habits, social and educational background as well as institutional advantages often simply do not allow them to relate to the citizens they are supposed to represent. As the students of Group 2 put it:

> STUDENT 1 – I remember something I watched on TV. It was Rocard [former French Prime minister] who was in the countryside. There was a woman saying "I don't understand why we have had these problems for a while with agriculture because we are doing what we've been advised to do". And he answered things like European interest rates, the debt and all of this was just so impossible to understand. He gave no reason but listed technical matters.
>
> S 2 – How, too brilliant… I didn't watch it but it's always like that. None of them tries to tell anything quite consistent and complete. They just bring twisted explanations, you know, things you just can't respond to. Even if there's something true in it, you can't get it. No one could get anything of it.
>
> S 1 – And that guy… he's been Prime minister!

A second reason why citizens perceive their representatives as neglecting them is that incumbents worry first and foremost about their political office which makes them tie primarily with their party. Politicians would then act from selfish motives. Strikingly, activists and ordinary citizens are equally critical of this behaviour.

Thirdly, representatives are seen by our groups to purposively avoid citizens, providing no opportunity for sustaining a collaborative and horizontal connection. This reason is obviously the most challenging one for representative democracy as it highlights patterns of behaviour which undermine the legitimacy that representatives are intended to provide through – borrowing the words of our focus group members – 'being close to people', 'going back to our level', 'having a true relationship with us', 'just being at our service' and 'having regard for us'. Once again, activists (Group 6) and ordinary citizens (Group 5) articulate very similar views:

> Conservative B1 – Sure, students have been moved to protest by rumours… they've been misinformed. Yet I saw none of our leaders on TV to explain what is right or wrong… and of course none of them in campuses or in lecture rooms so that they explain … and they could understand why students were so angry… So what we lack as conservative parties is the connection with people. Remember when I first talked of associations and volunteering, I was considered as a dangerous leftist! Sure, associations are more left oriented but leftists can use it to understand trends in society and so they basically stay tuned in…
>
> C B2 – To be in associations, well, we should get into it… You know, veterans or anything else… The leftists, they get in… they're in… They even run associations. We don't know how to do that…

C B1 – Sure but let's go back to what I said. Our guys should not only try to connect with the millions through television, but also get in touch with people directly, small groups of people so that we can understand what is going on. But you know what: it's so cool to be on television rather than meeting people…

TEACHER 1 – There are a lot of people who criticize the High Civil Servants' School, saying 'eh, all of those top graduates in Bureaucracy'. Well, I think it's not so bad that there is such a school teaching them how to manage institutions. Because we don't want to rely on anybody. At least, with that school, we know they are taught how to do it. Then we vote to choose those of them we want… politically. So, I'm satisfied about that. But their training has to be changed. They should be… they should get in touch with us, be on the spot, have internships… in business, why not? [Teacher 2 laughs]. Eh, it's true. I mean… I'm not against that School but…

T 2 – Oh yes, a factory internship. They will do their factory internship and… By the way, they already have to do internships…

T 1 – Eh, wait! What kind of internship? At the boss' office? [to the moderator:] Do they indeed have internships?

MODERATOR – Well, there are internships in districts and in administrations…

T 1 – I see! But, no… I didn't mean internships of that kind… not like a free guided tour at the Constitutional Court, no, no, no… That's not real life! They don't see anything there.

T 2 – You are joking?! They know everything they need. They know everything but they just want to balance their budget. Then, so that they have nothing to pay, they say 'I see no problem. No, I think there's no problem at all'.

T 1 – You think so?! That's… That's cynical…

T 3 – Well, we should have something which makes them… You know… Something that makes it impossible for these guys to say that there is no problem and that makes them come to the actual scene of problems to see what's going on.

This last excerpt, in particular, provides a synthesis of closely connected views which are to be found in all the groups. First, the division of political labour between a specially trained elite and the vast majority of citizens examining their work is accepted by the Communist activists as well as the less interested young workers. Citizens are even very demanding about this point, and there was no evidence of support for collective government of the country by lay people. The reactions of the groups' members to the TV excerpt where an extreme right representative says that 'a citizen who does not get involved in politics is a useless citizen' sheds some light on this preference. All groups regard this statement as unfair as it implies that political involvement ought to be compulsory. Some general information regarding this theme is also provided by opinion polls showing that the average citizen does not look like a possible representative: answering the question *Would you consider to get involved in politics yourself in order to make things change?* 75 per cent of the interviewees reject this proposal while 22 per cent felt tempted

(CSA-Reader's Digest, January 1999). Reasons for not considering political involvement seem to be mainly connected with politics itself, not with private life or professional career: 'I am not skilled enough' ('yes' 57 per cent vs. 'no' 41 per cent) and 'there is no party I am most inclined to join' (46 per cent vs. 51 per cent) are far ahead of 'I don't want to risk losing my job' (18 per cent vs. 78 per cent) or 'it's too difficult for a woman' (23 per cent vs. 74 per cent among women). Politics thus appears as a task not everyone can deal with. In line with this point, interviewees rather strongly support a high institutional status and a decent income for elected officials (68 per cent vs. 22 per cent).

The suggestion in last statement of the third teacher is closely related to accountability as it stresses responsiveness as a criterion for assessing the quality of politicians. This kind of reasoning occurs in all the groups and is connected with the view on accountability as well as the claim that politicians should keep their word ('Commitment'): representatives are expected to be loyal and responsive at any time. Whatever the policies which incumbents may pursue in accordance with their ideological alignment and which may more or less fail or succeed, citizens have two main expectations: not being fooled by election promises and being actually considered in a responsive way. What they claim is trustworthiness and responsiveness in terms of a direct connection. Citizens indeed want channels of continuous communication through which representatives can literally put their mandate into practice. This perspective is related to the type of responsiveness Eulau and Karps (1977) call 'symbolic' in contrast to the 'policy', 'service', and 'allocation' types which are related to government's performance. This kind of responsiveness emphasizes the critical importance of legitimacy as the first criterion to assess a regime as truly democratic. Some results from another research project using French focus groups back this view as they show how participants tend to assess policies not so much by what has been implemented (outputs) than by the extent to which the needs of the population have been taken into account (inputs) in the decision-making process (Balme et al. 2003).

This emphasis on legitimacy through the responsiveness and loyalty of representatives to their constituency is such that it ultimately leads most of our groups (apart from one Conservative activists group) to elaborate their view related to accountability as follows: just like bad employees can be fired by their employers, representatives be fired as well if they fail to be 'symbolically' responsive and loyal. Yet, this does not imply any intention to punish incumbents for failing to achieve efficient policies. Further exploration is required to establish how and why citizens claim a tighter control of representatives as a means of realising the division of political labour which they fundamentally approve of on the basis of strong reservations about direct democracy mechanisms.

6. Conclusion

The investigations above show that citizens are able to discuss abstract issues related to democracy once they are provided with practical examples and situations. Participants have high expectations of politicians and they still highly value representation. They subscribe to forms of direct participation only as an occasional and cautiously used extension of representative democracy, not as an overall institutional alternative to representation. Whilst explanations differ depending on the type of data, quantitative surveys as well as qualitative analysis of focus group discussions confirm that citizens clearly distinguish ordinary people from politicians. The former are not necessarily expected to be politically interested, able and committed, but the latter are expected to achieve their task to the highest standards with failure to do so entailing the risk of being 'fired' or recalled. This perception of difference between the ordinary citizen and the elected representative is in line with the views of the founding fathers of representative democracy. But does it mean that efficiency in the delivery of outputs, as it had originally been the major argument supporting representative government, is being approved by citizens as the core criterion for assessing the political system? The research presented in this chapter has provided some consistent evidence against this hypothesis, and there are two findings which are particularly important to reemphasise:

First, rather than supporting direct democracy in a blanket manner, members of our focus groups adopt a cautious approach which seeks to promote deliberation and is not in favour of referenda as a procedure symbolically expressing the sovereignty of the people. Whilst the deliberation which the focus groups are demanding could theoretically be connected to, and justified with, gains in *efficiency* ('Rationality'), our groups clearly connect it with *legitimacy* ('Fairness') which thus emerges as the primary criterion for assessing democracy.

Second, far from questioning political representation as a mechanism and suspecting an inescapable elite bias of representative democracy, our focus groups articulate high demands regarding the relationship between citizen and representative. Politicians are expected to remain closely connected to their constituencies and stay true to their values and promises. The relationship between citizens and representatives appears to be mainly a matter of accountability and could, as such, theoretically be related to efficiency ('Pragmatism'). Once again, however, most statements by the members of our focus groups relate it primarily to legitimacy ('Commitment').

By way of conclusion we may therefore state that in France democracy seems to be more consistently assessed by citizens on the basis of inputs (legitimacy) rather than outputs (efficiency). Whilst it is oftentimes criticized as unrealistic, classical theory of democracy thus seems to maintain its influence as a normative yardstick. The increase in societal complexity does not prevent citizens from framing their expectations and demands on the basis of norms and values underpinning classical democratic theory. Accordingly, the question whether what matters is only what works needs to be answered in the negative. And in response to Dahl's question what exactly it is that people value in democracy we may note: when French citizens say they support democracy, they are doing so primarily because they want their representatives to be accountable to and connected with them so as to make sure that the political system fairly *represents* their demands – even if they are not *fulfilled* in the end.

References

Balme, R./Marie, J.-L./Rozenberg, O. (2003): 'Les motifs de la confiance (et de la défiance) politique: intérêt, connaissance et conviction dans les formes du raisonnement politique', in: *Revue internationale de politique comparée* 10/3, pp. 433-61.

Barker, C. (1998): ''Cindy's a Slut': Moral Identities and Moral Responsibility in the 'Soap Talk' of British Asian Girls', in: *Sociology* 32/1, pp. 65-81.

Billig, M. (1989): 'The Argumentative Nature of Holding Strong Views: A Case Study', in: *European Journal of Social Psychology* 19/3, pp. 203-22.

Billig, M. (1998): *Talking of the Royal Family*, London: Routledge.

Blühdorn, I. (2007): 'The Third Transformation of Democracy: On the Efficient Management of Late-Modern Complexity', in: Blühdorn, I./Jun, U. (eds) *Economic Efficiency – Democratic Empowerment. Contested Modernization in Britain and Germany*, Lanham: Rowman & Littlefield (Lexington), pp. 299-331.

Bratton, M./Liatto-Katundu, B. (1994): 'A Focus Group Assessment of Political Attitudes in Zambia', in: *African Affairs* 93, pp. 535-63.

Dahl, R.A. (1999): 'The Past and Future of Democracy'. CIRCAP (Center for the Study of Political Change) Occasional Papers 5, at: http://www.unisi.it/ricerca/dip/gips/circap/circap.html

Daumard, A. (1987): *La bourgeoisie et les bourgeois en France depuis 1815*, Paris: Aubier-Montaigne.

Dennis, J./Owen, D. (2001): 'Popular Satisfaction with the Party System and Representative Democracy in the United States', in: *International Political Science Review* 22/4, pp. 399-415.

Diamond, L. (1998): 'Political Culture and Democratic Consolidation', CEACS Working Papers (Instituto Juan March de Estudios e Investigaciones) 118.

Easton, D. (1965): *A Systems Analysis of Political Life*, New York: John Wiley.

Eulau, H./Karps, P. (1977): 'The Puzzle of Representation: Specifying Components of Responsiveness', in: *Legislative Studies Quarterly* 2/3, pp. 233-54.

Farnsworth, S. (2003): *Political Support in a Frustrated America*, Westport: Praeger.

Gamson, W. (1992): *Talking Politics*, Cambridge: Cambridge University Press.

Gay, Peter (1993): *The Bourgeois Experience, Victoria to Freud. Vol. III: The Cultivation of Hatred*, Londres: Harper-Colins.
Hibbing, J.R./Theiss-Morse, E. (2002): *Stealth Democracy. Americans' Beliefs about How Government Should Work*, Cambridge: Cambridge University Press.
Hunt, D.M. (1997): *Screening the Los Angeles 'Riots': Race, Seeing, and Resistance*, Cambridge: Cambridge University Press.
Kavanagh, D. (1997): 'Crisis of Confidence: The Case of Britain', in: *Studies in Comparative International Development* 32/3, pp. 30-41.
Klingemann, H.D./Fuchs, D. (1995): *Citizens and the State*, Oxford: Oxford University Press.
Kriesi, H. (1995): *Le système politique Suisse*, Paris: Economica.
Lunt, P./Livingstone, S.M. (1996): 'Rethinking the Focus Group in Media and Communications Research', in: *Journal of communication* 46/2, pp. 79-98.
Manin, B. (1997): *The Principles of Representative Government*, Cambridge: Cambridge University Press.
Montero, J.R./Gunther, R./Loriente, M.T. (1997): 'Democracy in Spain: Legitimacy, Discontent and Disaffection', in: *Studies in Comparative International Development* 32/3, pp. 124-60.
Norris P. (ed.) (1999): *Critical Citizens. Global Support for Democratic Governance*, Oxford: Oxford University Press.
Nye, J./Zelikow, P./King, D. (eds) (1997): *Why People Don't Trust Government*, Cambridge: Harvard University Press.
Pitkin, H.F. (1967): *The Concept of Representation*, Berkeley et Los Angeles: University of California Press.
Romanelli, R. (1998): *How Did They Become Voters?: The History of Franchise in Modern European Representation*, The Hague: Kluwer Law International.
Schmid, C. (1981): *Conflict and Consensus in Switzerland*, Berkeley: University of California Press.
Scharpf, F.W. (1999): *Governing in Europe: Effective and Democratic?*, Oxford: Oxford University Press.
Zaller, J./Feldman, S. (1992): 'A Simple Theory of the Survey Response: Answering Questions versus Revealing Preferences', in: *American Journal of Political Science* 36/3, pp. 579-616.

Chapter 4
Re-engaging Citizens: Institutional Responses to Political Disengagement

Alexandra Kelso

1. Introduction

At the start of the new millennium, instead of celebrating their hopes and prospects for the future, western societies find themselves riddled with anxiety about the condition of their political systems, and immersed in dark introspection about what has gone wrong with the functioning of their democracies. As Stoker (2006: 1) notes, 'democracy as an idea is more popular than ever, but citizens in democracies appear disenchanted with the political process.' Across the advanced liberal democracies, electoral participation, which is widely regarded as the key measure of the health of a political system, has been in decline. In response to this phenomenon, political scientists have turned their attention to the task of describing, and more importantly, explaining democratic disenchantment (e.g. Dalton 2004; Gray and Caul 2000; Norris 1999; Pharr and Putnam 2000). Essentially, examination of the nature and cause of political disengagement is an examination of the relationship between legitimacy, efficiency and complexity in modern democratic societies. In attempting to construct solutions which are designed to re-engage citizens with their democracies, the task becomes one of increasing the legitimacy of modern political systems at a time when there is high, and rising, complexity, as well as an ever present need to make modern governance continually more efficient. If the 'problem' of engaging disaffected citizenries is a difficult one, it is because the exercise involves finding harmony between these highly divergent goals. Complexity impacts on the ability of societies to enhance input legitimacy – that is, participation in democracy – while also ensuring enhancing output legitimacy – that is, system performance and efficiency in the delivery of good governance. The goal may be to maximise both input and output legitimacy – to increase democratic participation and also increase governance efficiency. Yet, the complexity of the modern state and society makes this task profoundly problematical.

The United Kingdom provides an excellent case study for the purposes of analysing how political disengagement is understood and addressed, and one that highlights the kind of tension which exists between legitimacy, efficiency and complexity. In one respect, concern about the condition of representative democracy has been particularly prevalent in the UK, prompted largely by the pronounced decline in voter turnout in recent general elections. In 2001, turnout fell to 59.4 per cent, down from 71.6 per cent in 1997, with five million fewer voters participating between the two polls (Electoral Commission 2002). The figure was compounded by the evidence that just 39 per cent of 18-24 year-olds voted in 2001. The 2005 general election gave little hope that a corner had perhaps been turned: turnout barely increased to 61.4 per cent, with only 37 per cent of the 18-24 age group voting (MORI 2005). The UK works well as a case study for the additional reason that, in the Westminster system, the focus has traditionally been on facilitating a strong executive. Parliament is important in terms of providing legitimacy to executive actions, because it is the representational focus of the political system. Consequently, parliament's role is to facilitate strong government, and subject it to scrutiny and mechanisms of accountability. Parliament does not itself govern, but instead provides the legitimate forum for government. The Westminster system is therefore geared towards securing a high level of output legitimacy – that is, strong and efficient government – but with far less emphasis on the issue of input legitimacy, which has traditionally been understood as being fulfilled through the simple mechanism of representation of the public in parliament.

The figures on political disengagement in the UK have prompted much analysis and reflection of what has 'gone wrong', and a search for the causes of the apparent political disengagement has begun, with politicians and commentators alike expressing concern for the health of representative democracy in the UK (e.g. Bennett et al. 2000; Coleman 2003; Harrop 2001; Pattie et al. 2003; Phelps 2004). Public organisations and think tanks which are involved with issues related to democratic functioning have attempted to explore and explain the reasons for electoral disengagement, in order to find potential remedies. For example, the UK Electoral Commission (an independent body charged with fostering public confidence and participation in the democratic process), in its analysis of the 2005 general election, argued that 'there is a clear need to re-connect people with politics, and vice-versa, beyond moments of (relatively) high political drama such as general elections' (Electoral Commission 2005). The Electoral Commission also began working closely with the Hansard Society, an independent charity which promotes effective parliamentary democracy, to produce a series of Audits of Engagement, based on survey research, which attempted to measure participation in politics, knowledge of and interest in politics and satisfaction with politicians and the political process. Across the four Audits conducted between 2004 and 2007, the research uncovered little substantial change in the various indicators it measured, and thus found little evidence of short term significant change in levels of political engagement in the UK. In the 2007

Audit, while 54 per cent of those surveyed reported an interest in politics, just 49 per cent said they were knowledgeable about politics (although this was a remarkable 10 per cent increase on the 2006 Audit). Only 33 per cent of those surveyed agreed that by getting involved in politics, people could change the way the country was run, and a similar number agreed that the present system of governing works well. While 55 per cent of respondents said they would definitely vote at the next general election, 60 per cent of respondents claimed they had not discussed politics or political issues in the previous two or three years. Just 27 per cent of those surveyed said that they trusted politicians generally. While the figures appear gloomy, the authors of the Audit drew some comfort from the fact that, over the four year period in which these analyses had been undertaken, the stability of the figures uncovered suggested that engagement was, at least, not in an inexorable decline (Electoral Commission 2007: 60). This figure on trust is comparable to those found by the spring Eurobarometer 2007 survey, which discovered that only 34 per cent of UK respondents tended to trust the government, although this was itself up from 24 per cent from the autumn 2006 Eurobarometer. Similarly, 43 per cent trusted parliament, a figure that was also up from 29 per cent on the previous survey (Eurobarometer 67, 2007).

Along with these numerical analyses, there has also emerged a series of institutional analyses. Enquiries into the 'condition' of British democracy have been launched by public/civic organisations, by specially appointed public enquiry teams, and by political institutions themselves. Exploration of the documents produced by such enquiries affords us an insight into the real differences that can exist between how state and non-state actors perceive the challenges facing political institutions, and how each constructs solutions designed to help those institutions manage their changing role within modern representative democracy. Crucially, such an exploration helps us see how different actors understand political legitimacy, and how that legitimacy can be strengthened. This chapter therefore seeks to examine some of these documents in order to explore how they perceive the problem of disengagement and to probe the nature of the solutions which they propose. In so doing, the chapter aims to highlight the interesting differences and perspectives which exist with regards to the need for enhanced political legitimacy, and what this means for democratic participation and for the efficiency of political institutions.

We begin by examining two important reports from two different non-state Commissions, each of which sought to diagnose the 'problem' with democracy and to suggest solutions. The first is the *Hansard Society Commission on the Communication of Parliamentary Democracy*, which looked specifically at issues concerning how citizens engage with the Westminster parliament, and which reported in 2005. The second is the *Power Commission*, a group established by the Joseph Rowntree Reform Trust (an organisation committed to promoting the continued reform and improvement of the political system), and which reported in 2006. We then shift the analysis to explore how parliament, as the UK's institution of representative democracy, has responded to political disengagement. The Westminster parliament has made efforts in recent years to enhance the extent to which the public can interact with, and participate in, its work, and analysis of the changes secured reveals much about how parliamentarians conceptualise Westminster's role in the contemporary system of representative democracy. A focus on what parliament and parliamentarians think about political disengagement, and how we can find a balance between enhancing political legitimacy while still preserving the efficiency of the political system, provides an interesting insight into practical institutional responses to the proclaimed need to find a new way of 'doing' politics. The analysis reveals many different ideas about how political legitimacy can be recovered, even reinvented, in contemporary representative democracies, while also illustrating the practical difficulties associated with such a momentous project, particularly in terms of ensuring that, if legitimacy is to be maximised, it is not at the expense of efficiency.

2. Parliament and democracy

In the UK system, one of the most basic functions of parliament is that of linking government and governed. By providing a forum where the concerns of the electorate can be aired, and perhaps even addressed, and where governmental actions and decisions can be explained and scrutinised, parliament promotes the interest articulation and conflict resolution necessary for a healthy political system. The legitimacy that Westminster derives from its role as the representative and, more recently, the democratic focus of political life, is what also bestows legitimacy onto government (Judge 1993). Yet, parliament itself is most often described as a 'reactive' legislature, which provides a forum for government, but does not itself govern. Through its two separate Houses of Commons and Lords (with government being creatures of the former, lower chamber), parliament reacts to the strong and assertive executive to which it plays host. Parliament subjects government legislation to scrutiny in advance of approval, and has the opportunity to debate its key aspects and principles, although government, as a consequence of its majority in the House of Commons, is normally assured of securing its legislative agenda, even if it does sometimes concede some ground on the details (Cowley 2002, 2005; Russell and Sciara 2007). Parliament also has a system of select committees, which scrutinise the work of government departments, and conduct inquiries into government policy and administration. Yet, these committees do not have the power to direct government to abide by its conclusions, and are advisory only, with their main benefit coming from the oxygen of scrutiny and publicity to which they expose government activities. In the round, government controls parliamentary procedure in significant ways, and uses these procedures to preserve its dominance over parliament (Kelso 2007a). Consequently, the UK political system provides for high levels of output legitimacy, in terms of governance efficiency, precisely because input legitimacy, in terms of parliament's participation in the process of governing, is highly restricted.

The relationship between parliament and the electorate is crucial for the healthy functioning of the political system. By acting on behalf of the citizens they represent, parliamentarians 'can generate a latent body of support' for parliament specifically and the political system more broadly (Norton 2005: 11). As the UK's representative assembly, parliament facilitates linkage of government and governed, and provides a legitimation link between the two. In the historical development of the British state, representative government has always been valued as a way to secure a strong executive, and representative democracy has been but a recent newcomer to the political system. The historical nature of what representative government has meant in Britain has continued consequences for the practice of twenty-first century representative democracy. In Britain, 'representation both serves to include 'the people' in decision-making – indirectly and infrequently through the process of elections – yet, simultaneously, to exclude them from direct and continuous participation in the decision-making process' (Judge 1999: 19; also see Lefébure in the previous chapter).

Consequently, there are tensions inherent in efforts to marry representative and participatory mechanisms in the British system of democracy. The problem stems from the need to assimilate (often) inefficient democratic mechanisms into parliamentary structures built around the Westminster practice of representation, a practice that has thus far been highly efficient at securing consent for government actions, and thus maintaining political legitimacy. Yet, discussions about disengagement suggest fundamental problems with the way in which parliament fulfils its democratic functions, and also raise questions about how political legitimacy can be renewed at a time of falling engagement with even those limited opportunities for public participation. The *Hansard Society Commission on the Communication of Parliamentary Democracy* examined how the public's perceptions of parliament might be improved by enhancing the way in which parliament communicated with people.

3. Communicating parliamentary democracy

As the UK's national institution of representative democracy, the Westminster parliament tends to feature prominently in most accounts of the need for democratic renewal. In 2005, the *Hansard Society Commission on the Communication of Parliamentary Democracy* published its report which focused exclusively on the nature of the relationship between parliament and the public, and how it could be improved so as to enhance the legitimacy of the representational mechanisms embodied in the Westminster system. For this Commission, parliament's communication strategy mattered a great deal with respect to political disengagement:

> Because if people cannot understand what Parliament does, or why it does it, if people find its culture and language alienating, if voters cannot easily present their views and questions and believe they can make a difference, and if there is no continuing 'conversation' between Parliament and people, then Parliament cannot fulfil its purpose effectively. (Hansard Society 2005: 3)

The Commission report declared that 'a Parliament which involved and engaged the public more effectively in its work would respond to such increased attention with improved performance' (Hansard Society 2005: 7). The underlying assumption of the Commission, then, was that enhanced democratic performance (enhanced input legitimacy) could not but help increase the effectiveness of parliament's work – could not, in other words, do anything other than enhance output legitimacy. From this perspective, parliament's political legitimacy increases if public participation in and connection with its work is increased, because this necessarily improves the effectiveness of parliament overall. For the Commission, the relationship between input and output legitimacy was clear and simple: more participation would result in better governance. For the Commission there was no indication that more democratic participation might in fact impede governance efficiency because of the complexity of the relationships involved.

The Hansard Society Commission highlighted two broad sets of problems with parliament that contributed to political disengagement: levels of participation; and general political and social trends. In terms of the former, the Commission pointed to a number of likely issues for concern when analysing the downward trend in voting numbers. These included poor knowledge of parliament and how its works, low satisfaction with parliament along with a declining media profile, and the fact that people would be more likely to engage if they thought that their involvement actually affected outcomes. In terms of political and social trends, the Commission outlined a far more complex picture. This included a decline in party identification, an increase in the number of political institutions and processes, the development of a less deferential society, and the rise of a customer-focused approach to most aspects of life. Given its very specific concern with the way that parliament communicated with the public it represented, the Hansard Society Commission recommended that a systematic parliamentary communication strategy be developed, based on five key principles: accessibility and transparency, participation and responsiveness, accountability to the public, inclusiveness, and good practice in management and communication.

This idea for a communication strategy, geared towards improving the democratic responsiveness of parliament, immediately highlights the difficulties inherent in any programme for reconstructing the foundations of democracy and reinvigorating political legitimacy in the UK context. The executive requires parliament to approve its legislation efficiently and to engage with scrutiny that keeps interference and disruption of executive functioning to a minimum, but which also contributes to legitimising the actions of government. Yet, the Hansard Society Commission communication strategy clearly envisioned a parliament that would spend more time and resources on engagement mechanisms that might well result in a less efficient institution with respect to these executive priorities. The emphasis on enabling the public to participate in proceedings, and on parliament engaging in more meaningful dialogue and consultation with the public, flags up exactly how enhancing the democratic performance of an institution may impact on how efficiently that institution performs its various other functions.

Although the Hansard Commission made many recommendations for improving parliament's communication approach, a few in particular are of relevance in understanding the underpinnings of democratic renewal, how tensions between democracy and efficiency might be handled, and how this informs attempts to enhance political legitimacy. For example, in terms of the parliamentary website, the Commission argued that:

> It should be proactive as well as reactive – the purpose of the site should not be simply to provide information to those already in the know, but should invite participation from people who are not familiar with the workings of Parliament. (Hansard Society 2005: 54)

In this vein, the Commission advocated the use of the internet to enable interactive discussions and consultations, to foster more participative and two-way processes. Although individual MPs already engage with the public (to varying degrees) through their party and constituency bases, for parliament, as an institution, to do this as part of its normal routine is a new development. Parliament has traditionally been conceived as an institution of representation, and its role as a democratic institution is a modern one. While that role may well have been performed at the constituency and party level, it has not been so much in evidence at the institutional level of parliament itself.

Naturally, the Commission's recommendations involved more than simply updating the website, and also included changes to the rules for television coverage, enhancement of citizenship education, better strategies for engaging young people, and more besides. The Commission emphasised that the issue of enhanced engagement required attention:

> Piecemeal or incremental changes as a response to this report would go against the fundamental conclusions of our work – that the administration of parliament must be transformed, that the mindset of Parliament has to change to take into account the public's point of view and that communication has to be radically reorganised as a central democratic priority if parliament is to function effectively. (Hansard Society 2005: 90)

The proactive nature of the Hansard Commission recommendations may well be at odds with the executive's requirement that parliament work as an efficient institution that services its legislative and legitimation needs. The recommendations are also a challenge for parliament, a point acknowledged by the Commission, which advised that the more fundamental changes could be carefully considered while other, more easily achievable changes proceeded. Incremental change by itself, according to the Commission, would mean further disconnection between parliament and the public, 'with consequent damage to our democracy' (Hansard Society 2005: 9). The crucial premise on which the Hansard Society Commission report was based was that better communication between parliament and the electorate could at least partly address disengagement, and produce enhanced political legitimacy for parliament.

4. Power to the people

The Power Commission report of 2006 was a far-reaching inquiry into the functioning of British democracy, but it was not without its problems. The Commission's approach to researching the phenomenon of political disengagement was flawed, its methodology was questionable, and too much of the report relied on anecdotal evidence rather than on the findings of rigorous social science (Bale et al. 2006). The Commission in many ways fundamentally misunderstood much about the way that the British political system functions, and in particular, about the role of parliament as the UK's foremost institution of representative democracy. Nonetheless, the way this Commission approached the task of explaining disengagement, and providing solutions to it, is of interest from the perspective of understanding how difficult it can be to enhance legitimacy while maximising efficiency in the context of an increasingly complex societal background. The underlying assumption of the Power Commission was that if the political system was reoriented to be more participatory, and thus facilitate an increase in input legitimacy, this would necessarily lead to an increase in output legitimacy because the products of governance would be improved. As with the Hansard Society Commission, there was little sense that more participation might actually reduce the efficiency of the political system, because it would make the process of governing more, not less, complex.

The Power Commission outlined two sets of accounts for why people are disengaged from politics. The first set it termed 'Red Herrings' (Power Commission 2006: 57-72), because these accounts apparently offered dubious reasons for disengagement. The Commission felt satisfied that disengagement was not caused by: political apathy or a declining sense of civic duty; widespread economic and political contentment; a lack of competitive elections; an overly negative news media; or a lack of time on the part of citizens. More convincing was a range of complicated, and often interconnected, accounts. First, citizens felt they lacked influence over political decision-making, in addition to which the main political parties which provide citizen access to such decision-making were widely perceived to be too similar, and required citizens to commit to too broad a range of policies. This was compounded by an electoral system that produced unequal and wasted votes, and voting procedures that were inconvenient and unattractive. Finally, people simply lacked knowledge and information about formal political processes. The Power Commission pointed to deep-rooted social and political change, prompted by post-industrialisation, which led to citizens being unwilling to accept the deferential strictures of previous eras. For the most part, citizens perceived a political system that failed to take their views and interests into account, held political parties in contempt, and viewed voting as a waste of time because of the nature of the electoral system (Power Commission 2006: 29).

In response to these diagnoses, the Commission's recommendations were designed to 'create a political system which allows citizens a more direct and focused influence on the political decisions that concern them' (Power Commission 2006: 20), and comprised three key elements. First, there had to be a rebalancing of power away from the executive and unaccountable bodies towards parliament and local government. This rebalancing would involve enhanced powers for parliamentary scrutiny committees, an extension of parliamentary powers to initiate legislation and respond to public petitions, constraints on the powers of party whips in parliament, and the reconstitution of the House of Lords (the upper chamber of Westminster) on a substantially elected basis. Second, there had to be greater responsiveness and choice in the electoral and party systems, which would be secured by means of a reformed electoral system and changes to the basis of party funding. Finally, citizens had to have a more direct and focused say over political decisions and policies, which would involve, amongst other things, the right of citizens to initiate legislation, and more transparency with regards to the activities of MPs and government ministers.

Of all the recommendations issued by the Power Commission, those pertaining to the initiation of legislation perhaps pose the greatest challenge to the efficiency of the political system. Such a solution perfectly illustrates the tension which can exist in attempts to strengthen input legitimacy, by enriching democratic participation, while still preserving output legitimacy, in terms of the efficiency of political institutions. The Commission did apparently appreciate the difficulties involved in finding the right balance between input and output legitimacy, remarking that 'governments must be free to pursue their legislative programmes as efficiently as possible', and emphasising that parliamentary initiation of legislation should act purely as a 'safety valve' (Power Commission 2006: 147). However, in its recommendation that citizens should have the right to initiate legislation, the Power Commission not only sought to supplement representational mechanisms with those of direct democracy, but also prioritised the need to strengthen input legitimacy over the need to preserve output legitimacy. The Commission defended the use of the initiative on the grounds that it would enhance democracy, yet had little to say about how such a mechanism would impact upon the efficiency of the political system. The report in fact addresses this efficiency issue in a highly tangential way, stating that:

> … the power of the initiative is not the fact that it is used regularly – it is not – but its very existence exerts pressure on governments and other authorities to take account of public feeling, and address popular concerns, for fear that if they do not a citizens' initiative is always a possibility. (Power Commission 2006: 239)

Indeed, in discussing the 'serious concerns' associated with the power of initiative, the Commission did not mention those related to system efficiency at all. Similarly, in arguing that parliament should have the power to initiate public inquiries and to require action on public petitions, the Commission clearly appreciated the democratic utility of these mechanisms, but failed to augment it with a discussion of their resource implications, and their impact on system efficiency. The report argues that 'many people want more influence over political decisions, but regard elections as far too blunt a tool for the exercise of that influence' (Power Commission 2006: 200). The Commission, in short, failed to appreciate the 'embeddedness' of representational mechanisms within the UK political system, and the extent to which political legitimacy is already interlocked with those mechanisms. Although the idea of the initiative was forwarded as a way to enhance parliamentary legitimacy, the Commission failed to explore the possibility that it may in fact lead to the kind of institutional friction between parliament and the executive that could detrimentally impact upon the legitimacy of both.

5. Westminster's institutional response

As the UK's national representative assembly, the Westminster Parliament is the key institutional forum through which democratic participation is made manifest, and from which the actions of government can secure legitimacy. In recent years, far from being oblivious to the problems associated with declining political participation, parliament has been fairly proactive in approaching the matter, and has instituted a range of changes, all of which are designed to at least partially address the issue of disengagement and declining institutional legitimacy by encouraging the public to become more aware of, and involved with, its work (Kelso 2007b).

The House of Commons has a Modernisation Committee, comprising backbench MPs and a key government minister, which was set up when the New Labour government was elected in 1997 in order to ascertain how Commons' practices could be modernised, partly as a way to make the House more accessible to the public who elect it. However, unlike the Hansard Society Commission and the Power Commission, the Modernisation Committee has been far more willing to acknowledge that increasing input legitimacy might well reduce output legitimacy. The Committee has been clear that an expansion in participatory mechanisms might well mean that the efficiency of government is compromised, and has thus sought to delimit the kinds of solutions proposed on these grounds. In June 2004, the Modernisation Committee published a report on the issue of political disengagement, which remarked that 'lower levels of trust [in politicians] are translating into a disconnection from the institutions of democracy' (HC 368, 2003-4: para.3). The Committee's diagnosis is therefore far more short and sharp than that offered by either the Power Commission or the Hansard Society Commission, and identifies the problem firmly as one of a lack of trust. Part of the process of restoring that trust, for the Modernisation Committee, was to foster conditions that would encourage the public to 'understand and engage with parliament itself' (para.6). Consequently, parliament has clear responsibilities in facilitating engagement:

> It serves no-one if we make it difficult for voters to understand what their elected representatives are doing … the Commons can make itself more accessible to those outside, both as interested visitors and as citizens wishing to be more involved in proceedings, it can do more to make it easier for people to understand the work of parliament, and it can do more to communicate its activity to the world outside. (para.9)

However, as the Committee acknowledged that there is a point at which increased input legitimacy can cause a decrease in output legitimacy, its solutions are very firmly in the area of improved accessibility and information provision, rather than in the area of participatory innovations of the kind advocated by the Power Commission. Of the range of changes pursued by parliament in recent years, two areas in particular are of relevance for the themes explored here: provision of information to the public, and reform of the public petitions' procedure.

Public petitions have long been an example of a mechanism designed to add to the legitimacy of the political system – by ensuring that grievances are heard by parliament – but where its potential value in terms of democratic participation was compromised by the need to ensure the efficiency of Westminster working practices. While members of the public may well spend a long time collecting signatures for petitions, parliament traditionally had no productive way of dealing with them. In its 2004 report, the Modernisation Committee recommended that petitions should be referred to whichever House of Commons select committee was relevant to the topic (HC 368, 2003-4: paras. 96-104), an approach which was rejected by the Commons Procedure Committee on the grounds that select committees were overburdened enough without also having to respond to petitions (HC 1248, 2003-4). In this instance, the concern was that the efficiency of the House of Commons scrutiny systems might be compromised by the need to respond to public concerns that were directly communicated to it.

Crucially, the House of Commons has been reticent about learning how other institutions have managed to balance the need to be both democratically responsive and functionally efficient. The Procedure Committee examined how the devolved institutions in the UK, particularly the Scottish Parliament at Holyrood, approached its provisions for public petitions, where the system is far more open to and accessible by the public, and where there are institutional structures in place within Holyrood procedures in order to deal with those petitions in a way that is meaningful to those who submit them, and also manageable by the parliament (Kelso 2007b). However, the Procedure Committee rejected the opportunity to create a dedicated Petitions Committee along the lines of that used in the Scottish Parliament, primarily because this would enable the public to petition the parliament directly, rather than through their MPs, thus impacting on the representational link performed by MPs at Westminster. In this respect, while acknowledging the need for institutional change in order to better engage people and enhance the value of democratic participation, the Westminster parliament has largely eschewed approaches which might re-engineer the representational basis on which the political system operates, regardless of whether such re-engineering might enhance its democratic legitimacy.

While developments have been somewhat constrained in terms of public petitions, there have been more meaningful changes taking place with respect to online participation (Coleman 2004; Kelso 2007a). The UK parliament has had its own website since 1996, and although acknowledged as 'a highly informative resource', it nevertheless 'offer[ed] no opportunities for interactive communication between citizens and legislators' (Coleman 2004: 3). Recent attempts have been made to make more use of parliament's internet presence. In 2002, the House of Commons Information Committee explained that the internet could 'play an important role in influencing perceptions and helping to meet public expectations', and recommended that online consultation processes might be utilised so long as the public understood that their role was to 'inform the thinking of legislators', not 'to make policy' (HC 1065, 2001-2: para. 47). Several House of Commons committees have experimented with online consultations as part of their working practices. The Joint Committee on the Draft Communications Bill was the first committee to use online consultation mechanisms as part of its pre-legislative scrutiny, concluding that they had 'enhanced the openness of our deliberations' (HC 876, 2001-2: annex 5). Non-legislative select committees have also been relatively pro-active in experimenting with such innovations. During its enquiry into human reproductive technologies, the Science and Technology Committee concluded that online consultation had 'provided a useful context against which to consider the formal evidence' (HC 7, 2004-5: para.7). The Northern Ireland Committee also used an online consultation during its enquiry into hate crime, in the hope that it would 'widen the pool of people involved in the consultation process' (HC 548, 2004-5: annex A). The exercise did not attract the numbers of participants that the Committee had hoped for, although of those who did take part, 75 per cent had never contributed to such an exercise before. Clearly, valuable though online mechanisms may be, they need to enjoy sufficient publicity in order to attract the kind of participation levels that can offset concerns about the costs involved.

Yet, it is not simply participation levels that are an issue: the quality of the participation is problematic. Far from marking the beginning of a new deliberative platform, online consultations have been remarkably constrained in their impact. One inquiry operated by the House of Commons Defence Committee, for example, listed around 128 responses, but only twelve of these came from the Committee MPs themselves (Kelso 2007b: 367). Of those twelve responses, most were clearly written by the Committee clerks, and designed simply to prompt users for more information and to take the focus of contributions in a new direction. The responses were not, in other words, examples of genuine discussion and deliberation between parliamentarians and the public around the themes of the inquiry. Other online consultation exercises tell a similar tale. For example, in 2007, the House of Commons Joint Committee on the Draft Human Tissue and Embryos Bill used an online consultation which generated 153 posts. However, the consultation was no more than a message board, with very little deliberative discussion taking place either between the members of the public who made the posts, or between the public and the MPs engaging in the legislative scrutiny. In this respect, online consultations may well be utilised as a way to broaden the scope of a committee's knowledge basis, and use of such mechanisms may well add legitimacy to committee conclusions and recommendations, but they are far from fulfilling their potential effectiveness. For MPs, engaging with such mechanisms is time-consuming, and involves them interacting with users in what might well be prolonged debates. With so many pressures on their time, MPs may well be happy to leave the detail of such exercises to parliamentary clerks, and this almost entirely defeats the point of the exercise. Consequently, the recommendation from the Modernisation Committee that parliament could do a great deal more in this area is an understatement. It's declaration that the internet 'is an interactive medium that allows genuine two-way communication between politicians and the people they represent' is true (HC 368, 2003-4: para. 53), but such 'two-way communication' remains quite some distance off in the future.

6. MPs' perceptions of disengagement

While it is helpful to gaze briefly across the attempts made by the House of Commons to engage the public with its work, it is also useful to examine the views of individual parliamentarians with respect to this 'problem', what parliament might do about it, and what this tells us about the balance between efficiency and effectiveness at Westminster. The author conducted a short series of interviews with a range of House of Commons MPs and House of Lords peers in January and February 2006, and these help illustrate the difficulties experienced by parliamentarians in wanting to improve the functioning of democracy while still preserving the efficient operation of parliament as a primarily representative institution. These interviews further highlight the tension between input and output legitimacy, and how this impacts on the efficiency of the political system. Overall, enhancing democratic participation was viewed by MPs as a 'good thing', unsurprisingly, but the need to maintain system efficiency above all was broadly of more importance to them.

Almost all those parliamentarians interviewed indicated that political disengagement was an issue that troubled them, and most also attributed disengagement in large part to the lack of ideological divides between the two main political parties. Only a few interviewees argued the case made by the Hansard and Power Commissions: that people are disengaged because they feel they cannot influence political outcomes. In this respect, most MPs underplayed the complexity of the situation as outlined by the two Commissions, and tended to offer quite simplified versions of events. For one Labour MP:

> There's a discontinuity between the act of voting and any results that might come from it ... Even when someone's directly contacted their MP, they can't see how democratic politics actually makes a difference.

Another Labour MP explained disengagement in the context of:

> ... people think[ing] that parliament, not that it's irrelevant, but that nothing they can do can actually influence it ... all these things fuel this feeling that parliament is either irrelevant, it doesn't listen, or that there are more interesting things to do with your life.

A Labour peer also raised the issue of influence, arguing that people felt they lacked influence because public affairs had become far more complicated, resulting in 'a feeling of being overwhelmed and frustrated.' For one Liberal Democrat peer, the centralisation of government meant that 'people have a feeling of being remote from things.' Yet, this peer also linked disengagement with 'people [being] more engaged in a vast range of other things.'

A particularly varied range of solutions were provided to the 'problem' of disengagement. Crucially, none of the interviewees suggested changes specifically geared towards enabling people to be more involved in consultation or decision-making processes. Even those interviewees who pointed to a lack of influence as a reason why people were disengaged did not go on to mention any kind of deliberative or participative democratic mechanisms that could be used to complement representative democracy at Westminster. Responses ranged from 'blue sky' approaches designed to alter the institutional structure of the political system – such as overhauling the electoral system and radically reforming the select committee system – to rather more modest suggestions, such as running seminars between parliament and the media.

When parliamentarians were asked about how parliament might perform its democratic function in an ideal world, there was considerable pause for thought, and the answers produced were somewhat vague and general. For some, the democratic linkage function was best performed when parliament did more and better scrutiny, enjoyed more committee autonomy, and had better communication processes in place, all of which hint at a 'tick-list' approach to democratic enhancement. Yet, a small number of interviewees did place particular emphasis on the need for improved responsiveness in an ideal world scenario. A Labour MP, for example, stated that:

> It would have to be responsive, be seen to be relevant, it would have to address issues that concern people. I suppose it would have to deal with issues in a mature and considered way, and process and procedure is a huge part of what we do here. In an ideal world, laws are made when people have the opportunity to have an input, and what they say is considered. Of course, that doesn't happen, and that's why people get frustrated.

A Liberal Democrat peer made some similar points:

> There's a general perception that parliament and politicians don't listen, and if they don't listen, why engage? There have been some efforts to encourage politicians to be more active in their constituencies. But people don't think they're terribly consultative, and perhaps they could be more engaged with their constituents.

Yet, neither of these parliamentarians then went on to provide specific suggestions for just how this enhanced responsiveness might be brought about. This is not a reflection on the limited capabilities of the parliamentarians in question, so much as it is a general comment on the real difficulties which exist in balancing democratic participation with system efficiency. For some MPs, the internet was a perfect example of how efforts to enhance input legitimacy could impede output legitimacy: it simply encouraged people to contact MPs, most of whom would not have done so otherwise, and in so doing, made it harder for MPs to perform their various roles, because of the time taken to respond. Most MPs cited the internet and email as mechanisms which primarily enabled them to inform constituents of their activities, and did not view it as first and foremost an opportunity for two-way dialogue between politician and public. In this way, the internet, while it has the potential to provide for more deliberative interaction between MPs and constituents, was in fact used by most MPs as a way to constrain and delimit participation, by keeping interaction to a minimal level. While there may be compelling democratic grounds for the expansion of online tools as a way better to engage people with political processes, the fact remains that politicians themselves operate at the very fault-line where such democratic hopes are constrained by the practical requirement of ensuring that the political system functions efficiently.

7. Conclusion

In July 2007, the Labour government under the new Prime Minister Gordon Brown published a consultative document on *The Governance of Britain* (Cm 7170, 2007). This document declared that 'the nature of the relationship the Government has with its citizens, the credibility of our institutions, and the rights and responsibilities of citizens all determine the health of our democracy', and outlined the government's desire to 'forge a new relationship between government and citizen' and to secure a settlement 'that entrusts Parliament and the people with more power' (Cm 7170, 2007: 5). The government paper outlined a range of reforms, including: the surrender or limitation of many executive powers, such as requesting the dissolution of parliament and restricting parliamentary oversight of the intelligence services; a shift to securing more executive accountability to parliament, by expanding the opportunities for parliamentary debate and scrutiny; and a re-invigoration of democracy, through mechanisms such as those that enhance the public's role in local decision-making, as well as an assessment of national electoral practices. This *Governance of Britain* document therefore forms a key part of the response of the British executive to the issue of political disengagement and declining trust in political institutions. With respect to parliament, the paper states that 'low levels of public confidence, concentrated power in the executive and the growth of alternative centres of political power mean that further reforms are required to help Parliament reassert itself and establish a clearer identity' (Cm 7170, 2007: 40).

Quite whether such a parliamentary reassertion will be the outcome of the government's attempts to enhance democratic legitimacy in Britain of course remains to be seen. Yet, between the statement of its broad intentions and the production of actual institutional change lies the essence of the tension between stated desires to improve the functioning of democracy and the reality of how that then impacts on the efficiency of the political system. While there may be a genuine desire to decentralise power and expand the capacity of the institutions of representative democracy – that is, parliament – the fact remains that there are costs associated with this. Institutional change of this kind may well be geared towards enriching political legitimacy, but might only come about if the efficiency of the political system is also re-engineered. In this case, expanding the ability of parliament to scrutinise the executive and play a part in key decision-making processes will undoubtedly lead to a parliament which does just that, with consequent ramifications for the speed at which government can 'get its way.' Of course, a governmental approach to enhancing political legitimacy is quite unlike that taken by the public bodies examined here, and is also different from that pursued by parliament. The parliamentary and non-parliamentary actors examined here conceptualised disengagement in quite different ways, resulting in significantly different kinds of solutions being recommended and pursued.

However, in the final analysis, perhaps the most interesting aspect of all the reports and reforms examined here is that the actors involved believed that political disillusionment could be reversed, and that political legitimacy could be deepened significantly. The inference of the various diagnoses and the accompanying recommendations is that people will become more engaged, and thus more satisfied with the political system, if they are given opportunities to participate in decision-making and interact with politicians in new ways. Of course, as the evidence demonstrates, these 'new ways' must have a demonstrable impact on political outcomes. For example, the low participation rates in House of Commons online consultations is not just a reflection of the fact that the mechanism simply transplants old style participation into a new technological format without any qualitative change in the nature of the process, but that it also remains to be seen how such participation actually impacts upon subsequent political decision-making. While the various House of Commons committees involved in examining the expansion of consultation processes were clear that such processes would not involve participants directly making policy pronouncements and decisions, such participants nevertheless require some indication that involvement is not a waste of time and that their views and arguments do go on to inform policy makers in a meaningful and non-cosmetic way. Otherwise, participation of this kind may well contribute to a further de-legitimation of the political system, because while deliberation and debate are valuable underpinnings in democratic society, their value is determined by the responsiveness they promote from decision-makers.

Crucially, however, most of the reports and documents examined here paid scant attention to the delicate nature of the relationship between legitimacy, democracy and efficiency in modern Britain. Enhanced democratic functioning is almost too easy to argue in favour of, and clearly there are many different kinds of suggestions available about how such enhancement might be found, and how this will make the British system of governing more legitimate. However, the absence of sophisticated accounts of how improving input legitimacy might constrain output legitimacy – of how enhanced democratic participation might make it harder for the political system to produce decisions and societal conditions which are acceptable to the public – the tension between these two branches of legitimacy will remain. Ultimately, there is no easy answer to the problem of how to improve political legitimacy, deepen democracy and secure system efficiency, and until those actors interested in these issues acknowledge the depth of the complexity involved, the recommendations they produce will remain partial in their scope and unsatisfactory in their content. However, the fact that we continue to struggle incompetently with these issues is better than not struggling at all, and thus hope remains for our confused, well-meaning efforts at democratic governance.

References

Bale, T./Taggart, P./Webb, P. (2006): 'You Can't Always Get What You Want: Populism and the Power Inquiry', in: *Political Quarterly* 77/2, pp. 195-203.

Bennett, S. E./Flickinger, R. S./Rhine, S. L. (2000) 'Political Talk Over Here, Over There, Over Time', in: *British Journal of Political Science*, 30/1, pp. 99-119.

Cm 7170 (2007): *The Governance of Britain*, London: HMSO.

Coleman, S. (2003): 'A Tale of Two Houses: The House of Commons, the *Big Brother* House, and the People at Home', in: *Parliamentary Affairs* 56/3, pp. 733-58.

Coleman, S. (2004): 'Connecting Parliament to the Public via the Internet', in: *Information, Communication and Society* 7/1, pp. 1-22.

Cowley, P. (2002): *Revolts and Rebellions*, London: Politicos.
Cowley, P. (2005): *The Rebels*, London: Politicos.
Dalton, R.J. (2004): *Democratic Challenges, Democratic Choices: The Erosion of Political Support in Advanced Industrial Democracies*, Oxford: Oxford University Press.
Electoral Commission (2002): *Voter Engagement and Young People*, London: Electoral Commission.
Electoral Commission (2005): *Election 2005 Turnout: How Many, Who and Why?*, London: Electoral Commission.
Electoral Commission (2007): *An Audit of Political Engagement 4*, London: Electoral Commission.
Eurobarometer 67 (2007): *Public Opinion in the European Union: National Report*, United Kingdom, Brussels: European Commission.
Gray, M./Caul, M. (2000): 'Declining Voter Turnout in Advanced Industrial Democracies, 1950 to 1997', in: *Comparative Political Studies* 33/9, pp. 1091-1122.
Hansard Society (2005): *Members Only? Parliament in the Public Eye*, London: Hansard Society.
Harrop, M. (2001): 'An Apathetic Landslide: The British Election of 2001', in: *Government and Opposition* 36/3, pp. 295-313.
HC 7 (2004-5): *Human Reproductive Technologies and the Law: Fifth Report from the Science and Technology Committee*, London: HSMO.
HC 368 (2003-4): *Connecting Parliament with the Public: First Report from the Modernisation Committee*, London: HMSO.
HC 548 (2004-5): *The Challenge of Diversity: Hate Crime in Northern Ireland: Ninth Report from the Northern Ireland Committee*, London: HMSO.
HC 876 (2001-2): *Report from the Joint Committee on the Draft Communications Bill*, London: HMSO.
HC 1065 (2001-2): *Digital Technology: Working for Parliament and the Public: First Report from the House of Commons Information Committee*, London: HMSO.
HC 1248 (2003-4): *Public Petitions: Fifth Report from the Procedure Committee*, London: HSMO.
Judge, D. (1993): *The Parliamentary State*, London: Sage.
Judge, D. (1999): *Representation: Theory and Practice in Britain*, London: Routledge.
Kelso, A. (2007a): 'The House of Commons Modernisation Committee: Who Needs It?', in: *British Journal of Politics and International Relations* 9/1, pp. 138-57.
Kelso, A. (2007b): 'Parliament and Political Disengagement: Neither Waving nor Drowning', in: *Political Quarterly* 78/3, pp. 364-73.
MORI (2005): 'General Election Final Aggregate Analysis', at: http://www.mori.com/polls/2005/election-aggregate.shtml (accessed: April 2006).
Norris, P. (ed.) (1999): *Critical Citizens: Global Support for Democratic Governance*, Oxford: Oxford University Press.
Norton, P. (2005): *Parliament in British Politics*, London: Palgrave.
Pattie, C./Seyd, P./Whiteley, P. (2003): 'Civic Attitudes and Engagement in Modern Britain', in: *Parliamentary Affairs* 56/3, pp. 616-33.
Pharr, S./Putnam, R. (eds) (2000): *Disaffected Democracies: What's Troubling the Trilateral Democracies?*, Princeton: Princeton University Press.

Phelps, E. (2004): 'Young Citizens and Changing Electoral Turnout, 1964-2001', in: *Political Quarterly* 75/3, pp. 238-48.
Power Commission (2006): *Power to the People*, London: Power Commission.
Russell, M./Sciara, M. (2007): 'Why Does the Government Get Defeated in the House of Lords? The Lords, the Party System and British Politics', in: *British Politics* 2/3, pp. 299-322.
Stoker, G. (2006): *Why Politics Matters*, London: Palgrave.

Chapter 5
Informal Government: Complexity, Transparency and Legitimacy

Uwe Jun

1. Introduction

Informal government may be regarded as one key strategy in the governance of complexity and therefore needs to be considered within this volume. Germany is a good case study for this because a particularly wide range of forms of informal governing can be observed there. They fundamentally codetermine the everyday life of governance. This is because since 1961 national governments in Germany have always been coalition governments consisting of two or three parties (Saalfeld 1997). Yet, it is not only the coalition building process after general elections that is determined by informal instruments, processes and committees that mostly stay effective after the formation of a government. Informal but by now institutionalised ways of exchanging differences are rather common among the coalition parties, among the majorities of the two chambers of German parliament, i.e. the federal parliament (*Bundestag*) and the federal council (*Bundesrat*), and among the Cabinet and the heads of the governmental parties. They supplement formal provisions and procedures and have long been acknowledged to be functionally necessary and designed to improve efficiency (Rudzio 2002). Very complex forms of this government and coalition management have been established. However, different heads of government have used them in different ways. This chapter will identify, analyse and compare the ways in which the Kohl, Schröder and Merkel administrations have used, or are using, methods of informal governance. The focus shall be on defining central aspects of the patterns of informal governance characteristic of the respective governments, as well as on pointing out general tendencies and lines of development. Within the confines of this chapter it will, however, not be possible to analyse the informal aspect of governing in Germany in every detail.

When informal governance is mentioned, low transparency, fiddling behind closed doors and low political legitimacy of decisions due to a small circle of actors are often also mentioned. Formal institutions such as the Cabinet and the parliament are often seen as the *losers* of increasing informality because both are frequently confronted with accomplished facts by the decisions of informal committees, and it is difficult for them to defy the compromises or solutions initiated there without endangering the efficiency of governmental politics.

Therefore, it will have to be investigated to what extent informal committees really work in secrecy and whether they can guarantee a sufficient degree of transparency and legitimacy of the governmental proceedings. First, terms and definitions shall be clarified and the various dimensions of informality of the governmental proceedings shall be portrayed and placed in relation to one another. A distinction will be made between government-internal and government-external informality. In a second step the legitimacy of informal governmental proceedings will be briefly discussed. Following this, the forms of informality shall be analysed and compared with regard to transparency and legitimacy of the Kohl, Schröder and Merkel administrations.

2. Differentiation and dimensions of informality

Government in a parliamentary and federal system like that of the Federal Republic of Germany is a highly complex matter (e.g. Czada 2000; Schmidt 1992: 33ff). The governing process is subject to manifold factors of influence and context. To be named initially are formal institutional and structural factors, for instance the configuration of institutions and procedures prescribed under constitutional law, and those which result from the individual constitutional organs' rules of procedure (federal government, federal parliament, federal council).

However, viewed from a neo-institutionalist standpoint, these formal factors only shape fields of action in which political actors possess autonomy and room for manoeuvre. Here, institutional, structural and situational variables of context apply which are regulation-free, along with the formal and legally fixed institutions. The open fields of decision-making and formal action can be filled by informal actions, which take place within the scope of the specific rules of the game of the formal order, supplementing, changing, partially replacing or modifying the formal rules. To facilitate a closer examination of these informal aspects of governing it appears necessary to first conceptualise them. In this analysis, all actions in the political decision-making process which emanate from or involve the government and are aimed at reaching interim solutions and supplementing formal rules and procedures, shall be referred to with the term 'informalisation of governmental proceedings'. They have to be located outside of the decision-making procedures required by the Constitution or the rules of internal procedure. Furthermore, they primarily serve as a tool to make political decisions possible, i.e. to prevent potential blockades or to terminate already existing ones, and to conduct governmental politics more efficiently. Within the realm of 'informal governance' one must also include the formation of informal negotiation systems and/or the shifting of decision-making processes into informal committees involving governmental representatives. Informal negotiation systems or committees fulfil important functions by providing information and preparing the ground for agreement. They also serve as tools to identify political risks in the forefront of important political projects.

In political science research it is uncontroversial that informal components of modern governance are functionally necessary, and that they are even prerequisite for coordination, reaching agreements or for the enforcement of majority decisions by governments. Informality in this context stands for functional gain with regard to information, counselling, coordination and integration (Haungs 1991: 129) and is already viewed in some analyses as a key category of research into governmental systems and governmental actions (Kropp 2003: 24). According to Schultze-Fielitz's much-noted study of constitutional law, informal rules ensure the functioning of constitutional law and are, therefore, a relevant aspect of politics and of a country's specific political culture (Schultze-Fielitz 1984: 18). In terms of their function, they are regarded as an equally important main pillar of the state as formal rules (Schultze-Fielitz 1984: 159). Twenty-five years after Schultze-Fielitz's study, this observation assumes even greater importance: in light of constantly changing political, social, technological, environmental and other challenges, at the domestic level and internationally, formal arrangements alone appear insufficient to ensure appropriate problem-solving. If politics can actually still contribute to the solution of intra-society and/or global problems, it can hardly do so by sovereign decisions. Rather, it can do so by participating in pluralistic, corporatist and intergovernmental negotiation systems, in transnational regimes and international organisations (Scharpf 1993: 165; Risse 2007). Corporatist or intergovernmental negotiation systems themselves are already characterised by informality. Addressed are hereby informal processes of governing that can be found outside of the government's immediate institutions or organisations supporting the latter. These forms of governmental participation in negotiation systems, networks or corporatist arrangements can be conceptualised as *government-external informality*. A precondition for this is the direct involvement of governmental representatives in the respective committees and processes. Committees appointed by the government and exclusively serving as advisors to it shall be excluded if they are only acting upon governmental order, and if they have a low degree of decision-making authority or none at all (so-called exclusive advisory committees).[1] However, included will be all those committees in which the govern-

1 See Siefken (2003: 484) for a differentiation of decision-making and advisory bodies. He defines decision-making bodies as those committees whose decisions have a directly bind-

ment acts together with associations, NGOs, non-governmental parties or experts that are at least able to considerably influence the formally responsible institutions' preparations for decision-making, and in which the actors involved are making decisions that can also apply to those that are not involved.

However, governments also tend to develop informality within their organisation and structures. This kind of informal decision-making is especially evident in coalition governments which are the rule in the German political system (Manow 1996; Saalfeld 1997). I would like to term these forms of informality *government-internal informality*, and the analysis that follows will focus exclusively on the level of domestic politics. Figure 5.1 illustrates the distinction between government-internal and government-external informality. In order to grasp the informality of governmental actions and processes and thus of governments at large, it is not sufficient to only single out certain aspects, such as the personality of the incumbent and his or her style of government, single informal committees like commissions and alliances, or processes and decision-making bodies within governmental parties or coalitions. The analysis of individual incumbents' styles of government, for example, can explain a government's informality only to a very limited extent. For that reason situational variables of context, the field of policy and the cooperation with specific interest groups have to be included. Also, the concrete analysis of various informal committees, such as alliances, commissions and coalition roundtables, should only be viewed as one aspect of the informality of governments.

If one is to comprehensively analyse the informality of governments, one must examine four main dimensions of informality which are closely interrelated:

1. Actors: A distinction needs to be made here between individual and collective actors. Each group can be divided again into political actors with direct informal powers of decision, such as political parties or coalition committees, or with indirect informal power of decision, such as personal consultants, commissions, interest groups, NGOs etc.
2. Observers: Here too, one can differentiate between collective and individual actors who when acting as observing entities are either partially or wholly public. The more publicity that is generated via the mass media, the wider ranging is the circle of observers and under the more scrutiny is the informal process.

---

ing effect in dealing with third parties. This distinction leaves grey areas with regard to informality of governmental policies because it would need to be established in each case if a committee had made decisions which had influenced the government's decision in the run-up to the formal decision-making process.

3. Action Patterns: Included here are the particular strategies and tactics of actors in the informal process of preparation, production and implementation of decisions; in the chronological course of events (ad-hoc or planned) and in the choice of instruments as well as in the measures taken.
4. Fields of Action: The content of governmental policy can be differentiated into various areas, with each developing informal rules, processes and actors of their own.

Figure 5.1: Government-external and government-internal informality

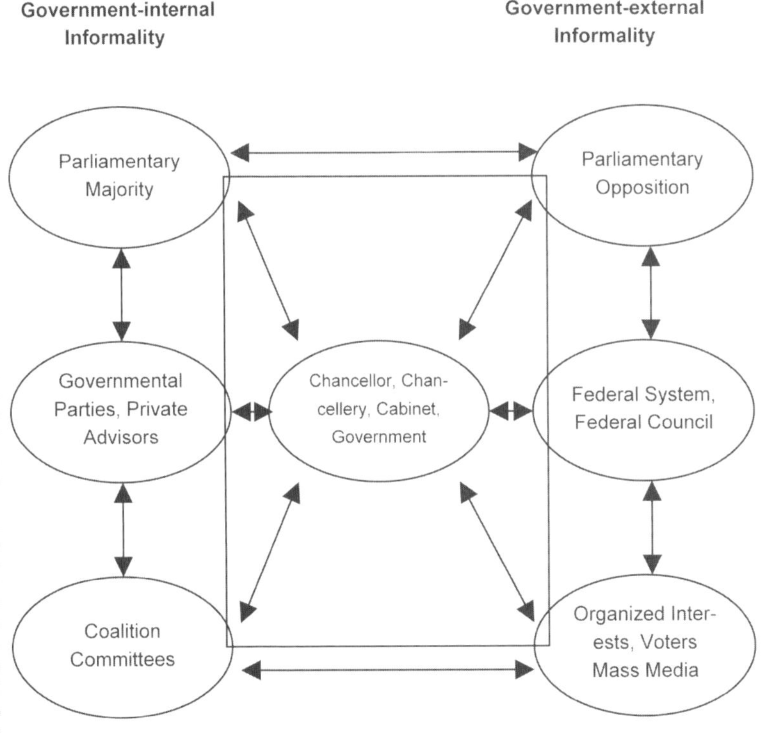

The different dimensions vary (actors the most, fields of action the least) depending on whether government-internal or -external informality is concerned.

3. Informality and transparency of governmental actions: More efficiency without losing legitimacy?

A government's recourse to informal rules, processes and committees can create more efficiency and better quality of governmental actions and also produce more legitimacy than decisions reached using the tools of traditional hierarchical governance. The use of informal structures and processes can achieve greater legitimacy, in that social or political problems are approached by involving relevantly affected groups in the process of finding a consensus or in reaching a compromise. By seeking coordination, consensus or compromise with government-internal and government-external actors, their values, interests and attitudes can be fed into the decision-making process. This grants a higher legitimacy both to the process and the result than would be achieved by leaving these actors out of the decision-making process. One can differentiate here between administrative and social legitimacy. The former can be increased by incorporating as many actors as possible on the governmental side (government-internal informality), the latter by consulting and cooperating with as many social groups as possible (government-external informality). These two types of legitimacy do not have to complement each other, but they also do not have to exclude each other. A government can accrue a high level of legitimacy for its political actions if both forms complement each other and form a higher total sum than the individual forms of legitimacy. The degree of transparency also contributes to the legitimacy of governmental actions, at least on the input side.

Ideally, therefore, informal procedures and committees can significantly strengthen input- and output-legitimacy, provided that the decision-making process (as defined by the political public) is transparent, and that the aspects of efficiency of governance are sufficiently accounted for. To gain more legitimacy, the actors involved should be granted insight into the decision-making process, to the extent that they can relate their interests to those of the other actors and that they accept the rules and procedures of the negotiation and decision-making process. The idea of 'good governance' essentially implies the incorporation of as many social groups and actors as possible. Depending on the subject-matter, the extent, and the need for regulation, they all have their participation guaranteed in a flexible way without fixed norms and forms of negotiating. Further, their involvement is not tied to formal rules of authority, to extensive disclosure of informal rules or to the topics under discussion and perspectives of success. The unclear regulation of authority in the case of informal practices allows both a concentration on the essentials, and, due to their flexibility, an adjustment to existing distributions of power and the actors' different needs for information.

Figure 5.2: Advantages and disadvantages of informal forms of governance

Advantages

- Absence of clear regulation of authority enables concentration on the essentials.
- Higher possibility to reach consensus due to unconstrained style of negotiating.
- Flexibility allows adaptation to distribution of power and needs for information.
- Often less effort in terms of transaction costs, time, labour, and effort of communication.
- Less resources required to gain, process and interpret information.
- Testing phase within a pre-legal frame offers orientation and allows for rational actions.
- Beneficial in relatively open situations.

Disadvantages

- Marked by exclusiveness; can impair generality and equality of participation.
- Informal networks are only transparent to a limited extent.
- Deparliamentarisation of the political process.

To ensure the efficiency of governance, however, it is necessary to limit the number of participants without having to accept major losses of legitimacy. This demand can be realized more easily inside the government, where such advantages of informal governance as flexibility, searching for a compromise without a legally fixed frame, the lowering of insecurity among the actors (see Wewer 1991: 25) or the possibility of tests in a pre-legal frame, could be used faster and without much effort. The incorporation of government-external actors calls for a clear selection of interests whose criteria should be disclosed by the government to rule out the suggestion of favouritism and patronage. In any case, informal acting has only limited visibility and comprehensibility. Legitimacy could be endangered by high exclusiveness and low transparency. Also, the decision-making outside of parliamentary committees could reduce the legitimacy of decisions if parliament is only able to agree to foregone decisions without having substantial scope of decision-making ability itself. These aspects of transparency and legitimacy shall be included in the analysis below of the informal components of governance of the Kohl, Schröder and Merkel administrations. Figure 5.2 summarises the advantages and disadvantages of informal governance.

4. From Kohl to Schröder to Merkel: or from party-and-coalition-democracy to commission-and-media-democracy and back?

On the basis of these conceptual considerations, a comparison of the different forms of informality during the Kohl, Schröder and Merkel administrations shall now be undertaken. At the beginning is the assumption that due to more recent developments in the governmental system of the Federal Republic of Germany, government-internal informality has become less important in favour of government-external informality. One should highlight, in particular, three courses of development: The change in politics towards more cooperative forms of engagement with the addressees; the necessity for at least a partial cooperation of government and opposition due to almost continuously contrary developments of *Bundestag* and *Bundesrat* majorities; and the notably increased mediatisation of politics (for the term of mediatisation of politics see Jun 2008). However, it should be stated explicitly that due to the special situation of the Grand Coalition since 2005, the government-internal dimension has experienced a clear gain in importance compared to the previous government. This is attributable to the increased complexity of the informal process of coalition management, due to the two main competitors' diverging politics, competition strategies and communication strategies in the German party system. Besides, the second aspect of change mentioned above (different majorities in the *Bundestag* and the *Bundesrat*) is currently irrelevant and the third one (mediatisation of politics) is less important in chancellor Merkel's style of governance than in that of her predecessor.

Informality, coalitions and cooperative forms of politics

The change in politics towards more cooperative forms of decision-making processes is hardly separable from an informalisation of politics. Indeed, one could also speak of the two sides of the same coin. At the centre of the argument is the idea that due to the increased complexity of political problems, the decreasing capacity for regulation of national politics, and an operational weakness of the established political institutions, decentralised structures and processes have to be created in which the arising problems can be solved in cooperation with the affected groups. Included can be experts and surveyors who can gain influence over decision-making through their knowledge and expertise (for more detail see Jun and Grabow 2008). In so-called pluralistic political networks or neo-corporatist arrangements, a high degree of openness of decision-making can be found in the ideal case, as well as a relatively thorough consideration of the participating social and political actors' interests whose divergent opinions are supposed to be accommodated through conflict management. The government primarily functions as a coordinator and moderator. Networks and cooperation forums mainly exist sectorally or regionally. It is the approaches taken toward solutions or the compromises reached during discussions or negotiations which are the decisive fundamentals of action, and not the decisions reached within the coalition government or between coalition (or rather, parliamentary) parties.

These developments are, at least at first glance, reflected in the informality of the Kohl and Schröder administrations. Whilst in the era of Schröder government-external actors had more access to governance and decision-making processes, the government-internal side played a very big role in the Kohl administration. During the first years of the Kohl administration, the main actors and venues of decision-making were the coalition summits between the party chairmen of the governing parties CDU, CSU and FDP, the coalition talks or roundtables consisting of the Cabinet's top politicians, the government's parliamentary parties and the parties themselves (Rudzio 1991; Korte 1998). Schreckenberger, the State secretary of the Chancellor's Office who was holding office at the beginning of the Kohl administration, called the coalition meetings, which took place on a weekly basis, a kind of guidance committee, in which procedures were coordinated and essential decisions or courses of decision established (Schreckenberger 1992: 152).[2] The coalition groups were mainly responsible for the preparation of decision-making, and it was in this context that the respective experts of the administration, government and their supporting parliamentary parties congregated. Government-internal circles were thus the main actors in the process of reaching a decision. The coalition roundtables' centrality to the decision-making process is also clear from the timing of their meetings prior to those of the Cabinet, and their preparation of the latter's decisions (Rudzio 1991: 136). As head of government, Helmut Kohl used coalition roundtables as a central management tool (Stüwe 2006: 550). Coalition roundtables and talks were the principal informal centre of power in which questions likely to cause conflict were addressed and binding agreements within the government reached. Whilst the circle of people fluctuated, it comprised party chairmen in only one decision-making round, and experts of the governmental parties in one other case.

In terms of the integration of different social interests, the first Schröder administration was less coalition- and more consensus-oriented. At the beginning of its term in office, it tried to grant various actors access to the government to put through reforms 'beyond the traditional ideological ditches'

---

2 Elsewhere Schreckenberger (1992: 147) pointedly remarks that there was no political evaluation, no measure and no bill by the federal government that could not be a matter of coalition debate or recommendation.

via 'a solution-oriented culture of dialogue' (Steinmeier 2001: 265). Guided by the motto of 'consensus and leadership' (Steinmeier 2001) it helped to develop numerous commissions, forums and alliances which primarily served the purpose of counsel and decision-preparation, but which also occasionally displayed a prejudicial effect on some of the federal government's decisions (e.g. nuclear energy consensus talks or the Hartz- and Rürup-commissions for the protection of the social security system; see Siefken 2006). The negotiation of political solutions in government-external, informal committees was supposed to exclude from the power struggle within the coalition problems that were controversial in particular amongst the coalition parties, as well as amongst various interest groups in society. These commissions were supposed to be excluded from party political competition as much as possible in order to contain critics of governmental politics, to annul departmental egotisms and to create a sufficient basis of legitimacy for governmental politics. On the one hand, this style of governance is based on the consensus of the people concerned, which is the reason why the participants have mainly been recruited as representatives of social groups and areas of operation, and only to a lesser extent because of their expertise. On the other hand, the attempt was made to create legitimacy beyond the formal participation of alliances, even in neo-corporate arrangements like the talks at the Alliance for Jobs (see for more detail Jochem 2007). A multitude of commissions were supposed to work out a broad consensus in the forefront of parliamentary debates and governmental decisions, to prepare their implementation and to generate acceptance for them (Korte 2007: 184). It is widely acknowledged that governance through commissions was the central characteristic of Gerhard Schröder's style of governing (for example Helms 2005: 88). One should, however, not dismiss those who voiced justifiable doubts about the limited legitimacy of the commissions due to their technocratic course of action and their few interactions with the representative organs (Decker 2007).

Governance through commissions does not mean that the SPD and the Greens' coalition committees during the Schröder administrations were meaningless. Nevertheless, they often were not in the centre of the decision-making process. Thus, they held their meetings more rarely during the first years and on the parliamentary party level, which from the very beginning did not attach central importance to the activities of coalition management. Although the coalition committee's power-political relevance increased in the course of the government, the same decision-political importance was never attached to it during the SPD and Greens' term of office as during the period in office of the coalition between the Christian Democrats and the Liberals.

It should be reiterated that this analysis endeavours to highlight different degrees of informality in the Kohl and Schröder administrations: Whilst during Kohl's terms of office, too, there had been manifold forms of cooperative politics, the federal government under Schröder intensified coalition management and put it more strongly into the foreground, mainly at the Greens' urging.

Since 2005 in the Grand Coalition of CDU/CSU and SPD, the coalition committee has won back its central position in the decision-making process (see Glaab 2007). According to the coalition agreement an immediate meeting of the committee must be held if one of the coalition parties requests it. The members are the federal chancellor and the vice-chancellor, the party chairmen, the chairmen of the parliamentary parties and the CSU's spokesman in the Bundestag (*Landesgruppenchef*). The relevant informal decision-making committee of the Grand Coalition forms the committee, since it is only in this environment that all central actors are gathered. In comparison, other channels of influence and decision-making appear subordinate. Although informal talks also take place at the centre of the decision-making process around the coalition committee within the coalition, the heterogeneous structure of power (within the CDU/CSU as well as the SPD) means that only talks in the coalition committee have a binding influence. Within the CDU, the party executive takes a leading role in managing government policy. This allows the minister-presidents of the CDU-governed state governments to provide input for the government's agenda. Regarding the SPD, former vice-chancellor Müntefering and his successor Steinmeier established a type of 'auxiliary governmental headquarters' within their ministries (respectively, Work and Social Affairs and Foreign Affairs) to organise and co-ordinate the SPD's work in the federal government. The coalition committee forms the Grand Coalition's strategic centre, whose protagonists are chancellor Merkel and the SPD's party chairman. In line with convention and with the central position of the chancellor in the German system, the federal government's strategic centre is still located in close proximity to the chancellor's position. As in the era of Kohl, coordinating talks take place not exclusively in the coalition committee on the parliamentary working level, but also in the committees and in the working groups that resolve numerous details in the individual fields of policy, so that only topics that are likely to cause conflict have to be solved within the coalition committee. The informal talks between the heads of the parliamentary parties in the *Bundestag* should also not be underestimated. The degree of informal parliamentary co-governance of governmental politics varies according to the field of policy, form of action and the coalition parties' interests. It is, however, to be ranked as substantial (for more details on the parliamentary co-governance see Schwarzmeier 2001).

Whereas the Schröder administration put the achievement of social legitimacy in the foreground, the preceding and following governments paid more attention to administrative legitimacy. This can be accounted for by the different roles of the respective governmental parties and the incorporation of the parliamentary opposition into the decision-making process.

Informality, governing Parties and opposition

A main factor in the promotion of government-external informality lies in the contrary majorities of the *Bundestag* and *Bundesrat*. Due to the high numbers of bills requiring the approval of the *Bundesrat*, the government is often forced into a measure of cooperation with the federal parliament's opposition (*Bundestagsopposition*) if it wants to achieve its political goals. In these cases, both the different majority proportions and the structure of the German federal system as a whole encourage informal negotiation and decision-making processes.

In the case of equal majorities, however, informal processes can be initiated more easily within the government because negotiation and coordination processes take place within the governing parties. In the years up until 1990, then-chancellor Kohl made use of this by closely linking the CDU's party organisation to informal processes. According to Peter Haungs (1991: 117), Kohl was not particularly fond of a more rigidly formalised structure and regarded it as superfluous. He expanded the CDU as a personal base of power alongside the chancellor's office by incorporating many office bearers and members of parliament, as well as functionaries in opinion-developing and decision-making processes (Schönbohm 1985: 16). Kohl used the support within the party through his network ('System Kohl') as a central resource of power, and expanded it in the course of his terms of office (Korte 2001: 58). 'After 1982 the network of CDU politicians that owed him their careers could be fortified. He could reward loyalists and recruit new ones – many high up in various federal states' branches – by granting them chancellery jobs, ministerial jobs or quasi-governmental posts' (Clemens 1998: 101). He used personal ties based on long-standing contacts, which he often maintained via phone from Bonn (Korte 1998: 30ff), as a kind of 'early-warning system' to recognize moods and opinions within his party and to guard himself against possible inner-party movements of rivalry. During the Kohl administration the inner-party process of voting became increasingly informal, because Kohl acted in a dual role as chancellor and head of his party to decide the agenda and frame the political debate. Udo Zolleis (2007: 193) talks about an 'informal style of decision-making' that was characterised by negotiation processes within the parties in which Kohl had the role of a facilitator attempting to gain information. The informants' network stretched across all party levels in a mostly non-hierarchical manner, although Kohl, during the whole of his government, attached a special importance to the party's chairmanship along with the coalition roundtables as a particularly important decision-making committee (Haungs 1989: 31). He especially used this to harmonise governmental policy with the minister-presidents of the CDU-governed federal states. It is widely agreed that these patterns of action and his close connection to the CDU as an actor in the informal process also shaped Kohl's subsequent governing; even in phases in which, because of a majority of SPD-governed federal states in the *Bundesrat*, inter-party cooperation between government and opposition became necessary in order to implement policy contents.

Unlike Helmut Kohl, Gerhard Schröder could not use his own party as a base of power, and it would never become one. When he was still minister-president of Lower Saxony, Schröder initially came forward as a critic of the party leadership in many instances, which won him only few favours within the party. At the beginning of his time as federal chancellor, the then party chairman and Schröder-adversary Lafontaine assigned the positions within the party. Meanwhile, during his almost five-year incumbency as party leader, Schröder was unable to construct the inner-party networks necessary to stabilise his position. In the end, Schröder had to put through his domestic reform package *Agenda 2010* as a top down endeavour against the resistance of many parts of the party (for more detail see Jun 2007). After sensing only low support from the majority of the population (serious defeats of the SPD in federal states' elections), the labour unions (public protests) and in his own party, he tried to effect re-elections by calling for a vote of confidence. Thus, the SPD never became a supporting pillar for the informality of Schröder's governmental politics.

Schröder instead preferred external informality, and thus in view of the majority proportions he included oppositional politicians in leading positions in governmental commissions. He also sought an inner-party consensus with minister-presidents of the CDU, and at the end of 2003 looked for consensus talks with the CDU/CSU leadership to pass the tax reform with regard to the procedure at the Conciliation Committee. Schröder often distinguished himself in these talks as facilitator and main actor of governmental politics who, on the one hand, clearly defined the direction of governance and on the other, attempted to synthesise different party political interests into a compromise. He conducted and coordinated several informal committees and roundtables such as commissions, the coalition committee and talks with the Union's party leadership. He achieved this by always providing the frame of the decision-making and by including both the political and social majorities necessary to find a solution through compromise. In order to break his party's resistance and to limit the coalition partner's room for manoeuvre, he attempted to centralise his power (Korte 2007: 173ff).

With regard to the aspects of inner-party structures and the attitude towards the parliamentary opposition, Angela Merkel's chancellorship is characterized to a great extent by the constellation of the Grand Coalition: First, the necessity of cooperation with the opposition does not apply since the parties in government have clear majorities in both chambers of parliament. Furthermore, her own party as a basis of power does not play such a central role as it did in the case of Helmut Kohl, for whom inner- and outer-party reasons applied. Merkel is fixed within the inner party less than Kohl. She either could not or did not want to create a balancing of interests within the party to the extent Kohl did, and as such could only use the party as a basis of power to a lesser extent. With regard to the outer party, the coalition partners, who are of approximate equality of power, must always find compromises and solutions of consensus. Merkel attempts to do justice to both by sometimes emphasizing her concurrent role as the CDU's party leader (for example, for a long time with regard to the topics of minimum wages and domestic security), and at other times, by opening up to social-democratic positions (for example, in the case of the extension of unemployment benefits (ALG I) or family policy) if they are close to those of the CDU. This strategic orientation is facilitated by her double role as chancellor and party leader, since it enables her to stabilize her power and to have a sufficient basis to put through governmental policy within the party. The party chairmanship offers central power-political resources with which to emphasize her position in relation to the powerful minister-presidents of the CDU. The party's federal executive committee serves Merkel as an informal panel of governmental politics, in which she can make arrangements and develop positions which the CDU represents towards its coalition partners.

The constellation of the Grand Coalition in particular marks the structural limits of the central governance of governmental politics through the Chancellery. More than in other coalition constellations, several individual and collective actors in the power triangle of executive, the majority of the Bundestag, and the governing parties define the results of the negotiation processes outside the formal decision-making mechanisms. The Grand Coalition's strategic centre of power can indeed be located close to the Chancellor, but is according to an assessment by Glaab (2007: 108) informal and to a large extent depending on context.

Informality, media-orientation and agreements among acquaintances

As an environment which surrounds politics, the media poses probably the most serious challenge to, and has the ability to effect far-reaching changes in, political communication and modern governance (see Kamps 2006). Increasing commercialisation and internationalisation has accelerated the process of media expansion. The media has thus taken on a life of its own barely controllable by politics on the national level. In spite of still existing structural deficits, political actors have largely succeeded in adjusting to the requirements of function and action as demanded by the media. This implies, inter alia, producing politics for the media and 'selling' contents to it. One of the main activities of the political parties has become the professional shaping of politics, according to the rules of media logic. In this context one can differentiate between the portrayal of politics and the creation of policy.

Whereas the creation of policy occurs in settings of complex, media-unfriendly negotiation and seeks to achieve 'legitimacy via procedure' (Luhmann), the portrayal pins its hopes on the production of images, on the media-appropriate implementation of politics and on the presentation by depiction- and conveyance-communication. The creation of decisions in the political domain and the portrayal of politics are incongruent and follow their own logic each. Nevertheless, media coverage (particularly in the electronic media) barely separates the two, thereby forcing political actors to recognise this temporary unison in the electronic media. Recently, a more often used and promising strategy consists of neutralising this separation with regard to the conceptualisation of politics, i.e. regarding self-portrayal, portrayal by third parties and creation as a uniform process. This results in paying major regard to the media's logic right from the definition of problems through to the evaluation of political actions. According to this view, access to the mass media and positive coverage for political actors are regarded as a power resource that is not to be underestimated.

This raises the consideration that informality in politics has to be made more transparent and carried out more systematically, since it cannot and should not avoid a portrayal at all. As a matter of fact, several differences can be seen between the Kohl and Schröder administrations: the government-external informality that was more pronounced with Schröder was also more transparent, since a greater number of actors were involved and the media gained access to the commissions that had already been set up with publicity effect. The appointment of commissions and the submission of final reports were widely and publicly debated. Moreover, they were media-compatible by being staged according to the rules of event management, and discussions within the commissions and committees were subjects of media coverage. This could be called a media-compatible functionalisation of informal advisory and consensus committees (Stüwe 2006: 557). This strategy of the Schröder administration has worked well: As an empirical survey shows, the coverage of the work of commissions increased significantly in the course of Schröder's term in office (Siefken 2003: 491). Besides, the appointment of these commissions requires long- or at least middle-ranged planning, thus to a lesser extent it allows for ad-hoc decisions. The commissions' intensified impact on the public was part of the strategy of mediatisation of governmental politics, which was overall clearly recognisable during Schröder's terms of office. He attempted for a long time to use the mass media to serve his purposes, and recognised the great importance of medial communication to governance. Further, he preferred a style of governing that had an effect on the public (Rosumek 2007: 227ff; Korte 2007: 186ff; Stüwe 2006: 552).

However, governmental reality had been different during chancellor Kohl's terms of office: many internal ad-hoc committees and strategy-roundtables dominated. A low degree of transparency of decision-forming channels and the spontaneous form of contact are patterns of action that characterised Helmut Kohl's style of governance: 'Instead the chancellor often upheld a spontaneous working method, grabbing the phone, having conversations in private, or taking someone aside' (former State-Secretary at the Federal Chancellery, Jenninger, quoted in Korte 1998: 33; see also Rudzio 1991: 136). The informal commissions and panels that Kohl appointed acted more in the background, fulfilling informational rather than public functions.

In Kohl's era, outside of the party- and coalition-committees, the so-called 'morning state-of-affairs discussion' was regarded as a central informal roundtable to aid decision-making, during which the chancellor consulted personal confidants from the Chancellery (special roles were played by the manager of Kohl's office, Weber, by the director of department 5 'Social and political analyses, communication and public relations', Ackermann, and since the appointment of Schäuble in 1984, by the respective minister of the chancellery). An additional venue, though of lesser importance, were the evening roundtables at the chancellor's bungalow that were set up more openly with regard to the circle of participants (Korte 1998: 25ff, Mertes 2003: 77). From the morning state-of-affairs discussion until the rounds of talks at the chancellor's bungalow in the evening, Kohl surrounded himself with a small group of advisors and people doing the preliminary work for him, chosen by the criteria of loyalty, solidarity and trustworthiness (Korte 1998: 25). 'Morning state-of-affairs discussions' with individual central actors from the federal government also existed in the Schröder administration, involving SPD-chairman Müntefering, secretary general Benneter, director of the Chancellery Steinmeier and government spokesman Anda. However, apart from Steinmeier and the manager of the chancellor's office, Krampitz, the circle of personal consultants was more fluid and only the two aforementioned individuals had a special proximity to the chancellor (according to Schröder in the programme 'Kerner' on ZDF on May 6, 2004).

Angela Merkel also organised such an intimate roundtable, notably including her office manager Beate Baumann, considered to be her closest confidant, and her media consultant Eva Christiansen. Numbering among her regular circle of consultants outside the cabinet are the former chairman of the Young Union, Hildegard Müller, the chairman of the Women's Union, Maria Böhmer, and government spokesman Ulrich Wilhelm (Rosumek 2007: 274). Merkel obviously draws the circle of people who have direct access to her rather narrowly: beside Baumann and the head of the Chancellery, Thomas de Maizière, the morning discussions belong to the head of the planning staff in the Chancellery Matthias Graf von Kielmannsegg, Hildegard Müller and Ulrich Wilhelm. The CDU/CSU's parliamentary party leader Kauder and the CDU's secretary-general Roland Pofalla occasionally join the talks. To a lesser extent Merkel counts on media-oriented forms of governance, which is particularly visible from the explicit non-staging of private aspects. However, her style of governance cannot withstand the increased demands of the media environment: Unlike Kohl's style of governance, Angela Merkel's government is clearly characterised by mass-medial, public characteristics as seen, for example, in the staging of policy and the highly public conflicts between the coalition parties. Merkel apparently pays attention to the principle that the staging of politics should at the same time convey contents in order to not be exposed as mere performance. However, the publicly recognizable, mass-medially communicated differentiation of the coalition parties is a central characteristic of the Merkel administration, and is implemented strategically by the actors involved in all controversial fields of policy, particularly in those areas of policy that are especially sensitive with regard to party politics. In terms of the Grand Coalition's more complex projects, the coalition parties, governmental parties and Cabinet are in a constant communicative trade-off, both behind closed doors and in front of the cameras or microphones. The mass media function as a mirror: the heads of parties, parliamentary parties and government use them not only as a platform, but also to take turns observing one another, and to test majority and communication capabilities of their projects as well as government-external and -internal reactions to them. In public communication, actors often test which position could permanently stay on the political agenda, what is accepted, what can be implemented and what cannot. The public is used to test political resonance and in this sense participates in defining the contents of governmental politics, as the levels of contents and conveyance have an interdependent relation (see Kamps 2006: 124).

The fact that Angela Merkel puts much less focus on the work of government-external commissions than her immediate predecessor can be attributed to the much greater role that formal aspects play in her style of governance than they did before. This is at least partially due to the constellation of the Grand Coalition, but probably also the result of an intentional distancing from Schröder's style of governing and a stronger turning towards parties, both their parliamentary arm and ministries as the central actors of governance. She often leaves – once an agreement has been reached in the coalition roundtables – large parts of the drawing up and implementation of governmental policy to the individual departments, particularly the ministries controlled by the SPD. Since her ability to interfere in these fields of policy is in any case restricted, she does not want to endanger the stability of the coalition. The ministries, on the other hand, are in close contact with their parliamentary parties or party headquarters. This proceeding became apparent in the cases of the health care reform, the labour market reforms, the pensions and the family policies. Even in departments controlled by the CDU, the individual ministers enjoy extensive self-contained room for manoeuvre within the agreements and understandings made between the coalition parties. The position of the Chancellery in everyday political decision-making appears less important than in the Kohl or Schröder administrations.

5. Conclusion

So this chapter has argued that in the Kohl, Schröder and Merkel administrations, different styles of governance, strategies and initial conditions have caused different forms of informal governance. During Helmut Kohl's administrations, greater value was attached to government-internal than to a government-external informality, whereas the opposite situation could be found during Schröder's administration.

Angela Merkel's administration ranges between these two poles. This can account for changes in politics, in particular a stronger emphasis on co-operative forms, the necessity of negotiations between the government and the parliamentary opposition due to a party-political difference of majorities in the *Bundestag* and *Bundesrat*, and the process of media-orientation. With regard to responsible governing, governance in Germany is tied to a permanent balancing of interests. This has led to high-publicity forms of governance due to the centrality of the mass media. The shifting of decisions into informal, government-external committees should also be understood as a reaction to the media's increased importance. It is constantly searching for up-to-date and accessible information, and receives it more easily if the discussion takes place publicly and outside of formal governmental institutions. The Schröder and Merkel administrations, with their informal forms of governing, were – or are – geared more to the tone and tenor of public communication and less to informal networks as was the case with Kohl. A relatively high level of transparency exists within the Grand Coalition and had existed in the red-green coalition, and a clear deficit of legitimacy cannot be ascertained. Unlike the red-green attempt to create more social legitimacy and direct legitimation, in the Grand Coalition the administrative search for consensus is (necessarily) more in the foreground. It is, however, also often exchanged in public. The differences presented here in the degree of informality between the Kohl, Schröder and Merkel administrations, and the explanations given, highlight general tendencies without claiming to have exhaustively dealt with the complex subject matter in all its aspects and details. It can, however, be concluded that informal governing in Germany is not only necessary, but also is a form of governance that barely limits legitimacy and substantially adds to the political decision-making capabilities and assertiveness. As such it is a key parameter in the governance of complexity.

References

Clemens, C. (1998): 'Party Management as a Leadership Resource: Kohl and the CDU/CSU', in: *German Politics* 7/1, pp. 91-119.

Czada, R. (2000): 'Konkordanz, Korporatismus und Politikverflechtung: Dimensionen der Verhandlungsdemokratie', in: Holtmaann E./Voelzkow, H. (eds), *Zwischen Wettbewerbs- und Verhandlungsdemokratie, Analysen zum Regierungssystem der Bundesrepublik Deutschland*, Wiesbaden: Westdeutscher Verlag, pp. 23-49.

Decker, F. (2007): 'Parteiendemokratie im Wandel', in: Decker, F./Neu, V. (eds) *Handbuch der deutschen Parteien*, Wiesbaden: VS Verlag, pp. 19-61.

Glaab, M. (2007): 'Strategie und Politik: das Fallbeispiel Deutschland', in: Fischer, Th./Schmitz, G. P./Seberich, M. (eds) *Die Strategie der Politik, Ergebnisse einer vergleichenden Studie*, Gütersloh: Verlag Bertelsmann Stiftung, pp. 67-115.

Haungs, P. (1989): 'Kanzlerprinzip und Regierungstechnik im Vergleich: Adenauers Nachfolger', in: *Aus Politik und Zeitgeschichte* B1-2/89, pp. 28-36.

Haungs, P. (1991): 'Parteipräsidien als Entscheidungszentren der Regierungspolitik – Das Beispiel der CDU', in: Hartwich, H.-H./Wewer, G. (eds) *Regieren in der Bundesrepublik II, Formale und informale Komponenten des Regierens*, Opladen: Leske + Budrich, pp. 113-23.

Helms, L. (2005): 'Die Informalisierung des Regierungshandelns in der Bundesrepublik: ein Vergleich der Regierungen Kohl und Schröder', in: *Zeitschrift für Staats- und Europawissenschaften* 3/1, pp. 70-96.

Jochem, S. (2007): 'From Corporatist Consensualism to the Politics of Commissions: German Welfare Reform and the Inefficiency of the Alliance for Jobs', in: Blühdorn, I./Jun, U. (eds) *Economic Efficiency – Democratic Empowerment, Contested Modernization in Britain and Germany*, Lanham, Maryland: Rowman & Littlefield (Lexington), pp. 147-64.

Jun, U. (2007): 'Radical Reformers – Defiant Electorates? Reform Policy and International Competitiveness under Schröder and Blair', in: Blühdorn, I./Jun, U. (eds) *Economic Efficiency – Democratic Empowerment, Contested Modernization in Britain and Germany*, Lanham, Maryland: Rowman & Littlefield (Lexington), pp. 31-67.

Jun, U. (2008): 'Professionalisierung der politischen Kommunikation in Großbritannien', in: Grabow, K./Köllner, P. (eds) *Parteien und ihre Wähler, Gesellschaftliche Konfliktlinien und Wählermobilisierung im internationalen Vergleich*, St. Augustin/Berlin: Konrad-Adenauer Stiftung, pp. 177-206.

Jun, U./Grabow, K. (2008): *Mehr Expertise in der deutschen Politik? Zur Übertragbarkeit des 'Evidence-based policy approach'*, Gütersloh: Verlag Bertelsmann Stiftung.

Kamps, K. (2006): 'Regierung, Partei, Medien. Meinungsfindung in der Mediengesellschaft', in: Kamps, K./Nieland, J.-U. (eds) *Regieren und Kommunikation,* Köln: Herbert von Halem Verlag, pp. 110-38.

Korte, K.-R. (1998): *Deutschlandpolitik in Helmut Kohls Kanzlerschaft: Regierungsstil und Entscheidungen 1982-1989*, Stuttgart: Deutsche Verlagsanstalt.

Korte, K.-R. (2001): 'Politisches Entscheiden im parlamentarischen System der Bundesrepublik Deutschland. Zum Entscheidungsspielraum des deutschen Bundeskanzlers', in: Dicke, K. (ed.) *Politisches Entscheiden*, Baden-Baden: Nomos, pp. 53-70.

Korte, K.-R. (2007): 'Der Pragmatiker des Augenblicks: Das Politikmanagement von Bundeskanzler Gerhard Schröder 2002-2005', in: Egle, Ch./Zohlnhöher, R. (eds) *Ende des rot-grünen Projektes. Eine Bilanz der Regierung Schröder 2002-2005*, Wiesbaden: VS Verlag, pp. 168-96.

Kropp, S. (2003): 'Regieren als informaler Prozess. Das Koalitionsmanagement der rot-grünen Bundesregierung', in: *Aus Politik und Zeitgeschichte* B 43/2003, pp. 23-31.

Manow, Ph. (1996): 'Informalisierung und Parteipolitisierung – zum Wandel exekutiver Entscheidungsprozesse in der Bundesrepublik Deutschland', in: *Zeitschrift für Parlamentsfragen*, 27/1, pp. 96-107.

Mertes, M. (2003): 'Bundeskanzleramt und Bundespresseamt. Das Informations- und Entscheidungsmanagement der Regierungszentrale', in: Hirscher, G./Korte, K.-R. (eds) *Information und Entscheidung. Kommunikationsmanagement der politischen Führung*, Wiesbaden: Westdeutscher Verlag, pp. 52-78.

Risse, Th. (2007): 'Governance in Räumen begrenzter Staatlichkeit: Reformen ohne Staat?', in: Wolf, K. D. (ed.) *Staat und Gesellschaft – fähig zur Reform?*, Baden-Baden: Nomos, pp. 231-45.

Rosumek, L. (2007): *Die Kanzler und die Medien. Acht Porträts von Adenauer bis Merkel*, Frankfurt am Main: Campus.

Rudzio, W. (1991): 'Informelle Entscheidungsmuster in Bonner Koalitionsregierungen', in: Hartwich, H.-H./Wewer, G. (ed.) *Regieren in der Bundesrepublik II, Formale und informale Komponenten des Regierens*, Opladen: Leske + Budrich, pp. 125-41.

Rudzio, W. (2002): 'Koalitionen in Deutschland: Flexibilität informellen Regierens', in: Kropp, S./Schüttemeyer, S./Sturm, R. (eds) *Koalitionen in West- und Osteuropa*, Opladen: Leske + Budrich, pp. 43-67.

Saalfeld, Th. (1997): 'Deutschland: Auswanderung der Politik aus der Verfassung? Regierungskoalitionen und Koalitionsmanagement in der Bundesrepublik 1949-1997', in: Müller, W. C./Strom, K. (eds) *Koalitionsregierungen in Westeuropa, Bildung, Arbeitsweise und Beendigung*, Wien: Signum, pp. 47-108.

Scharpf, F.W. (1993): 'Positive und negative Koordination in Verhandlungssystemen', in: Héritier, A. (ed.) *Policy-Analyse: Kritik und Neuorientierung*, PVS Sonderheft 24, pp. 57-76.

Schultze-Fielitz, H. (1984): *Der informale Verfassungsstaat, Aktuelle Beobachtungen des Verfassungslebens der Bundesrepublik Deutschland im Lichte der Verfassungstheorie*, Berlin: Duncker & Humblot.

Schmidt, M. G. (1992): *Regieren in der Bundesrepublik Deutschland*, Opladen: Leske + Budrich.

Schönbohm, W. (1985): *Die CDU wird moderne Volkspartei. Selbstverständnis, Mitglieder, Organisation und Apparat 1950-1980*, Stuttgart: Deutsche Verlags Anstalt.

Schreckenberger, W. (1992): 'Veränderungen im parlamentarischen Regierungssystem: Zur Oligarchie der Spitzenpolitiker in Parteien', in: Bracher, K. D./Mikat, P./Repgen, K./Schumacher, M./Schwarz, H.-P. (eds) *Staat und Parteien*, Berlin: Duncker & Humblot, pp. 133-57.

Schwarzmeier, M. (2001): 'Gouvernementale Kontrolle und parlamentarische Mitsteuerung. Wirkmechanismen informalen Einflusses zwischen Regierung und

Parlamentsmehrheit', in: Holtmann, E./Patzelt, W. (eds) *Kampf der Gewalten? Parlamentarische Regierungskontrolle – Gouvernementale Parlamentskontrolle: Theorie und Empirie*, Wiesbaden: Westdeutscher Verlag, pp. 55-83.

Siefken, S. T. (2003): 'Expertengremien der Bundesregierung – Fakten, Fiktionen, Forschungsbedarf', in: *Zeitschrift für Parlamentsfragen* 34/3, pp. 483-504.

Siefken, S. T. (2006): 'Regierten die Kommissionen? Eine Bilanz der rot-grünen Bundesregierungen 1998 bis 2005', in: *Zeitschrift für Parlamentsfragen* 37/3, pp. 559-81.

Steinmeier, F. W. (2001): 'Konsens und Führung', in: Franz Müntefering/Matthias Machnig (eds) *Sicherheit im Wandel, Neue Solidarität im 21. Jahrhundert*, Berlin: vorwärts Verlag, pp. 263-72.

Stüwe, K. (2006): 'Informales Regieren. Die Kanzlerschaften Gerhard Schröders und Helmut Kohls im Vergleich', in: *Zeitschrift für Parlamentsfragen* 37/3, pp. 544-59.

Wewer, G. (1991): 'Spielregeln, Netzwerke, Entscheidungen – auf der Suche nach der anderen Seite des Regierens', in: Hans-Hermann Hartwich/Göttrik Wewer (eds) *Regieren in der Bundesrepublik II, Formale und informale Komponenten des Regierens*, Opladen: Leske + Budrich, pp. 9-29.

Zolleis, U. (2007): *Die CDU. Das politische Leitbild im Wandel der Zeit*, Wiesbaden: VS Verlag.

Chapter 6
Delegated Authority: Legitimising the Regulatory State

Martino Maggetti

1. Introduction

Over the past two decades, a general trend has been observed in Western countries towards the reassignment of political power from representative institutions such as parliaments and governments to non-elected bodies (Gilardi 2002, 2005, 2008; Levi-Faur and Jordana 2005; Majone 1994, 1996; Thatcher 2002a, b) which are not democratically responsive to citizens by means of a chain of political delegation (Strom et al. 2003). This tendency corresponds, above all, to the decision of governments to delegate competencies to domestic independent regulatory agencies (hereafter IRAs) in order to increase the legitimacy and acceptance of policy outputs which have been undermined by the unprecedented level of societal complexity compromising the steering capacity of political decision-makers, whilst the citizens' demands for political action are continuously rising. Several types of independent regulatory agencies have, therefore, been established for enhancing sector-specific regulatory governance: competition authorities, communication agencies, financial markets commissions, and so forth.

From an organizational viewpoint, IRAs are governmental bodies which command some degree of specialised public authority, separate from that of other institutions, but which are not directly elected by the democratic sovereign and not directly managed by elected officials (Thatcher and Stone Sweet 2002). The formal independence of regulatory agencies is imposed in a set of statutory prescriptions that are supposed to insulate them from political pressures, ensuring credibility towards external actors (especially firms and shareholders) and guaranteeing that decisions and expertises are not politically biased. In a less formalised way, agencies are also presumed to be insulated from the potential influence of the representatives of the target sector, i.e. the 'regulatees'.

This chapter is devoted to discussing the extent to which delegating authority to independent regulatory agencies is a viable strategy for legitimising regulatory policies. The point is that IRAs are by definition non-majoritarian and non-democratic bodies, hence depoliticised, whilst legitimacy is widely believed to emerge, first and foremost, from democratic participation and procedures (see Chapter 1 in this volume). Hence, the central research questions are: How can institutions that are non-democratic be expected to increase the legitimacy of policies? Can such institutions really deliver what is expected of them?

As I will elaborate in detail below, the legitimacy of regulatory governance by independent agencies is supposed to derive from: (1) the expected high efficiency of IRAs, based on the assumption that they are faster and more proficient in producing qualitatively better policy output than democratic institutions; (2) the expected high procedural accountability of IRAs, i.e. the assumption that they operate in a transparent, open and fair way, more so than democratic institutions; (3) the expected high factual independence of IRAs from politics and organized interests, which should give them a higher level of credibility and policy time-consistency than democratic/political institutions normally have.

This chapter presents the argument that IRAs cannot really deliver in these three dimensions – at least not simultaneously – and that therefore delegating authority to IRAs is hardly a suitable strategy for regenerating the political legitimacy that has been undermined by the challenges of societal complexity. The chapter suggests that the politics of depoliticisation and the factual reliance by governments on IRAs which cannot really deliver what they are expected and supposed to do may be interpreted – based on Blühdorn's model of *simulative politics* (Blühdorn 2004, 2007a, b, c) – as part of a tendency towards a *simulative regeneration* of political legitimacy (see also the first chapter of this volume), i.e. as the performance of legitimacy in a context where legitimacy generation becomes increasingly difficult.

In the following section I will first of all present the logic of delegation to IRAs and the related phenomenon of depoliticisation. Section three will be devoted to outlining the expectations invested in IRAs as regards promoting legitimised regulatory governance. Then I will discuss the limits of legitimising IRA policies by output-oriented legitimacy, by procedural accountability and by reference to their effective independence (section four). In the concluding section I will interpret practices of delegation within the model of *simulative politics* and point towards some new perspectives for legitimising regulatory governance.

2. Delegation to independent regulatory agencies (IRAs)

Since the 1980s, a concomitant process of delegation and re-regulation has emerged in Western Europe. This development has been described as the rise of the *regulatory state* (Majone 1994) or, more generally, as *regulatory capitalism* (Levi-Faur 2005) by researchers who argue that the style of modern governance has considerably transformed. Indeed, the post-war settlements of 'welfare capitalism' have been severely challenged (Coen and Thatcher 2005), but in an unexpected way. While several studies emphasise how the spread of liberalisation and privatisation is reducing the power of the state by restraining the room for political manoeuvre, and other scholars point out the increase of deregulation, this approach underlines the expansion and intensification of increasingly strict regulatory arrangements (Levi-Faur 2005; Vogel 1996), whereby executive competencies are delegated to authorities that are formally independent from direct political control, i.e. IRAs. The reorientation of public priorities towards a more pro-market agenda indeed implied a new regulatory approach aiming to increase the allocative efficiency of markets and correcting market failures (Majone 1996).

Therefore, the institutional model of independent regulators has been extensively adopted in almost all OECD countries, and where older agencies had already been in place, their competencies and formal independence have been extended (Gilardi 2002). The diffusion of IRAs follows a similar trend in almost all regulatory domains. It reflects a mix of factors including cross-national policy learning, top-down initiatives – for instance EU policies and regulations – and pressures for improving credibility of national policies, and the need to cope with political uncertainty (Gilardi 2005, 2008). The shift of power towards these bodies is qualitatively and quantitatively impressive (Levi-Faur 2005). IRAs benefit from, and often accumulate, special powers: rulemaking and promulgation of rules, monitoring, control, supervision and prosecution of violations, adjudication of those violations, and sanctioning. According to a recent study covering 16 sectors and 49 countries over 39 years (1964–2002), more than 20 agencies were created per year from the 1990s to 2002, and by the end of 2002, autonomous regulatory agencies were in place in about 60 per cent of the possible cases (Jordana et al. 2007).

The logic of delegating authority to IRAs as a policymaking strategy to deal with conditions of unprecedented societal pluralism and complexity is consistent with other more general socio-political developments also elucidated in this book, such as the decline of parliaments (see Chapter by Kelso), the rise of informal government (Jun in this volume) or governance by committees (e.g. Heard-Lauréote or Kuitunen and Lähteenmäki-Smith in this volume). In particular, the proliferation of IRAs can be interpreted in the light of the functional and symbolic pressures for steering complex societies. Decision-makers have to cope with an environment perceived as increasingly uncertain, contingent and fluid, whilst external imperatives deriving from an internationalised economy and conditions of the *risk society* require quick adaptation, certainty and informed policy responses.

As noted in the first two chapters of in this volume, these developments are integrated in a structural transformation towards a Post-Fordist society in which the public/private and national boundaries become indistinct, political and economic power is fragmented and disseminated, and levels of decision-making become more and more entangled. On the one hand, the declining sovereignty of nation states in favour of less representative institutions such as international organizations (Dahl 1999; Held 2000) and supranational bodies (Follesdal and Hix 2006) seems to hollow out the substance of national policymaking setting up a structure of multilevel governance. On the other, the rising importance of international norms and standards is profoundly redefining the patterns of political authority and blurring the boundaries between states and markets. As a result, the provision and distribution of public goods is greatly affected by a transnational context that is increasingly shaped by private and quasi-state global actors (Drahos 2004; Graz et al. 2007). In this context, IRAs are the instruments of a technocratic approach, advocated in particular by the proponents of New Public Management who aspire to enhance the effectiveness of policy-making and the management of social complexity.

Above all, the rise of formally independent bodies is said to provide the specialised tools for improving the *efficiency* of the decision-making process, understood as the capacity to achieve a predetermined goal with the lowest costs possible, while also solving the time-inconsistency problem related to the political cycle. Indeed, as I will discuss in detail below, the contended legitimacy of IRA policies is normally based on a large array of 'non-representative' justifications, and principally in terms of the need to improve efficiency by means of technical expertise and credibility through insulation from day-to-day short-term politics (Thatcher and Stone Sweet 2002).

Finally, the decisions to delegate public authority to IRAs are in line with the broader phenomenon of *depoliticisation* as described by Blühdorn (2007c). Depoliticisation – and delegation to non-majoritarian regulators as one of its main strategies – is a means for managing complex systems by artificially reducing the conflicting nature of issues. It implies the elimination of alternatives and the circumvention of democratic veto players by claiming that certain matters are technical rather than political problems and are most suitably dealt with by technocratic approaches.

3. Depoliticisation and policy legitimacy

When regulatory practices are *depoliticised,* they are no longer considered to be objects of political struggle; IRAs are located outside the political arena because their activity is perceived as merely technical. In this context, IRAs' policies are uncontested by citizens, taken-for-granted by the political decision-makers, and usually accepted by those being regulated. Furthermore, political parties, associations, or social movements have hardly ever contested the existence of domestic IRAs. Indeed, they are normally regarded in a positive way, under the assumption that they are protecting the public interest from market failures and from unfair behaviour of economic actors (Cohen 2001).

Yet delegating power to IRAs was a deliberate political and hence reversible decision and can be considered as a governing strategy shaped by international factors and domestic conditions. This strategy has been described as a process of placing at one remove the political character of decision-making (Burnham 2001) that leads to the fragmentation of authority in response to public pressure 'to do something' about problems in society (Buller and Flinders 2005; Grant 2000). As a result, independent regulatory agencies can, in line with the Weberian/Schumperterian tradition, be considered as organizations exercising a specific – and advanced – form of rational legal authority in the context of a democratic order where the individual is – in contrast to participatory models of democracy – increasingly disconnected from the political process.

Moreover, the regulatory policies are themselves potentially highly controversial, as they may involve the redistribution of resources both between the public and private sectors and within the private sector. IRA policies could thus be challenged if their practice of regulation came to be perceived as adverse by the political decision-makers or regulatees. Indeed, regulatory action may affect the vital interests of the target sector, implying new costs and obligations for the regulated firms. Unsatisfied regulatees may decide to oppose the regulatory order. Also, the longer a particular IRA exists the more likely is it compromised by the inconsistent preferences of changing political elites which are exchanged in the political cycle, especially if the democratic deficit turns into a source of populist discontent (Mény and Surel 2000). If the technocratic sovereignty of experts tends to prevail over popular, parliamentary and governmental power, the argument concerning the impoverishment of democracy within the political system is likely to be taken up by political entrepreneurs and become politically salient (Papadopoulos 2003).

However, the politics of depoliticisation and the related delegation of regulatory competencies to IRAs appear at present to be a widely accepted solution to the challenges of an increasingly complex political system. IRAs and their policies are believed to derive their legitimacy from three different sources stemming from public interest theories about, and New Public Management approaches to, the superiority of regulatory governance by independent bodies for steering complex and increasingly internationalized societies. Speaking in Weberian terms, delegation to IRAs is conceived as a process through which legitimacy – the social acceptance of the existing order – is produced (Lagroye et al. 2002).

First, it is believed that specialized experts can ensure a more *efficient* regulatory process than democratic institutions. Politicians are believed to have neither the expertise to design technical policies nor the capacity to adapt them in case unexpected conditions or systemic crises emerge. Specialised agencies, in contrast, staffed by supposedly politically neutral experts, are said to possess the skills to improve the efficiency of the decision-making process and are viewed as having the capacity to achieve predetermined goals at the lowest possible costs (Majone 1999). This illustrates the shift from public management towards public governance, whereby the state is leaving its function as provider of services in favour of playing the role of their guarantor and coordinator.

Second, delegation to a specialized body is believed to imply enhanced procedural *accountability* of regulatory policies. This is a consequence of the improved transparency of rules, a legally specified assignment of functions, and the assumed high responsiveness to the stakeholders, through, for instance, regular consultations and appeals opportunities for producers and consumers. In addition, accountability refers not only to the legal basis upon which the regulator operates, but also to the shared understanding of the customs and practices of regulation that sustains a legitimate regulatory governance by means of an open regulatory process, the involvement of relevant parties, and the justification of the regulator's decisions and procedures (Stern 1997).

Third, governments decide to tie their own hands in order to create *credible* commitments, providing protection from erratic public moods and societal short-term interests, and ensuring isolation from the anticipated time inconsistency of policies due to the political cycle, so as to protect the common good and long-term public interest. This rationale for delegation stems from the theoretical framework that supports the independence of central banks. In this particular case, independence is seen as a necessary condition for price stability and low inflation rates, as it denies governments the discretionary use of monetary policy, so as to avoid a time inconsistency between monetary goals and actual results (Alesina and Summers 1993; Barro and Gordon 1983; Campbell and Peters 1988; Cukierman et al. 1992; Kydland and Prescott 1977). Otherwise, in collective negotiations private actors would anticipate expansive monetary policies adopted by governments, and incorporate ex-ante those anticipations into their strategies, thus triggering higher inflation rates.

4. Can regulatory agencies deliver on the expectation of improved legitimacy?

First of all, I will discuss the most important assumed source of legitimacy, i.e. the *efficiency* of delegating regulatory competencies from political decision-makers to independent agencies. In this regard, democratic systems can be conceptualised as chains of delegation from voters to parliament, to government, to ministers, to administration (Strom et al. 2003). Delegation to IRAs constitutes an additional step, which is, however, qualitatively different, as IRAs are not directly accountable to voters nor to elected officials.

The point is that IRAs are outside the chain of democratic delegation. In fact, delegation to IRAs should not be understood in terms of a principal/agent relationship, structured in order to minimize any possibility of an agent's shirking. Instead, the need for credibility requires that the agency be independent, according to a fiduciary mode of delegation (Majone 2001a). In this case, the principal's powers and competencies are factually delegated to the agency. In other words, regulatory agencies are intrinsically and irremediably insulated from democratic responsiveness because independence is seen as the precondition for high-quality regulatory outcomes. The role of elected representatives is becoming less relevant, in favour of influence connected to specialized experts (Papadopoulos 2003). As a consequence, it is generally accepted that the regulatory state dramatically suffers from a deficit of democratic legitimacy (Majone 1999; Scott 2000).

In response to the criticism of this democratic deficit it has been argued that the lack of input-oriented legitimacy might be compensated by a positive evaluation of the policy outputs and results by citizens (Scharpf 2000). The legitimisation of IRA policies relies on the capacity of IRAs to produce regulatory outcomes which are highly satisfactory: this is the substantive component of IRA legitimacy (Majone 2001a). After all, regulatory agencies are cut off from the chain of democratic delegation precisely with the purpose of obtaining *better* results from the regulatory action, because a certain amount of autonomy is supposed to be necessary to perform certain tasks in a complex society (Majone 2001a/b). The expected higher quality of regulatory results *necessitates* the absence of input legitimacy.

Yet, two major drawbacks are challenging this form of legitimacy pertaining to IRAs. Firstly, there is still no clear-cut empirical evidence for the superior efficiency of the regulatory action performed by IRAs. This is because: (a) it is difficult to assess the impact of IRAs because their constitutional goals are varied, mixed, broad, and sometimes ambiguous or at least blurred, and in most cases much less clearly defined than those of central banks (e.g. market competition authorities are uneasy about deciding whether the task of promoting the public interest can be narrowly defined as the reduction of market prices in the sector under investigation, or whether they should encompass broader public concerns); (b) the assessment of regulatory *quality* is always relative to the subjective understandings of the different actors involved, such as political-decision makers, civil servants, experts, producers, consumers, and citizens (Radaelli and De Francesco 2007), which implies fundamental difficulties in attempting to reach a general agreement on the measurement of regulatory quality (e.g. a process of market concentration can be interpreted as indicating oligopolistic, reduced competition in the investigated sector or, alternatively, as normal adjustment where lower-performing firms are evicted from the market); and (c) even if we could confidently assess the implementation of regulatory policies, it would still be arduous to persuasively verify the causal relationship linking the regulatory action of IRAs with the broad outcomes for society and societal well-being at large. As a matter of fact, the vague notion of 'x-efficiency' is occasionally used in order to denote this somewhat undefined type of outcome (Button and Weyman-Jones 1993; Stennek 2000).

Secondly, there is a more fundamental critique of reliance on IRAs that concerns a theoretical problem. It is not certain that a deficit of input legitimacy indeed can be compensated by the 'better' quality of the outcomes. In fact, ex-post legitimacy cannot be conceptually separated from input legitimacy, notably because the positive evaluation of results depends firstly on the political consensus about the existence of a specific problem (see Blühdorn 2007d). Furthermore, such a form of legitimisation requires that the regulatory process is perceived as a win-win game (Papadopoulos 2003). However, the relevant actors tend to conceive of this process differently. They normally understand the game as competitive, and they fight to obtain the most favourable compromise, as the regulatory action often also has significant redistributive effects.

The literature on governance arrangements that deals with these problems proposes a way to resolve the legitimisation dilemma: it emphasises the relevance of *procedural* legitimacy, i.e. an enhanced *accountability* of the political process (Papadopoulos 2003). The basic idea is that political actors, even if they disagree with a particular decision, may be able to accept it as legitimate if it has been taken in a way considered fair, namely if it originates from an open and inclusive political process, ideally based on openness, transparency, equal access, and deliberation. Similarly, one can make good the democratic deficit if the regulatory agencies in charge engender the belief among the relevant actors that procedures are appropriate. Indeed, according to some scholars – and most IRA professionals – it is possible to legitimise regulation by independent agencies on the basis of the throughputs, whatever costs the decisions may entail (Stern 1997). This is the procedural component of IRA legitimacy (Majone 2001a).

Yet, once again a twofold criticism of IRA legitimacy by throughputs has to be considered: Accountability and efficiency may be in conflict, undermining the underlying assumption that justifies the delegation to IRAs. Indeed, it has been argued that a participative and deliberative process would weaken the efficiency of the regulatory action (Majone 1994), as it would significantly increase the political transaction costs of the process. A minimal version of accountability, however, probably cannot secure the legitimacy of the IRA towards the relevant political actors. In fact, when participation is reduced, and legitimacy is only based on Schumpeterian procedural correctness, the regulatory order will risk being considered barely legitimized and at best weakly democratic (Barber 2004).

This puzzle is inherent to all scenarios in terms of procedural accountability, as stated by Sosay (2006). In the participatory scenario, the diffusion of power is emphasized and public involvement is improved. The management of social complexity is accomplished by decentralizing power and opening channels of access to decision-making. This scenario is in line with the Habermasian ideal of communicative and collective deliberation. Yet, apart from the criticism of its overly idealistic assumptions – the prospect that only certain powerful interest groups are actually able to influence the process, excluding ordinary citizens and less well organised groups such as consumer associations (Olson 1971) – it is plausible that the participation of an increasing number of actors does undermine the decision-making capacity of the agency, reducing its efficiency (Majone 1999), i.e. its *raison d'être*. Conversely, the technocratic scenario represents the merely procedural way to legitimise IRAs. The instrument is the implementation of a strict, rule-based system providing expertise in order to maximise the efficiency of regulatory action. It corresponds to the Weberian process of rationalisation and bureaucratization that follows the development of a complex and differentiated society. This scenario implies the minimization of the involvement of political representatives and public participation, generating the supremacy of technocratic rule over democracy.

Given the aforementioned substantial inconsistencies, the criteria of efficiency and accountability appear to be unsatisfactory for securing legitimacy for of regulatory policies. Another way commonly adopted by scholars and professionals refers to the value of the agencies' *independence* itself (Spence 1997). This point is crucial in the theory of delegation to IRAs (Majone 1996). The argument is that administrative bureaucracies in general, and regulatory agencies in particular, have often been described as the fourth branch of government. In this context, the legitimacy of the regulatory order does not derive only from the quest for efficiency or enhanced accountability, but, above all, from another more fundamental aspect: the intrinsic value of the separation of powers, a concept that enjoys a long history and characterises the modern constitutional state. Separation of powers refers to the conception of the rule of law and reliance on checks and balances in order to help prevent the abuse of power (Persson et al. 1997).

This view of legitimacy is consistent with the Madisonian model of democracy, prescribing the fragmentation and limitation of political power in order to avoid a tyranny of majority: IRAs are believed to protect some pre-established *basic principles* from the populist component of democracy and from the potentially arbitrary use of power by political decision-makers (Riker 1982). Therefore, the claim of effective independence of agencies from political decision-makers is a crucial feature of legitimising regulatory governance by independent agencies, especially because it could supplement the other – and defective – avenues of legitimacy generation discussed above. Once again, however, two shortcomings may undermine this form of legitimisation:

First, in theory, regulation by factually independent agencies can reduce the efficiency of the political process again. In fact, according to the literature on delegation, the pursuit of efficiency and the need for independence imply two utterly different relational structures that come between the political decision-makers and the agency. Following the principal/agent model, policy efficiency requires a close alignment between principal and agent preferences and/or behaviour, because the principal should minimize any possibility of an agent's shirking (Braun 2003; Braun and Guston 2003). Yet, following Majone (2001b), factual independence in the long term requires a substantial differentiation between the principal and the trustee, implying that the agency benefits from a fiduciary mode of delegation, i.e. the possibility of self-determining its preferences and implementing a factually autonomous activity of regulation (Maggetti 2007).

Nonetheless, one may argue that, particularly in sensitive, unpredictable and globalized economic sectors such as financial markets (Baker et al. 2005), the need for credible regulation derived from the expected enhanced time-consistency of independent regulatory policies is so crucial for the functioning of the system that the choice of an independent regulator could be considered as per se legitimate. However, even in this extreme case – this is the second point – the legitimacy of the regulatory order cannot be simply deduced from the existence of a formally independent regulator (Maggetti 2007). When discussing the reliability of this form of legitimacy, it first and foremost needs to be investigated whether agencies in fact really are as independent from political decision-makers as prescribed in their statutes.

In this regard, the level of formal independence should only partially explain the variations in effective independence from politicians (Stern 1997; Thatcher 2002a; Wilks and Bartle 2002; Yesilkagit 2004). Given that any institutional framework allows a certain amount of discretion (Friedberg 1997; March and Simon 1958), *de facto* independence from politicians will not necessarily be consistent with statutory prescriptions. Empirical evidence, based on a survey inquiry of 16 West-European agencies (Maggetti 2007), suggests that formal independence alone is insufficient for explaining variations in the *de facto* independence of IRAs. In other words, prescriptions of formal independence cannot guarantee a factually autonomous regulatory action.

This means that formal independence may not always be effective; hence, legitimising the regulatory order in this way may not work. Indeed, especially if the relevant stakeholders perceive the outcomes of regulatory policies as adverse (Landry et al. 1996), a lack of *de facto* independence from the elected politicians is likely to be criticised by those being regulated. This reduces the sustainability of regulatory governance and in the long run criticism from the public at large will build up, too, because the regulator's independence is supposed to justify the democratic deficit. If, however, the opposite is the case, i.e. if there is a very high level of factual independence, uncontrolled agencies may develop their own strategies, thereby rerouting the strategic aims of delegation (Braun 2002) and hardly providing any additional legitimacy beyond what political decision-makers could claim. Furthermore, a lack of political support could facilitate a capture process by the regulated industries (Bernstein 1977), which would in turn seriously challenge the efficiency of the regulatory action.

The consequences of this puzzle are critical for the study of the consequences of delegating authority to agencies, as a lack of effective independence will render the formal separation from the representative institutions and hence the democratic deficit problematic. At the same time, the capacity to deliver 'better' regulatory outputs might be compromised because independence is seen as the precondition for high-quality regulation.

5. On the simulative (re)generation of legitimacy

So it has been argued that the delegation of public authority to independent regulatory agencies is a currently favoured solution for governments confronted with contradictory demands deriving from a situation of unprecedented societal complexity, in order to regenerate the legitimacy of the political process. The solution both presupposes and engenders the belief that regulatory policies can be enhanced if they are delegated to specialised bodies which are insulated from democratic institutions. IRAs are in fact by definition depoliticised, non-majoritarian, and non-democratic bodies. Yet legitimacy is widely believed to emerge, first and foremost, from democratic participation and procedures. How can institutions that are non-democratic be expected to increase the legitimacy of policies? As discussed above, the legitimacy of regulatory governance by independent agencies is expected to derive from a supposedly superior capability of IRAs in comparison to democratic institutions related to: the higher efficiency of IRAs, based on expertise; their higher procedural accountability, based on transparency, openness and fairness; the higher independence of IRAs from politics, organised interests, and the democratic masses, which provides a higher level of credibility.

But can such institutions really deliver what is expected of them so as to legitimise regulatory policies? The argument developed in this chapter is that delegating to IRAs is hardly a suitable strategy for regenerating the legitimacy that has been undermined by the challenge of societal complexity because: the expected superiority of independent agencies is difficult to assess – if it exists at all; there are serious trade-offs concerning the delivery in any of the three dimensions of legitimacy; and the reliance on one single dimension is hardly sufficient to legitimise the political process. Indeed, agreement on a positive evaluation of results is hard to achieve, and in any case it cannot substitute for input-oriented legitimacy. Moreover, the procedural legitimacy, in terms of accountability, may be in conflict with the IRAs' *raison d'être*, that is their assumed efficiency. Furthermore, it has been demonstrated that legitimisation in terms of effective independence does not work either. It appears that formal independence is neither a necessary nor a sufficient condition for explaining variations in the *de facto* independence of agencies from political decision-makers (Maggetti 2007). But any lack of *de facto* independence would render the democratic deficit unjustified and may lead to the contestation of the regulatory order.

As a consequence, the delegation of public authority to independent regulatory agencies appears as a rather unreliable and unsatisfactory means of policy legitimisation. Delegation emerges as a way of dealing with the contradictions of complexity that relies on depoliticisation as an end in itself rather than a means. In this sense, delegation can be interpreted as a way to reduce social complexity by eliminating some demands from the political system. So, the reliance by governments on institutions (IRAs) that cannot really deliver what they are expected and supposed to, may be interpreted – based on the model of *simulative politics* – as a process of simulative regeneration of political legitimacy, i.e. as the performance of legitimacy in a context where legitimacy becomes increasingly difficult to generate (Blühdorn 2007c; also see Chapter 1 in this volume).

In this context, simulation is a way of managing systemic contingency, by attempting to reconcile, or at least to permit the coexistence of, two contradictory needs. On the one hand, delegation relies on the *metaphysics of efficiency* (Blühdorn 2007d: 75-82) in a context presented as complex, differentiated, flexible and competitive, in order to answer dramatic social demands for public action and intervention, whereby the assessment of actual improvements to the quality of regulatory governance remains an uncertain and intricate process. On the other hand, following many structural transnational developments – particularly the liberalisation and internationalisation of the markets – delegation to independent regulators is crucial to secure credibility in the eyes of global actors such as foreign firms, international investors, and consumers. Accordingly, the simulative nature of the politics of delegation is particularly significant if there is a discrepancy between formal and factual independence. Other modes of regulation are likely to continue operating to a certain extent, in order to avoid an abrupt and perilous transition to the new regulatory order.

At present, this reconciliation of conflicting goals seems successful. Regulatory issues are depoliticised, and delegation to agencies is widely adopted as the taken-for-granted solution to the challenges of complexity. However, regulatory governance by independent agencies, although momentarily uncontested, can hardly secure legitimacy for the policy process. Depoliticisation is thus a fragile political strategy, and the new regulatory order is likely to be challenged, especially in cases of a systemic crisis or paradigm shift.

Some recent trends, however, open up new perspectives on legitimising regulatory governance by independent agencies. The emergence and ongoing consolidation of transnational networks of regulators might configure a new potential source of legitimacy for regulatory policies, if these institutional arrangements prove to be effective. For instance, European networks (Coen and Thatcher 2008) – where domestic independent regulatory agencies, scientific committees, member states, the Commission, and the European parliament are involved – could provide agencies with incentives and means for the development of an independent and efficient regulatory process (Majone 2001c) because of the lasting cooperation among agencies and the requirement of international reputation, ideally also making the agencies reciprocally (horizontally) accountable (Moe 1985). Further research will have to look carefully at the consequences of these new institutional developments, especially from the point of view of the potential improvements of regulatory governance.

References

Alesina, A./Summers, L. (1993): 'Central Bank Independence and Macroeconomic Performance: Some Comparative Evidence', in: *Journal of Money, Credit and Banking* 25/1, pp. 151-62.

Baker, A./Hudson, D./Woodward, R. (2005): *Governing Financial Globalization. International Political Economy and Multi-Level Governance*, Oxon: Routledge.

Barber, B.R. (2004): *Strong Democracy. Participatory Politics for a New Age*, Berkeley: University of California Press.

Barro, R./Gordon, D. (1983): 'Rules, Discretion and Reputation in a Model of Monetary Policy', in: *Journal of Monetary Economics* 12/1, pp. 101-21.

Bernstein, M.H. (1977): *Regulating Business by Independent Commission*, Westport: Greenwood Press.

Blühdorn, I. (2004) 'Post-Ecologism and the Politics of Simulation', in: Wissenburg, M./Levy Y. (eds) *Liberal Democracy and the Environment. The End of Environmentalism?*, London/New York: Routledge, pp. 35-47.

Blühdorn, I. (2007a): 'Self-description, Self-deception, Simulation: A Systems-theoretical Perspective on Contemporary Discourses of Radical Change', in: *Social Movement Studies* 6/l, pp. 1-19.

Blühdorn, I. (2007b): 'Sustaining the Unsustainable: Symbolic Politics and the Politics of Simulation', in: *Environmental Politics* 16/2, pp. 251-75.

Blühdorn, I. (2007c): 'The Third Transformation of Democracy: On the Efficient Management of Late-modern Complexity', in: Blühdorn, I./Jun, U. (eds) *Economic Efficiency – Democratic Empowerment. Contested Modernisation in Britain and Germany*, Lanham, Maryland: Rowman & Littlefield (Lexington), pp. 299-331.

Blühdorn, I. (2007d): 'Democracy, Efficiency, Futurity: Contested Objectives of Societal Modernization', in: Blühdorn, I./Jun, U. (eds) *Economic Efficiency – Democratic Renewal. Contested Modernization in Britain and Germany,* Lanham, Maryland: Rowman & Littlefield (Lexington), pp. 69-100.

Braun, D. (2002): 'Debate: State Intervention and Delegation to Independent Regulatory Agencies', in: *Swiss Political Science Review* 8/1, pp. 93-96.

Braun, D. (2003): 'Lasting Tensions in Research Policy-making – a Delegation Problem', in: *Science and Public Policy* 30/5, pp. 309-21.

Braun, D./Guston, D.H. (2003): 'Principal-agent Theory and Research Policy: An Introduction', in: *Science and Public Policy* 30/5, pp. 302-08.

Buller, J./Flinders, M. (2005): 'The Domestic Origins of Depoliticisation in the Area of British Economic Policy', in: *British Journal of Politics and International Relations* 7/4, pp. 526-43.

Burnham, P. (2001): 'New Labour and the Politics of Depoliticisation', in: *British Journal of Politics and International Relations* 3/2, pp. 127-49.

Button, K./Weyman-Jones, T. (1993): 'X-inefficiency and Regulatory Regime Shift in the UK', in: *Journal of Evolutionary Economics* 3/4, pp. 269-84.

Campbell, C./Peters, B.G. (1988): *Organizing Governance, Governing Organizations*, Pittsburgh: University of Pittsburgh Press.

Coen, D./Thatcher, M. (2005): 'The New Governance of Markets and Non-Majoritarian Regulators', in: *Governance: An International Journal of Policy, Administration, and Institutions* 18/3, pp. 329-46.

Coen, D./Thatcher, M. (2008): 'Network Governance and Multi-Level Delegation: European Networks of Regulatory Agencies', in: *Journal of Public Policy* 28/1, pp. 49-71.

Cohen, E. (2001): *L'ordre économique mondial*, Paris: Fayard.

Cukierman, A./Webb, S./Neyapti, B. (1992): 'Measuring the Independence of Central Banks and Its Effects on Policy Outcomes', in: *World Bank Economic Review* 6/3, pp. 353-98.

Dahl, R.A. (1999): 'Can International Organisations Be Democratic? A Skeptic's View', in: Shapiro, I./Hacker-Cordon, C. (eds) *Democracy's Edges*, Cambridge: Cambridge University Press.

Drahos, P. (2004): 'The Regulation of Public Goods', in: *Journal of International Economic Law* 7/2, pp. 321-39.

Follesdal, A./Hix, S. (2006): 'Why There is a Democratic Deficit in the EU: A Response to Majone and Moravcsik', in: *Journal of Common Market Studies* 44/3, pp. 533-62.

Friedberg, E. (1997): *Le pouvoir et la règle. Dynamiques de l'action organisée*, Paris: Editions du Seuil.

Gilardi, F. (2002): 'Policy Credibility and Delegation to Independent Regulatory Agencies: A Comparative Empirical Analysis', in: *Journal of European Public Policy* 9/6, pp. 873-93.

Gilardi, F. (2005): 'The Institutional Foundations of Regulatory Capitalism: The Diffusion of Independent Regulatory Agencies in Western Europe', in: *Annals of the American Academy of Political and Social Science* 598/l, pp. 84-101.

Gilardi, F. (2008): *Delegation in the Regulatory State: Independent Regulatory Agencies in Western Europe*, Northampton, MA: Edward Elgar.

Grant, W. (2000): 'Globalisation, Big Business and Blair Government', CSGR Working Paper, University of Warwick.

Graz, J.C./Hartmann, E./Heires, M./Niang, N./Sutlian, A. (2007): 'The Emerging Power of Services Standards in the Global Political Economy', paper presented to *ECPR Standing Group on International Relations* at the *6th Pan-European Conference on International Relations,* Turin (unpublished).

Held, D. (2000): 'Regulating Globalization? The Reinvention of Politics', in: *International Sociology* 15/2, pp. 394-408.

Jordana, J./Levi-Faur, D./Fernandez i Marin, X. (2007): 'The Global Diffusion of Regulatory Agencies: Institutional Emulation and the Restructuring of Modern Bureaucracy', *IV ECPR General Conference,* Pisa (unpublished).

Kydland, F./Prescott, E. (1977): 'Rules rather than Discretion: The Inconsistency on Optimal Plans', in: *Journal of Political Economy* 85/3, pp. 473-91.

Lagroye, J./Bastien, F./Sawicki, F. (2002): *Sociologie politique*, Paris: Dalloz Fondation nationale des sciences politiques.

Landry, M./Banville, C./Oral, M. (1996): 'Model Legitimisation in Operational Research', in: *European Journal of Operational Research* 92/3, pp. 443-57.

Levi-Faur, D. (2005): 'The Global Diffusion of Regulatory Capitalism', in: *Annals of the American Academy of Political and Social Science* 598/l, pp. 12-32.

Levi-Faur, D./Jordana, J. (2005): 'Globalizing Regulatory Capitalism', in: *Annals of the American Academy of Political and Social Science* 598/1, pp. 6-9.

Maggetti, M. (2007): 'De Facto Independence after Delegation: A Fuzzy-Set Analysis', in: *Regulation & Governance* 1/4, pp. 271-94.

Majone, G. (1994): 'The Rise of the Regulatory State in Europe', in: *West European Politics* 17/l, pp. 77-101.

Majone, G. (1996): *Regulating Europe*, London/New York: Routledge.

Majone, G. (1999): 'The Regulatory State and Its Legitimacy Problems', in: *West European Politics* 22/l, pp. 1-24.

Majone, G. (2001a): 'Nonmajoritarian Institutions and the Limits of Democratic Governance: A Political Transaction-Cost Approach', in: *Journal of Institutional and Theoretical Economics* 157/1, pp. 57-78.

Majone, G. (2001b): 'Two Logics of Delegation: Agency and Fiduciary Relations in EU Governance', in: *European Union Politics* 2/l, pp. 103-22.

Majone, G. (2001c): 'Regulatory Legitimacy in the United States and the European Union', in: Nicolaidis, K./Howse, R. (eds) *The Federal Vision. Legitimacy and*

Levels of Governance in the United States and the European Union, New York: Oxford University Press, pp. 252-76.

March, J.G./Simon, H.A. (1958): *Organizations*, New York: Wiley.

Mény, Y./Surel, Y. (2000): *Par le peuple, pour le peuple: le populisme et les démocraties*, Paris: Fayard.

Moe, T.M. (1985): 'Control and Feedback in Economic Regulation: The Case of the NLRB', in: *The American Political Science Review* 79/4, pp. 1094-1116.

Olson, M. (1971): *The Logic of Collective Action; Public Goods and the Theory of Groups*, Cambridge, Mass.: Harvard University Press.

Papadopoulos, Y. (2003): 'Cooperative Forms of Governance: Problems of Democratic Accountability in Complex Environments', in: *European Journal of Political Research* 42/4, pp. 473-501.

Persson, T./Roland, G./Tabellini, G. (1997): 'Separation of Powers and Political Accountability', in: *The Quarterly Journal of Economics* 112/4, pp. 1163-1202.

Radaelli, C.M./De Francesco, F. (2007): 'Regulatory Quality in Europe: Concepts, Measures and Policy Processes', Manchester: Manchester University Press.

Riker, W.H. (1982): *Liberalism against Populism: A Confrontation between the Theory of Democracy and the Theory of Social Choice*, San Francisco: W.H. Freeman.

Scharpf, F. (2000): *Gouverner l'Europe*, Paris: Presses de Sciences Po.

Scott, C. (2000): 'Accountability in the Regulatory State', in: *Journal of Law and Society* 27/1, pp. 38-60.

Sosay, G. (2006): 'Consequences of Legitimizing Independent Regulatory Agencies in Contemporary Democracies. Theoretical Scenarios', in: Braun, D./Gilardi, F. (eds) *Delegation in Contemporary Democracies,* Abingdon, Oxon, New York: Routledge, pp. 171-90.

Spence, D.B. (1997): 'Agency Policy Making and Political Control: Modeling Away the Delegation Problem', in: *Journal of Public Administration Research and Theory* 7/2, pp. 199-219.

Stennek, J. (2000): 'Competition Increases X-efficiency: A Limited Liability Mechanism', in: *European Economic Review* 44/9, pp. 1727-44.

Stern, J. (1997): 'What Makes an Independent Regulator Independent?', in: *Business Strategy Review* 8l, pp. 67-74.

Strom, K./Bergman, T./Müller, W.C. (2003): *Delegation and Accountability in Parliamentary Democracies*, Oxford, New York: Oxford University Press.

Thatcher, M. (2002a): 'Delegation to Independent Regulatory Agencies: Pressures, Functions and Contextual Mediation', in: *West European Politics* 25/1, pp. 125-47.

Thatcher, M. (2002b): 'Regulation after Delegation: Independent Regulatory Agencies in Europe', in: *Journal of European Public Policy* 9/6, pp. 954-72.

Thatcher, M./Stone Sweet, A. (2002): 'Theory and Practice of Delegation to Non-majoritarian Institutions', in: *West European Politics* 25/1, pp. 1-22.

Vogel, S.K. (1996): *Freer Markets, More Rules: Regulatory Reform in Advanced Industrial Countries*, Ithaca, N.Y.: Cornell University Press.

Wilks, S./Bartle, I. (2002): 'The Unanticipated Consequences of Creating Independent Competition Agencies', in: *West European Politics* 25/1, pp. 148-72.

Yesilkagit, K. (2004): 'The Design of Public Agencies: Overcoming Agency Costs and Commitment Problems', in: *Public Administration and Development* 24/2, pp. 119-27.

Chapter 7
Delegation to the EU: Participation *versus* Efficiency in German EU-Policy

Timm Beichelt

1. Introduction

In the political space of the European Union we can distinguish between the levels of national and EU politics. From the perspective of nation-state governments, domestic preferences or interests need to be first delegated to and then negotiated at the EU level. This process itself represents a considerable challenge of cross-linking several different arenas within the European political system. In some member states, notably in Germany, a federal structure of the nation state adds a further dimension of political action. Against the background of this multi-level-system, the process of delegating domestic demands to the EU level is a particularly complex exercise of steering politics. An enquiry into the ways in which the involved delegation networks respond to societal needs and expectations is therefore able to produce valuable insights into the overall question of this volume, namely how governments seek to generate legitimacy for their policies and for themselves. In this chapter, German EU delegation will be analysed as a case study for legitimacy generation in the EU context. It will be demonstrated that two dominant strategies have evolved to secure legitimacy: actor inclusion and policy effectiveness/efficiency. Yet, contrary to what Dahl's famous dilemma of participation and effectiveness may suggest (Dahl 1994), the two strategies are not mutually exclusive but even seem to imply each other.

In the EU, the character of democracy is peculiar. Nowadays, minimum standards of democracy are firmly established almost all over Europe, and most certainly throughout the EU. Several years ago, when the formula of the 'ever closer Union' dominated not only the preamble of the Maastricht Treaty but also many expectations about the future dynamics of European integration, nation-state democracies seemed to be very close to a conversion. Dahl (1989) speculated about a 'third transformation' of democracy beyond the nation state. With some blend of idealism, authors like David Held or Ernst-Otto Czempiel proposed models in which national sovereignty was given up in favour of a 'world domestic policy' (Czempiel 1998) or transferred into a 'cosmopolitan model' of democracy (Held 1995). The capacity of nation-state democracy to deal with problems beyond the national territory seemed limited. Thus, national democracy was theoretically expected to be superseded by a model in which regional issues were to be tackled by regional institutions and global issues by global institutions. Yet, as we know after the constitutional process, for the time being even the European Union, the world's most integrated regional organization, stopped short of merging into a new democracy on a higher, transnational level. Because of the limited success of transnational democracy, political actors in the European polity still have to refer to the procedures of the nation state when having to cope with transnational problems.

The EU is not a democracy but consists of nation democracies, and these national political systems need legitimacy in order to survive. Seymour M. Lipset once described legitimacy as a concept closely linked to the ability of a political system to create those institutions which are adequate for a society (Lipset 1960: 64). If we follow the definition, open societies that are ruled democratically link legitimacy to participation, transparency, and accountability. These are elements of democratic regimes which have evolved in a long struggle of parliaments against executives (Friedrich 1953) and of publics against the political sphere as a whole (Habermas 1962). If democracies want to remain stable, their political processes furthermore need to produce outcomes which relate positively to societal expectations and to the resources used. In short, political actors in a democracy have to secure their legitimacy through both participation and effectiveness. Early political system theory (Easton 1965) as well as more recent research (Fuchs 1989; Dalton 2004) tell us that none of the two dimensions may be neglected in the long run without serious consequences for the political regime.

With regard to the EU as a 'political system' (Lindberg and Scheingold 1970; Hix 2005), a specific relationship of politicians' quest for effectiveness and participation has been identified. By distinguishing between the two dimensions of input and output legitimation, Fritz Scharpf has shown that EU level actors are by far more able to seek support through providing output than by including citizens, groups, or parties into the European political process (Scharpf 1999). Efficiency and effectiveness in output delivery can therefore be regarded as major goals of EU political practice.

The strengthening of input legitimation, on the other hand, is confronted with serious obstacles: the lack of a common culture and language, which result in segmented European publics and an altogether weakly developed European identity (Giesen 2002; Kastoryano 2005). If the political actors of the EU want to secure legitimacy, they have to rely almost exclusively on the output side of the political system. Of course, this does not mean that the dimension of input legitimacy is completely absent from EU politics. But it remains closely tied to one particular level of the system: the nation state. Except for the members of the Commission, almost all important EU political actors are seeking re-election in their national constituencies. Altogether, the EU political system is therefore characterized by a preponderance of the national level with regard to input legitimation, and by a competition of arenas with regard to output legitimation: actors that mainly draw their legitimation from domestic sources have the choice of placing outputs on either the national or the European level.

The aim of this chapter is to shed light on the challenges EU related national policy makers have to confront in trying to secure the different categories of legitimacy. I use the arena of the delegation of German demands to the EU; a process that is sometimes also called EU policy coordination (Kassim et al. 2000; Kassim et al. 2001).[1] It takes place on two levels, namely within national government and in the arena of negotiation in Brussels and other EU capitals. The major finding that will be revealed is that strategies of effectiveness and efficiency achievement have been implemented in addition to steps to improve the inclusion of relevant institutions for the gathering of societal demands.

In the context of the whole volume, a study on the practices of EU delegation represents a special case because of the exceptionally complex nature of decision-making. Three different layers of complexity need to be distinguished (also see the introductory chapter in this volume): complexity with regard to different levels of decision-making, i.e. generating legitimacy under conditions of multi-level governance; complexity of institutional structures and organisational procedures within national governments, i.e. distribution of decision-making competencies between various government branches; and complexity as a quality of the issues which are being negotiated and implemented. The conclusion will offer a tentative assessment of the extent to which these problems of complexity are the underlying cause of the difficulties of legitimacy generation in a transnational setting.

2. Legitimacy attainment in the EU multi-level system

The concept of legitimacy has been of major concern for the theoretical branch of political and social science. However, this is barely reflected in the existing theory of European integration which focuses much more on the foundations, reasons and driving forces of integration than on the relationship between the governing and the governed (see Rosamond 2000; Wiener and

1 Delegation seems the more adequate notion when questions of legitimacy are concerned (as opposed to the organizational focus of the literature on EU policy coordination). Delegation is about the delivery of demands, and the EU-level actors of a national government will be judged by the extent to which domestic demands are eventually fulfilled.

Diez 2004). In fact, Rosenau's verdict of 'governance without government' (Rosenau and Czempiel 1992) made it difficult even to distinguish the two entities which are supposed to be interlinked by the concept of legitimacy. Where the distinction has been made, the thesis of the 'third transformation of democracy' led social theory to invocations of a European unity on the societal level that, at least at present, hardly exists in reality (Beck and Grande 2004; Delanty and Rumford 2005). The weak basis of legitimation for European actors translates into a systematic burden on the legitimacy of two regimes: The nation state is losing support because the problems national politicians are facing are hard to cope with, and the EU is facing poor acceptance because its decision-making processes seem inaccessible and fail to enable national politicians to deliver the results demanded by their respective publics.

At this point, the differentiation between input and output legitimation can be used instructively. As regards the input side, Dahl (1971, 1994) has described democracy as a matter of participation, with the size of the territory determining the potential for effective participation. Sartori (1987) and Tsebelis (1995) have argued along similar lines when relating the size of representative bodies to their potential to include many group representatives with decision-making capacity. Hence, their variable of reference is inclusion. These considerations show that in the democratic nation state normative elements of *how* to reach decisions are political aims in themselves. Notably participation and inclusion are necessary conditions of acquiring democratic legitimacy.

When turning to a transnational regime, however, things look different. Transnational regimes pursue aims that are to a much lesser extent linked to the input dimension. NATO, for example, was founded to increase security in Europe and elsewhere, and the European Community aimed at economic prosperity. The governments which founded these transnational organisations allowed for assemblies rather than parliaments, and in the case of the EC/EU the European Parliament had to struggle for decades to play a significant role in European decision-making. Up to the present the EP can only add suggestions on the basis of a Commission proposal; it is designed primarily as a preventive power. On this basis, the EP's legitimation basis has to compete with that of the Council and is therefore both in empirical and normative terms heavily circumcised. Thus, at the level of EU politics participation and inclusion are much weaker features of democracy than is the case in nation states.

In itself, this does not represent a normative problem as long as the democratic legitimation of the remaining actors in the game is upheld. However, this is exactly one of the dimensions where the democratic deficit of the EU is rooted. The input functions which are not fulfilled by the EP and the European public are absorbed by the executives of national governments who, mainly in the Council, negotiate the output of the EU. In practical terms many of the elements of nation-state democracy like control, transparency, or openness therefore suffer from an executive overweight in EU decision-making. The inclusion of national interests or demands into the EU political system in fact marginalises exactly those institutions which are responsible for the inclusion of societal interests into national politics, namely parties and (national) parliaments. All this makes the inclusion of societal interests into EU politics extremely complex and in many respects unable to meet democratic standards.

Legitimacy is, of course, also attained through output legitimation. In the EU system, however, the delivery of demanded outputs is not only constrained by limited resources – a factor which political actors in any regime have to live with – but the complexity of the multi-level system limits the potential for efficient policy-making. In public policy, the politics of efficiency has been defined as 'the process by which diffuse, ill-organized, broadly encompassing interests sometimes succeed in overcoming particularistic and well-organized interests' (Majone 1996: 620). The definition puts efficient policy-making into a context of a specific set of policies, namely those with an 'aim (...) to improve (with respect to the status quo) the position of all, or almost all, individuals or groups in society' (ibid.: 612). Efficient policy-making in this way is a 'key criterion of public policy making (...) Administrators should combine ethical discourse and policy analysis to make decisions that are substantively correct as well as democratically legitimated' (ibid: 613).

While efficiency therefore stands for the relationship between resources used and the public good achieved, the term needs to be distinguished from the notion of effectiveness (see Blühdorn 2007). The latter has a stronger focus on pre-defined goals of actors – the more goals one achieves, the higher the level of effectiveness. Effective policy-making presumes an institutionally determined political space in which decisions are undertaken (and their implementation assured) in order to reach goals which have to exist as a necessary condition. Wright (1996: 165) has reminded us that looking merely at the 'machinery' of a delegation process is not enough for judging its efficiency; at the same time policy objectives have to be taken into consideration.

In the output dimension, policy actors aiming to gain legitimacy have to take account of both efficiency and effectiveness. This needs to be done against a background of complex interests and demands. Interest settings in the EU vary from policy field to policy field and from institution to institution. The differing goals in the system make the same procedure appear efficient or inefficient depending on the point of view. Proposals by the Commission are often linked to national or sub-national interests that inform the proposition or at least the negotiated changes which are the subject of EU policy coordination. Goal attainment in EU delegation thus bears a competitive element: what may be effective for German officials may not be efficient for British officials at all.

However, regardless of the issues discussed all actors in the game do usually have a common interest in saving time and other resources. Therefore, attaining efficiency and effectiveness in EU delegation inevitably bears a target conflict. Goals usually bear a pan-EU dimension – otherwise a policy area would not have been incorporated into EU policy making but would have remained under national auspices. Where transnational goals have been achieved, they can be translated into measurable legitimacy only on the nation level. This makes the transnational level very dependent on the national one. If no sufficient output is achieved, the EU level's legitimacy is damaged. If output is satisfactory with regard to demand, it is the national level which controls how much legitimacy is ascribed to transnational actors. Of course, there will always be a tendency that national actors – seeking for re-election – will claim as much legitimacy as possible for themselves.

Are there formal or informal rules for the allocation of legitimacy in the EU? From the beginning of EU integration, member state governments opted for a double strategy of routing legitimation. On the one hand, the Commission and the Court of Justice were equipped with autonomous sources of legitimation. They were given the function of 'guardians of the treaties', and as institutions they were able to monitor and enforce the member states' compliance with the general rules of the treaties. Also, the growth of European parliamentarism – the first direct elections in 1979 as well as the continuous upgrading of the co-decision procedure – can be seen in this line. On the other hand, national governments were keen to keep the final power of decision to themselves. The deepening of integration was pushed forward on intergovernmental conferences, mostly without any participation from societal groups or parties. Despite the growth of majority voting, consensual decision-making survived in the form of the Luxembourg compromise.

There are two kinds of problems with this structure. The first has been picked up by Fritz Scharpf: the over-reliance on output legitimation. The second has been dealt with to a lesser extent (see, however, Wessels et al. 2003). It is the shift of legitimacy generation at the national level from the legislative towards the executive. National parliaments only come into the process of European decision-making at a stage where the capacity to induce substantive changes to pre-drafted legislation is heavily restricted. According to the Nice Treaty, national parliaments possess competencies in three areas: ratification of treaty revisions and accession decisions, the conversion of directives into national law, and the adaptation of national orders as a consequence of regulations.[2] All three forms of authority have reactive character.

2 The ratification of treaty revisions follows from the international law character of the TEU and the TEC but is also put down in Art. 48 TEU. Accession ratification is regulated by art. 49 TEU. The rules concerning directives and regulations are in Art. 249 TEC.

This means that acquiring legitimation is quite difficult for parliamentary actors. In the nation-state model, political parties, interest groups and national parliaments contribute to input legitimation to a great extent. Due to the structure of EU policy-making, in the EU regime this function is largely transferred to the main actors of the EU policy cycle: the Commission and the Council. On the input side, these two institutions may open up to group pressure in the pluralist sense that voicing particular interests in the end helps rationalise decision-making as a whole. Their nature, however, barely allows for making interest articulation or aggregation transparent. As bureaucracies, their main intent continues to be to produce effective decisions regardless of the way in which these decisions have been generated (as is well known from the sociology of organizations, see Crozier and Friedberg 1977; Weber 1980; Michels 1989/1908).

Altogether, therefore, participation/inclusiveness and efficiency/effectiveness become issues in EU delegation in ways that differ from national regimes. The input dimension of EU regime legitimation is for contextual and institutional reasons underdeveloped. National delegators can do little but to make sure that technical processes are running smoothly in order to affiliate group or sectoral interests with those parts of the European executive (Council and Commission) which are ready to include them in one way or another. The output dimension of EU regime legitimation is not as underdeveloped but suffers from imbalances as well. In comparison to transnational organizations less sophisticated than the EU, actors need to pay much more attention to the internal structure, i.e. the parliamentary institutions which possess autonomous legitimation sources. The legitimacy of the EU regime thus rests to a considerable degree on the management of the procedures leading to outputs on the EU level. Legitimacy is attained through output legitimation, and high levels of output legitimation depend highly on the efficiency and effectiveness with which national interests or demands are collected, catalyzed, and transposed into EU decisions.

3. Case study: EU delegation in Germany

The principle inherent to German government organization is departmental responsibility (*Ressortprinzip*) which usually leaves much independence to the ministry in charge of any particular piece of legislation. The role of the administrative delegation units therefore is to ensure a smooth transmission of departmental positions and instructions to the Brussels arena and to the relevant German actors there. When trying to reach solutions by taking over the function of interest aggregation, EU delegators in the German system have to deal with three structural domestic conflicts:

- *Political* conflicts including not only disagreements between government and opposition forces in the *Bundestag* but also conflicts within coalition governments which appear at times even more severe;
- *Societal* conflicts which evolve between interest groups or between one interest group and non-organized interests of society;
- *Federal* conflicts which emerge between the *Länder* and the federal government in the many policy areas where both levels share competence.

This conflict structure – which is more complex than in other big member states like France or Great Britain (Kassim 2000; Menon 2000) – is dealt with by the 'iron triangle' of the Foreign Office (*Auswärtiges Amt*, AA), the Ministry for Economic Affairs (*Bundesministerium für Wirtschaft und Technologie*, BMWi) and the Chancellor's Office (*Bundeskanzleramt*, BK). Within this triangle, the AA is responsible for preparation of the more political and 'general' committee COREPER II which does the preliminary work for the General Affairs and External Relations Council and therefore also for the European Council. The BMWi deals with the more economic and 'technical' COREPER I.[3] The BK only gets involved in situations where the Chancellor has to use his/her guideline competency (*Richtlinienkompetenz*) to avoid conflicts getting out of hand or to make political use of his/her capacity to intervene. However, as domestic political issues in German politics often interfere with coalition politics, involvement of the Chancellor is a sensitive matter and therefore does not occur very frequently.

In view of this at times confusing structure, many judgements on the country's EU delegation mechanisms have been rather dismissing in the past. Several authors have pointed to the great extent of fragmentation and over-hierarchisation of German EU coordination, leading to imprecise inputs, tardy proposals and incoherent position taking (Regelsberger and Wessels 1984; Wessels and Rometsch 1996; Bulmer et al. 2001; Sturm and Pehle 2006). Some judgements are more benevolent in stating that many problems of coordination have to be attributed to Germany's complex internal structure rather than to the delegation procedure itself (Maurer 2003). In other words, while there is agreement on the existence of efficiency problems, these are sometimes excused by the requirement to include many different demands into the delegation process.

In recent years, however, the German EU delegation process has undergone steps of considerable efficiency enhancement (Beichelt 2007a,b).[4]

---

3 COREPER = Committee of Permanent Representatives. COREPER I deals with questions of the Internal Market; COREPER II covers institutional, financial, and trade policy as well as matters traditionally related to the second and third pillar, that is Common Foreign and Security Policy (CFSP) and Justice and Home Affairs (JHA).

4 The findings of these two texts are quite different from those of most other recent literature on the topic (e.g. Bauer et al. 2007; Große Hüttmann 2007). Whilst the latter rely on the

Within the delegation system, two important institutional reforms have been implemented in recent years in order to enhance effectiveness and overcome the shortcomings of a system which for cultural and constitutional reasons has been rather fragmented: firstly, the creation of a dedicated coordination unit and, secondly, the establishment of a Parliamentary State Secretary with coordinating function. As regards the first reform, policy makers in the Foreign Office separated in 1999 the two tasks of providing general guidelines for European policy and of organizing the delegation process. The coordination unit (named 'E-KR', 'E' standing for the European Affairs division, 'KR' for *Koordinierung*) is directly responsible to the head of the European Division who in turn is one of the highest-ranking officials in the ministry. This affiliation equips E-KR with considerable trouble-shooting potential and makes the unit an active player, whereas the related unit in the Economics ministry is more restricted to a relay and information function.

As regards the second reform, the coordinating Parliamentary State Secretary was established in 2002. Since then, the most important Committee of European Affairs State Secretaries (EStS) has been coordinated by a Parliamentary State Secretary, a position that is called *Staatsminister* in the Foreign Office. When the reform was first implemented, then Chancellor Gerhard Schröder gave further significance to the process by nominating Hans Martin Bury, former Parliamentary State Secretary of his own Chancellor's Office, to this new position. As a result, Germany did much better in implementing EU legislation in the years that followed. Despite the complexity of the process, the goal of timely preparation, deliberation and decision-making was most generally achieved.

Beyond enhancing effectiveness and efficiency, a further aim of the reform was to bring parliament – especially the lower chamber, the *Bundestag* – closer to EU affairs. Martin Bury had been a parliamentarian since 1990, with intermediary leading positions within the SPD faction of the *Bundestag*. Bringing such a person into the 'administrative' delegation process was intended to make the inclusion of the parliamentary arena into the core of EU delegation possible. This objective, however, was not really achieved. While a strong chair of the EStS Committee is good for internal coordination, it makes the body a competitor to long-established decision-making centres within both the leading and the coordinating ministries. In doubt, the delegation bodies would lean towards these regular structures – for example, regular State secretaries – to whom they will be nominally responsible if serious conflicts emerge. Moreover, if conflicts between parliament and government arise, these are more likely to be brought to the Cabinet via the leaders of the

study of secondary literature (including some fairly old sources), my own results are based on an extended period of research within the *Auswärtiges Amt* during 2005/06 (participant observation and interviews).

parliamentary party factions than through a medium-level Committee. Therefore, the head of the EStS can only secure his power when he aligns with the executive, which means upholding parliament's distance to EU matters.

Still, in other fields parliament has been more effective in securing its interests. The German constitution (Articles 23 and 45) grants consultative and participating functions ('*mitwirken*', Art. 23) to both chambers of parliament. For many years, this right existed exclusively on paper, partly because of a limited cooperation attitude by the government, partly because of the self-understanding of many national parliamentarians (Hölscheidt 2001; Töller 2004; Auel 2006). In 2005 and 2006, however, with the EStS experiment not producing the expected results, further reform steps have been taken to empower the *Bundestag*: An inter-institutional agreement between the *Bundestag* and the government ensures that the parliament is informed on all government initiatives at the EU level (Schäfer et al. 2007). Moreover, the *Bundestag* has established an own office in Brussels, enabling the parliamentary party factions to formulate their particular positions on EU issues at a much earlier stage. The office does not aim to feed *Bundestag* positions into pre-council decision-making in Brussels. Nevertheless, its mere presence is a signal to all EU institutions that a transposition of any EU directive will be linked to the preferences of the German *Bundestag*. In that sense, the *Bundestag* has managed to enhance its inclusion into the EU delegation process at least to some degree.

4. Lessons from German EU delegation reform: The compatibility of inclusion and efficiency strategies

In his 1994 article Robert Dahl hypothesized an inverse relationship between 'system effectiveness' and 'citizen participation' in transnational regimes (Dahl 1994). Dahl's theoretical expectation was that the enhancement of effectiveness would inevitably impair inclusion; the two aims were essentially regarded as irreconcilable. In a way modifying Dahl, the terminology of Fritz Scharpf (1999) puts a weaker focus on the incompatibility of both targets. In his writings, input and output legitimation constitute different focal points of actor attention. In a context of limited resources, it may be difficult to enhance both; there is however no categorical reason why reaching input and output legitimation at the same time should be impossible.

The example of German EU delegation has shown that strategies of increasing both efficiency/effectiveness and participation/inclusion are not only reconcilable, but follow a logic of appropriateness of the institutions involved in the EU political system. On the domestic level, national parliaments are the most important legislative decision-making institution. There is no reason to expect that in the multi-level system they willingly surrender that role. Nominally, big parts of EU legislation go to the Council of Ministers, and therefore to national governments. Still, these governments depend on domestic parliaments who exert a control function regardless of the number of levels involved. Therefore, governmental strategies of enhancing efficiency and/or effectiveness will sooner or later trigger a response by parliament which has to keep an eye on input legitimation – which in a transnational regime is the only dimension a national parliament is able to keep control of.

What results is an interesting division of labour. The German government has tried to generate output legitimacy by adapting, institutionally, to the complexity of decision-making in the multi-level system. On the one hand, the structure of German EU delegation shows that governments reach out to fulfil a core function of parliament, namely the aggregation of territorial interest. On the other, the *Bundestag* – more by trial-and-error than by proactive planning – has been keen to maintain its position as a major player in decision-making in general. As is typical of legislative institutions, this concerns both input and output legitimation. Whereas the *Bundestag* cannot do much about outputs on the EU level, it evolves as an aggregation institution that potentially competes with the government. The change is in the relationship between government and parliament in affairs that are not exclusively domestic. Usually, parliament is expected not to challenge its own government in external affairs. Yet, the more parliaments define EU affairs as internal politics, the more likely are they to use their power to actively control government.

All this does not mean, however, that the quality of democracy as a whole is automatically upheld in a transnational regime. Two different institutions are formally responsible for decision-making on the different system levels: government on the EU level, parliament on the domestic level. Even if the threats to system legitimacy emanating from this bifurcation have been detected, there is still no effective institutional mechanism for resolving conflicts between these competing legislative bodies. While some prominent EU issues – e.g. the directives for a European arrest warrant, for the service sector, or for the usage of chemicals (REACH) – have been discussed in German parliament and in public political debate, the transparency of the delegation system remains altogether limited. Most decisions are still prepared, taken and implemented by the executive which does not regard broad interest inclusion as a major goal. The control function of the legislative does exist but is curbed by the logic of coalition government and the Chancellor's guideline competency. Effectiveness is assured by a mechanism that favours administrative coordination to public deliberation. Due to the complexity of the system, inclusion often takes place on informal channels.

In sum then, the case study reveals that there is no necessarily negative correlation in transnational regimes between complexity and legitimacy.

EU delegation stands in a paradigmatic way for the legitimation choices of political actors in a transnational arena. The institutions of the national and the EU level are closely interlinked, but European publics have only to a limited extent switched their attention to the new centre of political decision-making. This makes it possible for both the executive and the legislative to act within their traditional lines of action: government is responsible for the output, whereas parliament serves, beyond this, as an arena of interest aggregation and representative decision-making. However, the problems of very long chains of legitimation remain, and so does the issue that the different forms of complexity which were distinguished in the introduction can negatively affect the representativeness of power. While the system has worked for the last two decades of deepening European integration, it has not yet proven its stability in situations of serious conflict in European political life.

References

Auel, K. (2006): 'The Europeanisation of the German Bundestag: Institutional Change and Informal Adaptation', in: *German Politics* 15/3, pp. 249-68.

Bauer, M. W./Knill, C./Ziegler, M. (2007): 'Wie kann die Koordination deutscher Europapolitik verbessert werden? Folgerungen aus einem Leistungsvergleich institutioneller Arrangements in Deutschland, Finnland und Großbritannien', in: *Zeitschrift für Parlamentsfragen* 38/4, pp. 734-51.

Beck, U./Grande, E. (2004): *Das kosmopolitische Europa*, Frankfurt: Suhrkamp.

Beichelt, T. (2007a): 'Die europapolitische Koordinierung der Bundesregierung: besser als ihr Ruf', in: *Zeitschrift für Parlamentsfragen* 38/4, pp. 751-64.

Beichelt, T. (2007b): 'Over-efficiency in German EU policy coordination', in: *German Politics* 16/4, pp. 421-32.

Blühdorn, I. (2007): 'Democracy, Efficiency, Futurity: Contested Objectives of Societal Reform', in: Blühdorn, I./Jun, U. (eds) *Economic Efficiency – Democratic Empowerment. Contested Modernization in Britain and Germany*, Lanham, Maryland: Rowman & Littlefield (Lexington), pp. 69-98.

Bulmer, S./Maurer, A./Paterson, W. (2001): 'The European Policy-Making Machinery in the Berlin Republic: Hindrance or Handmaiden?', in: *German Politics* 10/1, pp. 177-206.

Crozier, M./Friedberg, E. (1977): *L'acteur et le système*, Paris: Seuil.

Czempiel, E. O. (1998): *Friedensstrategien*, Opladen: Westdeutscher Verlag.

Dahl, R. A. (1971): *Polyarchy. Participation and Opposition*, New Haven/London: Yale University Press.

Dahl, R. A. (1989): *Democracy and its Critics*, New Haven: Yale University Press.

Dahl, R. A. (1994): 'A Democratic Dilemma. System Effectiveness versus Citizen Participation', in: *Political Science Quarterly* 109/1, pp. 23-34.

Dalton, R. (2004): *Democratic Challenges, Democratic Choices: The Erosion of Political Support in Advanced Industrial Democracies*, Oxford: Oxford University Press.

Delanty, G./Rumford, C. (2005): *Rethinking Europe. Social Theory and the Implications of Europeanization*, London: Taylor & Francis.

Easton, D. (1965): *A Systems Analysis of Political Life*, New York, London, Sydney: John Wiley & Sons.

Friedrich, C. J. (1953): *Der Verfassungsstaat der Neuzeit,* Berlin: Springer.

Fuchs, D. (1989): *Die Unterstützung des politischen Systems der Bundesrepublik Deutschland*, Opladen: Westdeutscher Verlag.

Giesen, B. (2002): 'Europäische Identität und transnationale Öffentlichkeit', in: Kaelble, H./Schmidt-Gernig, A./Kirsch, M. (eds) *Transnationale Öffentlichkeiten und Identitäten im 20. Jahrhundert*, Frankfurt: Campus, pp. 67-84.

Große Hüttmann, M. (2007): 'Die Koordination der deutschen Europapolitik', in: *Aus Politik und Zeitgeschichte* 10, pp. 39-45.

Habermas, J. (1962): *Strukturwandel der Öffentlichkeit*, Darmstadt, Neuwied: Luchterhand.

Held, D. (1995): *Democracy and the Global Order: From the Modern State to Cosmopolitan Governance*, Cambridge: Polity Press.

Hix, S. (2005): *The Political System of the European Union* (2nd ed.), New York: St. Martin's Press.

Hölscheidt, S. (2001): 'The German Bundestag: From Benevolent 'Weakness' Towards Supportive Scrutiny', in: Maurer, A./Wessels, W. (eds) *National Parliaments on their Ways to Europe: Losers or Latecomers?*, Baden-Baden: Nomos, pp. 117-36.

Kassim, H. (2000): 'The United Kingdom', in: Kassim, H./Peters, B.G./Wright, V. (eds) *The National Co-ordination of EU Policy: The Domestic Level*, Oxford, New York: Oxford University Press, pp. 22-53.

Kassim, H./Peters, B.G./Wright, V. (eds) (2000): *The National Co-ordination of EU Policy: The Domestic Level*, Oxford, New York: Oxford University Press.

Kassim, H./Menon, A./Peters, B.G./Wright, V. (eds) (2001): *The National Co-ordination of EU Policy: The European Level*, Oxford, New York: Oxford University Press.

Kastoryano, R. (ed.) (2005): *Quelle identité pour l'Europe?*, Paris: Les Presses de Sciences Po.

Lindberg, L./Scheingold, S. (1970): *Europe's Would-Be Polity: Patterns of Change in the European Community*, Englewood Cliffs: Prentice Hall.

Lipset, S.M. (1960): *Soziologie der Demokratie*, Neuwied: Luchterhand.

Majone, G. (1996): 'Public Policy and Administration: Ideas, Interests and Institutions', in: Goodin, R.E./Klingemann, H.D. (eds) *A New Handbook of Political Science*, Oxford: Oxford University Press, pp. 610-27.

Maurer, A. (2003): 'Germany: Fragmented Structures in a Complex System', in: Wessels, W./Maurer, A./Mittag, J. (eds) *Fifteen into One? The European Union and its Member States*, Manchester: Manchester University Press, pp. 115-49.

Menon, A. (2000): 'France', in: Kassim, H./Peters, B.G./Wright, V. (eds) *The National Co-ordination of EU Policy: The Domestic Level*, Oxford, New York: Oxford University Press, pp. 79-98.

Michels, R. (1989/1908): *Zur Soziologie des Parteiwesens in der modernen Demokratie. Untersuchungen über die oligarchischen Tendenzen des Gruppenlebens*, Stuttgart: Kröner.

Regelsberger, E./Wessels, W. (1984): 'Entscheidungsprozesse Bonner Europa-Politik: Verwalten statt Gestalten?', in: Hrbek, R./Wessels, W. (eds) *EG-Mitgliedschaft: Ein vitales Interesse der Bundesrepublik Deutschland?*, Bonn: Europa Union Verlag, pp. 469-99.

Rosamond, B. (2000): *Theories of European Integration*, Houndsmills: MacMillan.

Rosenau, J.N./Czempiel, E.O. (eds) (1992): *Governance without Government: Order and Change in World Politics*, Cambridge: Cambridge University Press.

Sartori, G. (1987): *The Theory of Democracy Revisited*, Chatham: Chatham House Publishers.

Schäfer, A./Roth, M./Thum, C. (2007): 'Stärkung der Europatauglichkeit des Bundestages', in: *Integration* 30/1, pp. 44-49.

Scharpf, F.W. (1999): *Governing in Europe: Effective and Democratic?*, Oxford: Oxford University Press.

Scharpf, F.W. (2000): *Interaktionsformen. Akteurszentrierter Institutionalismus in der Politikforschung*, Opladen: Leske + Budrich.

Sturm, R./Pehle, H. (2006): *Das neue deutsche Regierungssystem* (2nd ed.), Wiesbaden: VS Verlag.

Töller, A. E. (2004): 'Dimensionen der Europäisierung – Das Beispiel des Deutschen Bundestages', in: *Zeitschrift für Parlamentsfragen* 35/1, pp. 25-50.

Tsebelis, G. (1995): 'Decision Making in Political Systems. Veto Players in Presidentialism, Parliamentarism, Multicameralism and Multipartism', in: *British Journal of Political Science* 25, pp. 289-325.

Weber, M. (1980): *Wirtschaft und Gesellschaft*, Tübingen: J.C.B. Mohr.

Wessels, W./Rometsch, D. (1996): 'German Administrative Interaction and European Union. The Fusion of Public Policies', in: Mény, Y./Muller, P./Quermonne, J. L. (eds) *Adjusting to Europe. The Impact of the European Union on National Institutions and Politics*, London, New York: Routledge, pp. 73-109.

Wessels, W./Maurer, A./Mittag, J. (eds) (2003): *Fifteen into One? The European Union and its Member States*, Manchester: Manchester University Press.

Wiener, A./Diez, T. (2004): *European Integration Theory*, Oxford: Oxford University Press.

Wright, V. (1996): 'The National Co-ordination of European Policy-Making: Negotiating the Quagmire', in: Richardson, J.J. (ed.) *European Union: Power and Policy-Making*, London: Routledge, pp. 148-69.

Chapter 8
The Legitimacy of EU Decision-Making: Theory and Practice of the Open Method of Co-ordination and the European Employment Strategy

Peter Bursens

1. Introduction

Much has been said and written on the issue of legitimacy of the European Union (EU). In their answer to Majone (1998, 2000) and Moravcsik (2002), Follesdal and Hix (2006) present an overview of the charges brought against an undemocratic EU. They see five accusations. Firstly, the European integration process has led to a decrease in national parliamentary control, essentially pointing to the fact that national executives' actions in the European arena are beyond systematic scrutiny of domestic parliaments. Secondly, the powers of the European Parliament (EP) are too weak, both regarding political control vis-à-vis the EU-level executives (Council and Commission), and regarding its legislative and budgetary competencies. Thirdly, true European elections don't exist: EP elections are second order national contests, hence depriving the European public from direct impact on EU policy outcome. Fourth, the European level is institutionally and psychologically too far from the European voter who therefore is unable to identify with it. Finally, EU policy outcomes are not supported by a majority of European citizens. Rather, a substantial part of the electorate contest the often right of centre output of social-economic policies and the disproportional impact of private actors in particular.

Most of these criticisms can be traced back to the complexity of the EU's multi-level political system. More than any national political system, the EU has to cope with a multitude of governance levels, public institutions, private actors and intertwined policy sectors. The EU faces a substantial challenge to organize its policy-making democratically and to deliver effective policies in such a complex environment. As such, the EU is a relevant case when assessing the capacity of modern political systems to perform in a legitimate way, while being increasingly challenged by their own complex governance setting. Unlike Beichelt who in the previous chapter has looked at one particular country's EU policy co-ordination; and unlike Follesdal and Hix who holistically focus upon the EU as a political system, this chapter focuses on the question of how the EU seeks to secure legitimacy for its policies. Working on the policy level implies that the analysis needs to depart from the political system level variables and to translate the system variables to a lower level of analysis. Taking up Blühdorn's discussion in Chapter 1 of this volume (also see Blatter's and Beichelt's contributions), the following section therefore first develops a conceptualisation and operationalisation of the input and output dimensions of legitimacy. This first section will develop the application of these concepts, not only within the specific EU context, but also to the level of policy instruments in particular. The subsequent empirical test will deal with one particular governance tool, the Open Method of Coordination (OMC). The OMC suits the chapter's purposes very well, as it was explicitly introduced to upgrade participation in the policy-making process and to ameliorate EU policy output. To make a sufficiently detailed assessment possible, the empirical test focuses on one particular policy sector that is governed by the OMC: the European Employment Strategy (EES). Hence, the central puzzle of this contribution can be defined as exploring whether the introduction of the OMC as a governance tool helps the EU to increase the legitimacy of its employment policies.

2. Input and output legitimacy in the European Union

The five problematic domains identified by Follesdal and Hix essentially cover two core dimensions of the legitimacy concept. The first three refer to democratic participation of the European public in EU politics through national and European parliamentary elections, and subsequent parliamentary control of the various executive actors within the EU political system. The latter two point to the general public's identification with the European political level as a whole and its acceptance of specific EU policy outcomes in particular. These dimensions clearly refer to the concepts of input and output legitimacy as introduced in the first chapter of this volume. In this section, I operationalise both dimensions in such a way that they become applicable to assess the legitimacy of EU policies.

The distinction between input and output legitimacy in an EU context has been explicitly used by Scharpf (1999). He defends this dichotomous conceptualization, arguing that 'while both dimensions of legitimacy are generally complementary, they differ significantly in their preconditions and their implications for the legitimacy of the EU, when each is considered by itself' (Scharpf 1999: 6). In other words, for analytical purposes both dimensions can best be separated, but an overall assessment of the EU's legitimacy should take both dimensions into account, paying attention to how they interrelate (Cini and Rhodes 2006: 465).

Input legitimacy, or 'government by the people' (Scharpf 1999), refers to the idea that citizens attribute legitimacy to a political system if they consider themselves sufficiently involved in delivering 'input' into the decision-making processes (Smismans 2004a: 72f). For a long time, the input legitimacy debate in the EU has been framed within the national democratic rhetoric, often suggesting that the EU can only become 'input legitimate' after a transformation into a nation state-like parliamentary democracy. However, a political system's legitimacy cannot be exclusively judged by the democratic dimension alone, and even less by using the ideal type of national parliamentary democracy (Jachtenfuchs 1997). If this were to be the case, the EU would never qualify as a legitimate political system since the EU is simply not a nation state, nor are its tasks those of a nation state (Majone 2000; Moravscik 2002). How then can input legitimacy be conceptualized to make it a suitable instrument for evaluating specific EU policies? Inspired by the broad literature on legitimacy, I propose four criteria, and suggest that the more they are met by the EU, the more its policies can be regarded as legitimate on the input side (see Zandstra 2007 for a different operationalisation of preconditions). In the following I apply the criteria of participation, representation, transparency and accountability to the analytical level of EU policies. Note that the EU is regarded as a political system with direct links between European level authorities and EU citizens, hence implying that input legitimacy needs to come from both the Member States and the individual citizens (Amato 2006).

Participation refers to the idea that citizens whose concerns and interests are affected by certain policies should have an equal and effective opportunity to represent their views during the consecutive stages of the EU decision-making process (De la Porte and Nanz 2004: 272). The more encompassing the participation of actors that are affected by the policy in the EU decision-making process, the higher the input legitimacy of the specific EU policy (Heritier 2003: 108).

The criterion of *representation* comes close to that of participation, but can nevertheless be distinguished. Unlike participation, representation does not necessarily mean direct involvement of every single affected citizen. It rather refers to the representation of affected citizens' interests by interest organizations and democratically appointed actors like the members of the EP (Engelen and Sie Dhian Ho 2004: 21). The better the interests of citizens are represented during the EU decision-making process, the more input legitimacy is achieved.

Transparency implies that interested citizens, stakeholders and civil society organizations as well as European, national, sub-national and local actors, should have access to all relevant information and policy documents at all stages of the EU decision-making process. In addition, there must be an active communication from the EU institutions and the Member States to the general public (Dyrberg 2002: 81; De la Porte and Nanz 2004: 272). Transparency also refers to the clearness of the decision-making process, which should be relatively simple for interested actors to grasp (Dyrberg 2002: 84). The higher the degree of transparency, the higher the level of input legitimacy.

Finally, in order to establish input legitimacy, it must be possible for affected EU citizens to hold the decision-makers *accountable* for their actions. This means that EU decision-makers should be able to give explanations for the decisions they take and should be prepared to accept responsibility for their actions (Arnull and Wincott 2002). The more the criterion of accountability is met, the more the input legitimacy of an EU decision-making procedure is established.

Output legitimacy or 'government for the people' (Scharpf 1999) connects the legitimacy of a political system with its (perceived) performance. It attributes legitimacy to a political system based on its capacity to achieve citizens' goals (effectiveness) and to solve their problems (problem-solving capacity) (Höreth 1999). Scharpf's key point is that – in at least some cases – the EU can be conceived as legitimate by reference to its output, even if input legitimacy is largely lacking (Scharpf 1999: 11). Also, other authors argue that the EU, given the fact that it is only a partial state and given the tasks it fulfils, is more based on output than on input legitimacy (Majone 2000). Applied to specific EU policies, effectiveness and problem solving capacity can be operationalised as follows.

First, output legitimacy refers to the acceptance that decisions or structures of governance at the EU level 'work', 'perform', or are able to 'deliver the goods'. EU policies should be *accepted as effective*. With respect to the EU, this idea stems from (neo-)functionalist theorists who argue that supranational institutions should be judged by how well they perform: EU policies are granted more legitimacy if they perform well.

Secondly, the EU's output legitimacy is derived from its *capacity to solve problems* that require collective solutions. This is because these problems cannot be solved through action at the individual state level, through market exchanges or through voluntary cooperation by civil society actors. This concept touches upon the principle of subsidiarity, which states that decisions should be taken as closely as possible to citizens. Actions by the EU level should therefore be motivated to prove that the supranational level is more capable than the national, regional or local level of tackling certain social problems. The concept also refers to the idea that a common European level should trigger a learning process. Bringing Member States together and making them discuss each others' policy achievements should raise the bar by setting the best national practices as examples and explicitly pointing to lagging Member States. The more the EU succeeds in implementing this learning process and in delivering solutions for social problems that other governance levels fail to tackle, the more its policies can be considered legitimate.

3. The Open Method of Coordination (OMC) and the European Employment Strategy (EES)

While the EU in itself can serve as an excellent illustration of a complex political system, an assessment of the legitimacy of complex governance environments can better take place at a lower level of analysis. In the following, I argue why the Open Method of Coordination (OMC) suits this purpose very well. After all, the OMC was introduced to enhance the effectiveness and the legitimacy of a policy sector that is confronted with several features of complexity (Zandstra 2007: 251).

For a long time, EU governance could be associated with two clearly different modes: the intergovernmental procedure and the supranational or Community decision-making procedure. The former, mainly used in the second and third pillar, clearly favours the central position of the member states (mainly through the Council of Ministers) while the latter grants substantial decision-making powers to supranational institutions such as the European Commission and the European Parliament. Both are operational more than ever, but now enjoy the company of a third, somewhat hybrid mode of governance in the form of the OMC.

The OMC is a flexible and open regulatory method, which contrasts with the traditional Community method by means of its non-compulsory character of rules and the plurality of involved actors (Dehousse 2002; Goetschy 2003). It aims to keep competences at the national level whenever possible (Borrás and Jacobson 2004: 197), and at the same time to complement existing European level instruments such as legislation, collective agreements, social dialogue, etc. (Goetschy 2003: 6 and 79). Policy-makers hope to generate solutions which are appropriate to the complex nature of particular policy problems, for instance through self-regulation of private actors or co-regulation involving both public and private partners (Heritier 2003: 103).

The principle of the OMC was originally introduced in the Maastricht Treaty (Art. 98-104 TEC) for the purpose of coordinating national economic policies through the Broad Economic Policy Guidelines (BEPGs) (Borrás and Jacobson 2004; Zeitlin et al. 2005). It was extended to other related policy fields through the European Employment Strategy (EES), formally designed in the Amsterdam Treaty (1997) and the Lisbon Summit Conclusions (2000). It is now used in several policy fields (budget, macro-economic policy, employment, social inclusion, pensions, health care, research and innovation, education and training) (Cini and Rhodes 2007: 468) and aims to accomplish the transition to 'the most competitive and dynamic knowledge-based economy' (European Council, 2000). In reality, OMC procedures vary according to policy fields with regard to ambitions, functioning and legal bases (De la Porte and Pochet 2002: 47; Goetschy 2003: 6).

Issues of effectiveness, democracy and complexity gave rise to the introduction of the OMC. With respect to *effectiveness*, Member States recognized that, due to the intergovernmental character of decision-making in some sectors (such as employment, social policy, migration, criminal prosecution), the EU had become increasingly unable to deliver acceptable output. At the same time, however, many Member States failed to support the harmonization of legislation in these sectors by means of the Community method. A new approach of flexible and open coordination among Members States was seen as a way out of this dilemma (Scott and Trubek 2002: 2; Heritier 2003: 105f; Radaelli 2003: 21f; Borrás and Jacobson 204: 186). Regarding *complexity*, it should be noted that by the late 1990s the idea of a 'Social Europe', as agreed upon in the Maastricht Social Protocol, was lagging behind 'Monetary Europe'. The introduction of the OMC was seen as a solution for the integration of economic and social dimensions of the EU (Goetschy 2003: 7; Radaelli 2003: 21; Borrás and Jacobson 2004: 186). Finally, at about the same time, the alleged *democratic deficit* of the EU generated a window of opportunity to create a new governance tool that would increase the number of participants in the decision-making process and speed up the creation of a European model of social policy (European Commission 2001; Goetschy 2003: 10; Radaelli 2003: 7; Borrás and Jacobson 2004: 186f; Schäfer 2004). The question then becomes, to what extent can the OMC be considered a legitimate governance tool in the complex governance environment of the EU?

While the OMC is a useful case to assess the legitimacy of EU governance, its relative newness in many areas, and hence empirical deficit, makes an overall assessment difficult (Radaelli 2003). Zeitlin (2002: 4) adds to this that the 'growing political salience, proliferation and variety of OMC processes has elicited a bewildering array of contradictory assessments from both academic researchers and EU policy actors alike'. For these reasons I limit the assessment to the European Employment Strategy (EES). EES is the oldest and most developed form of OMC (Heritier 2003: 117; Trubek and Trubek 2005: 54). It was introduced in Art. 130 of the Amsterdam Treaty (1997) in order to achieve employability, development of entrepreneurship, adaptability and equal opportunities in the EU (Goetschy 2003: 66-7; De la Porte and Nanz 2004: 274). In comparison to other OMC-processes, EES is not loosely structured (Zeitlin et al. 2005) but includes detailed guidelines to be achieved by Member States, which have to present National Action Plans (NAPs) that become subject to mutual surveillance and peer review by Member States' representatives in the Employment Committee (EMCO). In addition, programmes for mutual learning through the exchange of good practices have been organized within the framework of the EES.

4. Does the OMC increase the legitimacy of the EES?

According to the Lisbon Summit Conclusions, the OMC is 'an important tool to improve transparency and democratic participation' (European Council 2000: 7). This section assesses these ambitions with regard to the input and output legitimacy preconditions of participation, transparency, representation, accountability, effectiveness and problem solving capacity.

Participation

The qualification 'open' in OMC refers to the idea that 'the Union, the Member States, the regional and local levels, as well as social partners and civil society, will be actively involved, using varied forms of partnership' (European Council 2002: 38). The argument goes that in the case of employment policy, the context – in terms of involved actors, levels and sectors – is too complex to be handled either by the Member States on an intergovernmental basis or through the Community method on a EU level. By involving most of the affected public and private actors in a loose policy-making process without binding legislation, both support for and output of a particular policy initiative should be generated, and ultimately input legitimacy should be increased (Heritier 2003: 107). Several authors (as referenced throughout this chapter) have investigated the actual participation of the above-mentioned actors during both the negotiation and implementation stages of the EES. The general conclusion is that, although EU employment authorities stress the inclusion of many and different actors, real participation is not that prevalent.

Participation of European labour and management organizations has been fairly limited (Goetschy 2003: 68). There seems to be a lack of commitment to the EES from the European Trade Union Confederation (ETUC) and even a reluctance to become involved from the Union of Industrial and Employers Confederation of Europe (UNICE) (De la Porte and Nanz 2004: 279). Although efforts have been made to increase participation of national social organizations, their actual participation is rather weak, mostly because national actors fail to reach agreement amongst themselves with respect to the National Action Plans (NAPs) (Trubek and Trubek 2005: 52). In a comparative study, De la Porte and Nanz (2004: 279f) found that satisfaction with the participation conditions among the social partners was low. Radaelli (2003: 40) reports that attempts to explicitly include civil society during the formulation of EES, or to strengthen the involvement of regional and local actors in the Commission's proposals for the 2003 Employment Guidelines, were watered down by national representatives within the Employment Committee (EMCO). In addition, Goetschy (2003: 67) concludes that the EES often remains a purely national governmental issue. Although the Lisbon Council Conclusions encourage participation at all levels, in most Member States the involvement of the local level reflects the dynamic that existed before the EES, suggesting that the OMC has not given new stimuli for local involvement in European employment policies (De la Porte and Nanz 2004).

With respect to parliamentary involvement, the EP is consulted in the ESS process (in contrast to other OMC-procedures), but in practice its role in the first five years was rather marginal. Due to time constraints, the EP was hardly able to formulate positions or opinions that could be influential. At the national and regional level, even parliamentary debates on the EES were quite rare. De la Porte and Nanz suggest that national parliamentarians have too little knowledge about the EES to draft relevant opinions (2004: 278). Nevertheless, national parliamentary involvement is a crucial condition for effective parliamentary participation because the EES remains largely a national issue: decisions on concrete reform plans and allocation of financial resources ultimately take place at the national level (Dehousse 2002: 19).

The conclusion for the participation dimension reflects a definite cleavage between theory and practice. While the principles of the OMC clearly encourage the participation of a diversity of actors in the EES and emphasise the involvement of sub-national and local actors in the formulation and the implementation of NAPs, empirical assessments point out that actual participation is fairly weak. The practice of OMC does not seem to meet the ideal of an 'open and deliberative mode of governance' (Smismans 2004a). Telo (2003: 138) even concludes that the lack of effective participation leads to a 'social legitimacy deficit' in contrast to the openness that was originally announced by the Lisbon Council Conclusions. The more nuanced conclusion would be that the rather weak participation of social partners in the EES process differs substantially from the expectations that have been raised.

Representation

The representative potential of the OMC refers to the representation of citizens' concerns by social partners, regional and local governments, rather than to direct citizen representation in the EES at the EU level. The argument goes that the policy issue at stake touches upon a large number of actors and therefore asks for the aggregation of interests and channelling of participation. In practice, however, the limited participation of social partners (see above) already points to the weak representation of affected citizens such as the unemployed. And what about the 'democratic' representation of the general public? Neither national nor regional parliaments are actively involved during the NAP preparation (Zeitlin et al. 2005): this process is clearly dominated by executive and bureaucratic institutions. This is quite worrying from a representation perspective, since parliaments are the most important channels for the democratic representation of citizens.

Some authors say that even if parliamentary scrutiny of national executives' actions in the European Council or Council of Ministers were substantial, representative legitimacy would remain insufficient. They argue that much of the real work is carried out within the EMCO, which is composed of national civil servants and EU officials and is little controlled by elected bodies. In addition, the EMCO's decisions are rarely overturned by the political level (Zeitlin et al. 2005). Smismans (2004a) even brands the OMC as nothing more than transgovernmental exchanges between national civil servants and EU officials, hardly offering any guarantee for the representation of citizens' concerns.

In short, representation is closely linked to participation and their assessment runs parallel. The rather weak participation of social partners, regional and local actors in the EES has a negative effect on the representation of citizens' interests in the EU employment policies. This low level of representation itself leads to problems in terms of input legitimacy: the OMC type of representation clearly does not secure the legitimacy of the EES.

Transparency

Improved transparency is an explicit aim of the OMC procedure. De la Porte and Nanz (2004) analyzed the information transparency of the EES at the EU level. They argue that access to key documents regarding the EES has improved considerably since a website dedicated specifically to the EES has been launched in 2003. Prior to this initiative, information was available all over the website of DG Employment, making it difficult to obtain clear information. Whilst the evaluation of the strategy in 2002 was initially secret, the documents were ultimately made available for the larger public on the web, including specialized programs on the exchange of experiences, midterm reviews and expert reports (De la Porte and Nanz 2004: 276-7).

However, with regard to the decision-making process itself, transparency has not improved. The EES has introduced new decision-making mechanisms combining supranational and intergovernmental procedures, which does not make it any easier to grasp the process in all its details. Complexity of decision-making has increased rather than decreased. An illustration is the empowerment of the Commission and Council to issue joint recommendations to Member States on the implementation of the EES and the BEPG, but not on other OMC processes. Consultation of the European Parliament is only formally required in the case of the EES (Zeitlin et al. 2005).

In addition, the deliberations of the committees who draft the EES guidelines, objectives and recommendations, take place behind closed doors. Information on the proceedings of these meetings is difficult to acquire.

Therefore, a potential learning effect does not sufficiently find its way beyond the meeting room (De la Porte and Nanz 2004): only some bureaucrats, experts and politicians gain an insight into the best practices of national employment processes (Radaelli 2003: 50). This contrasts with the idea that the OMC is supposed to stimulate learning processes, meaning that exactly the exchange of best practices is meant to lead to a more open and transparent approach by national employment policies. The theoretical argument adds that peer review and yearly evaluation mechanisms will lead to more transparency of employment policies and to opportunities for public debate. However, public debate on employment policy evolving from the EES process is very weak (De la Porte and Nanz 2004: 277). For citizens, it remains vague whether employment measures result from EES agreements or from national initiatives. At the level of social partners, the introduction of more opportunities to get involved has no doubt created more transparency for these particular actors. At the same time, it can be argued that increased involvement of social partners has also made the decision-making processes as a whole more complex, hence making it even less clear for the general public (Goetschy 2003: 78).

The overall assessment of the transparency dimension is rather ambivalent. With regard to the access to documents and information of the EES, transparency has been largely improved, but with regard to the clearness of the decision-making procedure, transparency has not been increased.

Accountability

How accountable does the OMC make the decision-makers who are responsible for the EES? Accountability as such is only implicitly suggested in the OMC through the principle of 'democratic participation', which assumes that organized civil society, social partners and national parliaments give voice to affected citizens' preferences (De la Porte and Nanz 2004: 273). Should accountability, as a substantive aspect of input legitimacy, not be made more explicit? Several authors think it does, building on Majone's (1996) argument that since employment is a largely redistributive issue, input legitimacy from an accountability perspective can only be accomplished if democratically appointed actors take decisions and not technocratic, bureaucratic networks. Radaelli (2003) argues in this respect that there is no clear demarcation between decision-making and implementation within the OMC process, which makes the process susceptible to problems of judicial and political accountability. With regard to the judicial accountability, the European Court of Justice is not competent, neither for the definition of the initiative nor for the implementation or practical application of the NAPs (De la Porte and Pochet 2002; Radaelli 2003). As far as political accountability is concerned, I refer to the earlier discussion on participation and representation of social partners and parliaments, which concluded that the OMC reshuffled the conventional balance of power between EU institutions favouring executive actors, therefore also raising the accountability question (Borrás and Jacobson 2004: 199). Benz (2007) warns that accountability in complex multi-level games such as the OMC can run into problems as there are too many principles (national parliaments, the European Parliament, interest groups) and too many agents (the Commission, the Council, national executives) involved. Some authors are even more explicit: 'As a network of (closed) networks, the EES tends to resist any type of accountability: management by objectives and procedural routines tends to remove decisions from electoral cycles' (Ferrara et al. 2000: 84). Others even make the case that the OMC should be seen as a threat for the 'accountable' Community method: the OMC is seen as a soft law option which may overrule the (more) democratically elaborated hard law (Goetschy 2003; Trubek and Trubek 2005).

Opposing these criticisms, however, Rodriguez (2001) argues that the OMC enhances accountability because by opening the decision-making process to input from civil society and sub-national actors, national governments must justify to a broader public their performance in meeting common European objectives (see also Telo 2003). Other authors argue that the 'naming, shaming and blaming' mechanisms, included in the 'soft' EES process by annual peer review and discussions, create a pressure on Member States to meet their agreements. That way, governments can be held accountable in a 'soft' way (Zeitlin et al. 2005).

I would argue that the latter is above all theoretical or presumed accountability, especially with respect to the EES which consists of voluntary agreements without hard sanctions. De la Porte and Pochet (2002: 296) note in this respect that 'because it is open, it also leaves the possibility for everyone to not engage at all'. Concluding with Radaelli (2003: 50), the question of accountability seems to be a Damocles' sword hanging over the OMC in general. It is a handicap for the input legitimacy of the EES.

Increasing input legitimacy was an important motivation in the Lisbon European Council Conclusions. The OMC, however, was mainly prompted by output legitimacy motivations, in particular by becoming 'the most competitive and dynamic knowledge-based economy in the world capable of sustaining economic growth with more and better jobs and greater social cohesion' (European Council 2000). In other words, to assess the legitimacy of the OMC, output legitimacy must also be taken into account: the EES' goal is to reduce unemployment by affecting policies and programmes at the national level. In the following paragraphs, I discuss whether the EES plays a role in changing these policies (problem-solving capacity) and whether it effectively reduces unemployment (effectiveness).

Effectiveness

To assess the effectiveness of the EES it is best to look at the three EES priorities: employability, investment in human capital and adaptability. Firstly, with respect to attracting and retaining people in employment, the EES seems to deliver, but too slowly and in too fragmented a fashion. The Council reports increasing attention of Member States for labour market reforms, resulting in modest policy successes in terms of falling unemployment, increasing employment rates, narrowing gender gaps and increasing employment for older workers. Youth employment, on the other hand, is stagnating. Despite progress in some domains, the overall assessment is that Member States are still far below the 2010 targets, especially with respect to employment rates and older workers' employment (European Council 2007: 7). A similar evaluation is presented regarding Member States investment in education and skills. Despite the introduction of specific policies in this area, only piecemeal progress is reported. Especially worrisome are results regarding issues such as early school-leaving and adult participation in lifelong learning (European Council 2007: 6 and 15-6). Adaptability of workers and enterprises to technological progress and increasing global competition is delivering least of all. According to the Joint Implementation Report, Member States' measures to meet the flexicurity challenges are insufficient (European Council 2007: 13). One striking leitmotiv in the consecutive Joint Implementation Reports is the observation that Member States still take too many isolated and fragmented measures and do not succeed in designing, let alone implementing, a comprehensive strategy which effectively combines education, employability and flexicurity. Employment policies are intrinsically multi-faceted, touching upon a wide range of intertwined issues. While the EES was deliberately designed to provide a coherent answer to the societal complexity of the employment policy domain, it fails to deliver thus far. Trubek and Mosher (2003: 41) add to this assessment that the EES does not embrace all relevant side-policies affecting employment. Important areas such as monetary, fiscal and wage policies, which critically affect growth and job creation in the EU, are left outside the scope of the EES strategy. As a result, the EES has to develop largely as a supply side strategy focusing on altering structural impediments to employment.

The effectiveness of the EES seems to be largely affected by its 'soft governance' features (Jacobsson and Schmid 2002). Since there are no 'hard' sanctions to ensure compliance by the Member States to the guidelines, 'soft' measures such as evaluation, peer review and naming-and-shaming-mechanisms must encourage Member States to implement the agreed guidelines and comply with the agreed targets. Scholars tend to have different opinions on the EES' 'hard' versus 'soft' characteristics, and their consequences for the effectiveness of EES. On the one hand, the 'softness' of the EES is contested by scholars who believe that soft law mechanisms make it more likely that Member States will comply, because divergent domestic systems cannot be steered with rigid harmonization instruments (Goetschy 2003: 77; Trubek and Mosher 2003: 39). There is evidence that soft measures – peer pressure and associated practices such as recommendations and ranking (naming, shaming and blaming) – have influence on the behaviour of Member State governments. Member States feel pressure to reach common targets and to carry out agreed commitments, and they want to avoid EU recommendations and low ranking (Zeitlin et al. 2005). Critics of the method, however, argue that the benefits of the OMC crucially depend on the willingness of national actors, who are in control of the policy choices, to get themselves involved in processes of European coordination. Some plead to attribute the OMC with the capacity to impose binding sanctions (Heritier 2003). Also, Dehousse (2002) argues that soft EES mechanisms are not sufficient when convergence of national employment policies is imperative. Goetschy (2003: 77) points out that while the adoption of guidelines is easier in the case of 'soft' mechanisms, the implementation is far more difficult because monitoring and follow-up must compensate for the weak legal density of the guidelines.

Also, there is a mixed assessment with respect to the involvement of stakeholders. It is correctly argued that effectiveness is theoretically enhanced by large participation (Zeitlin 2002; Heritier 2003; Radaelli 2003). Formulating policy goals, as well as choosing instruments to reach these goals, may stimulate involved actors to support policy measures that they might have opposed under the traditional legislative mode of governance (see also Börzel 2002). As discussed earlier, however, participation of social partners and democratically elected actors is in practice fairly weak, potentially leading to problematic implementation of NAPs: outvoted actors seek to recuperate their interests during the implementation phase, particularly when redistributive issues, such as employment, are at stake (Heritier 2003: 112).

To conclude, the EES can claim a measure of effectiveness with respect to some isolated employment issues but, overall, its promises are not quite fulfilled. While the EES created an employment policy which would otherwise not have been possible at EU level, its effectiveness – measured by the achievement of the targets – is not very high, hence raising doubts about its output legitimacy.

Problem-solving capacity

Expectations were high with respect to problem-solving capacity at the start of the OMC instruments' application. Biagi (2000: 159), for instance, writes that 'consistent application of the Luxembourg exercise might lead to a convergence of Member States' employment and labour policies, not dictated by

Brussels but based on a growing consensus on effective solutions through a process of trial and error'. Problem-solving capacity of the EES would emerge through policy learning about employment policies through information exchange, benchmarking and peer review, deliberation and blaming and shaming.

In practice, however, the hoped-for bottom-up and cross-country learning has been limited to problem-recognition rather than to the actual adoption of foreign best practice solutions, as for example lifelong learning, gender segregation and labour market integration of immigrants and ethnic minorities (Zeitlin et al. 2005). Also, other authors argue that, due to the poor participation of social actors and to the safeguarding of the political power of the Member States, the problem solving-capacity of EES remains restricted to the convergence of ideas on employment policy across the Member States instead of the adaptation of national employment policies themselves (Radaelli 2003: 45). Although there is evidence that participants in the EMCO are willing to learn from each other and to alter their visions (De la Porte and Nanz 2004: 282), not much more than selective borrowing and adapting of foreign programs to the peculiarities of own domestic contexts has happened.

Concluding on this dimension, one has to recognize that the attitude of Member States has not yet changed sufficiently to reach cross-national and bottom-up learning, again putting question marks to real output legitimacy effects of the EES.

5. Conclusion

Does the EES live up to its legitimacy expectations? Is the OMC an effective instrument to cope with the complex governance environment and to make EU employment policies more legitimate? A mixed evaluation seems appropriate. It is clear that the EES has promising features, encompassing all dimensions considered to contribute to input legitimacy. In comparison with more traditional decision-making at the EU level, the OMC can in theory raise the overall input legitimacy of the EU. It envisages more participation of a whole range of public and private actors during decision-making and implementation stages, a better representation of the interests of the affected actors, a relatively high level of transparency of the decision-making processes, information and documents, and accountability to a multitude of affected actors. In short, the OMC was meant to achieve some kind of *Open Management of Complexity*[1]. So far for the theory. In practice, this contribution has, by means of an empirical assessment, shown that input legitimacy of

1 Thanks to Ingolfur Blühdorn for suggesting this alternative reading of the acronym and interpretation of the OMC.

the EES is contested with respect to all preconditions: participation, representation, transparency and accountability. With Zeitlin, I can conclude that the EES is essentially 'a narrow, opaque and technocratic process involving high-level domestic civil servants and EU officials in closed policy networks, rather than a broad, transparent process of public deliberation and decision-making, open to the participation of all those with a stake in the outcome' (Zeitlin et al. 2005: 446). It is not enough to recognize that the complexity of current policy issues, such as employment, necessitates innovative governance models. It is not even sufficient to design these models on paper and to approve the related policy guidelines. The proof of the pudding is, ultimately, in the eating. The EES pudding, however, will need quite some cooking time in order to pass the taste contest of input legitimacy.

Assessing the OMC and the EES with regard to output legitimacy is an even more delicate exercise. How to determine the extent to which national employment changes are really inspired by the EES? The EES is not really external to national policy making because many indicators are uploaded from the Member State level to the EU (Börzel 2002). The EES is also very clearly not the only external impact on national employment policies: in a globalizing world, other imperatives and guidelines can also trigger domestic policy change (Zeitlin et al. 2005), especially in social-economic domains. Finally, it is important to note that the process is still fairly recent. Taking all this into account, the Commission's Report on the OMC and the yearly Council Reports on the EES strategy nevertheless show that the EES has produced genuine impact and achievements at both EU and Member State level. At the same time, however, it has clearly also not yet fully realized its theoretical promises: the EES' output legitimacy is in practice rather mediocre.

Overall, the empirical conclusion should be that the EES has much potential to live up to expectations in both input and output legitimacy dimensions, but that the current EES processes and results do not yet meet these expectations. Using a slightly different list of preconditions, Zandstra (2007: 266) comes to a similar, yet slightly more optimistic, conclusion. 'While the OMC may seem to be a panacea for the democratic flaws of EU policy-making in sensitive policy areas in theory, a closer examination of how the method is implemented in the case of the EES presents a somewhat different image. (…) Certain hindrances might, however, be overcome as growing pains are dealt with over time'. One might even think of a paradoxical effect of introducing the OMC: while increasing participation and transparency through the involvement of more actors was one of the main motivations to install the OMC, exactly the incorporation of more players has introduced more complexity, resulting in less legitimate instruments and policies. The struggle of the EU with its own level of legitimacy serves as an excellent illustration of the challenges modern political systems have to cope with. They are increasingly confronted with the complexity of the act of governance. Decision-makers are increasingly aware of this, and introduce a diverse set of solutions to overcome the vices of complexity. For the moment, however, their efforts do not seem to necessarily lead to the envisaged results. The management of complexity is an intricate undertaking, as the European experience clearly illustrates.

References

Amato, G. (2006): 'Constitutional Developments in Europe', in: Bel, J./Kilpatrick, C. (eds) *The Cambridge Yearbook of European Legal Studies 2005-6*, Oxford: Hart, pp. 1-8.

Arnull, A./Wincott, D. (eds) (2002): *Accountability and Legitimacy in the European Union*, Oxford: Oxford University Press.

Benz, A. (2007): 'Accountable Multilevel Governance by the Open Method of Coordination?', in: *European Law Journal* 13/4, pp. 505-22.

Biagi, M. (2000): 'The Impact of European Employment Strategy on the Role of Labour Law and Industrial Relations', in: *International Journal of Comparative Labour Law and Industrial Relations* 16/2, pp. 155-73.

Borrás, S./Jacobsson, K. (2004): 'The OMC and New Governance Patterns', in: *Journal of European Public Policy* 11/2, pp. 185-208.

Börzel, T. (2002): 'Pace-Setting, Foot-Dragging and Fence-Sitting: Member State Responses to Europeanisation', in: *Journal of Common Market Studies* 40/2, pp. 193-214.

Cini, M./Rhodes, M. (2006): 'New Modes of Governance in the European Union: A Critical Survey and Analysis', in: Jörgensen, K./Pollack, M./Rosamond, B. (eds) *Handbook of European Union Politics*, London: Sage, pp. 463-82.

Dehousse, R. (2002): 'The Open Method of Coordination: A New Policy Paradigm? The Politics of European Integration: Academic Acquis and Future Challenges, Paper presented at the ECPR Joint Sessions, Bordeaux 2002 (unpublished).

De la Porte, C./Nanz, P. (2004): 'OMC: The Cases of Employment and Pensions', in: *Journal of European Public Policy* 11/2, pp. 267-88.

De la Porte, C./Pochet, P. (2002): *Building Social Europe through the Open Method of Coordination*, Brussels: Peter Lang.

Dyrberg, P. (2002): 'Accountability and Legitimacy: What is the Contribution of Transparency?', in: Arnull, A./Wincott, D. (eds) *Accountability and Legitimacy in the European Union*, Oxford: Oxford University Press, pp. 81-96.

Engelen, E.R./Sie Dhian Ho, M. (2004): *De Staat van de Democratie: Democratie voorbij de Staat*, Amsterdam: Amsterdam University Press.

European Commission (2001): 'European Governance, a White Paper', Luxembourg: European Commission.

European Council (2000): 'Conclusions of the Lisbon European Council', Luxembourg: European Commission.

European Council (2007): 'Joint Employment Report 2006/2007', Luxembourg: European Commission.

Ferrera, M./Hemerijck, A./Rhodes, M. (2000): *The Future of Social Europe: Recasting the European Welfare State*, Oeiras: Celta Editora.

Follesdal, A./Hix, S. (2006): 'Why there is a Democratic Deficit in the EU', in: *Journal of Common Market Studies* 44/3, pp. 533-62.

Goetschy, J. (2003): 'The European Employment Strategy, Multi-Level Governance and Policy Coordination', in: Zeitlin, J./Trubek, D. (eds) *Governing Work and Welfare in a New Economy: European and American Experiments*, Oxford: Oxford University Press, pp. 59-87.

Heritier, A. (2003): 'New Modes of Governance in Europe: Increasing Political Capacity and Policy Effectiveness?', in: Börzel, T./Cichowski, R. (eds) *The State of the European Union*, Oxford: Oxford University Press, pp. 105-26.

Höreth, M. (1999): 'No Way out for the Beast? The Unsolved Legitimacy Problem of European Governance', in: *Journal of European Public Policy* 6/2, pp. 249-68.

Jachtenfuchs, M. (1997): 'Democracy and Governance in the European Union', at: *European Integration Online Papers* 1/2, http://eiop.or.at/eiop/texte/1997-002a.htm.

Jacobsson, K./Schmid, H. (2002): 'Real Integration or just Formal Adaptation? On the Implementation of the National Action Plans for Employment', in: De la Porte, C./Pochet, P. (2002) *Building Social Europe through the Open Method of Coordination*, Brussels: Peter Lang.

Majone, G. (1996): *Regulating Europe*, London: Routledge.

Majone, G. (1998): 'Europe's 'Democratic Deficit': The Question of Standards', in: *European Law Journal* 4/1, pp. 5-28.

Majone, G. (2000): 'The Credibility Crisis of Community Regulation', in: *Journal of Common Market Studies* 38/2, pp. 273-302.

Moravcsik, A. (2002): 'In Defence of the 'Democratic Deficit': Reassessing the Legitimacy of the European Union', in: *Journal of Common Market Studies* 40/ 4, pp. 603-34.

Radaelli, C.M. (2003): *The Open Method of Coordination: A New Governance Architecture for the European Union?*, Stockholm: SIEPS.

Rodriguez, M.J. (2001): 'The Open Method of Coordination as a New Governance Tool', in: *Europa Europe* 10.

Schäfer, A. (2004): 'Beyond the Community Method: Why the Open Method of Coordination Was Introduced to EU Policy Making', at: *European Integration Online Papers* 8/13, http://eiop.or.at/eiop/texte/2004-013a.htm.

Scharpf, F.W. (1999): *Governing in Europe: Effective and Democratic?* Oxford: Oxford University Press.

Scott, J./Trubek, D. (2002): 'Mind the Gap: Law and New Approaches to Governance in the European Union', in: *European Law Journal* 8/1, pp. 1-18.

Smismans, S. (2004a): 'EU Employment Policy: Decentralisation or Centralisation through the Open Method of Coordination', *Law Department Working Papers 2004/01*, Florence: European University Institute.

Smismans, S. (2004b): *Law, Legitimacy and European Governance. Functional Participation in Social Regulation*, Oxford: Oxford University Press.

Telo, M. (2003): 'Strengths and Deficits of the Open Method', in: Weiler, J./Begg, I./Peterson, J. (eds) *Integration in an Expanding European Union*, Oxford: Blackwell, pp. 135-39.

Trubek, D./Mosher, J. (2003): 'New Governance, Employment Policy and the European Social Model', in: Zeitlin, J./Trubek, D. (eds) *Governing Work and Welfare in a New Economy. European and American Experiments*, Oxford: Oxford University Press, pp. 33-58.

Trubek, D./Trubek, L. (2005): 'The Open Method of Coordination and the Debate over 'Hard' and 'Soft' Law', in: Zeitlin et al. (eds) *The Open Method of Coordination in Action: The European Employment and Social Inclusion Strategies*, Brussels: Peter Lang, pp. 83-103.

Zandstra, P. (2007): 'The OMC and the Quest for Democratic Legitimization: The Case of the European Employment Strategy', in: Bekkers, V.J.J.M./Dijkstra, A.G./Edwards, A.R./Fenger, H.J.M. (eds) *Governance and the Democratic Deficit: Assessing the Democratic Legitimacy of Governance Practices*, Aldershot: Ashgate, pp. 249-68.

Zeitlin, J. (2002): 'Opening the Open Method of Coordination', Brussels: Presentation for the Committee of the Regions (unpublished).

Zeitlin, J./Pochet, P./Magnusson, L. (eds) (2005): *The Open Method of Coordination in Action: The European Employment and Social Inclusion Strategies*, Brussels: Peter Lang.

Chapter 9
Advisory Committees in EU Agricultural Policy: A Suitable Source of Political Legitimacy?

Karen Heard-Lauréote

1. Introduction

Throughout its half-century existence and in the face of various challenges, the European Union (EU) has often had the task of rethinking its political legitimacy. Most significantly, the crisis sparked by the Maastricht Treaty's difficult ratification process led to a substantial deviation from an EU legitimised primarily by its capacity to deliver efficient and effective collective decision-making and problem-solving, towards a system based on greater direct public consent. The European Commission (CEC) has had to undertake a similar rethink of its legitimacy resource. Initially founded on the basis of technocratic administration and efficiency gains, it has had to readjust these features underpinning its legitimacy – largely as a result of the politicisation of the integration process and its 1999 institutional crisis, which have resulted in increased pressure on the CEC to justify itself. In response, it has advanced the increased participation of organised civil society in its activities as an important means to justify and gain public consent for its institutional role and activities. CEC committees such as the Agricultural Advisory Groups (AAGs[1]) have been drawn into this discourse, representing as they do an institutionalised mechanism for civil society's participation and consultation.[2]

This chapter asks whether the AAGs can deliver what they are increasingly being used for and promoted as; that is, do they constitute a source of additional legitimacy for the CEC? The core argument is that whilst CEC advisory committees have historically been used to increase output legitimacy (efficiency, performance), and continue to fulfil this role currently; more recently, as the need for input legitimacy has increased and become more visi-

1 Entitled Agricultural Advisory Committees up until a reform of their statutes in 2004.

2 The Commission is represented on three main types of committee: 'management', 'regulatory' and 'advisory'. The former two were created in 1962 and 1968 respectively and comprise mainly member state civil servants and operate principally during the implementation phase of the policy cycle. The first AAGs were established in the early 1970s, are composed of representatives of relevant socio-economic interest groups and operate primarily during the preparatory stage.

ble, they have also been presented by the CEC as a source of input legitimacy and thus a means to counter its difficulties in securing public consent. Arguably however, at least from the perspective of normative political theory, they are ill suited for this purpose. Given that they are, nevertheless, used and presented as a source of input legitimacy, two explanations offer themselves. Either the CEC is dabbling in a bit of deception, and should thus stop presenting advisory committees as something they cannot be, acknowledge output legitimacy as committees' primary contribution to European integration and disassociate them from the CEC's legitimation via civil society participation discourse. Or alternatively it may be the case that, as Blühdorn indicates in the early parts of this volume, prevalent understandings and expectations of legitimacy are silently changing in response to the challenge of societal complexity and the CEC is simply being swept along in this trend.

The discussion is divided into three parts. The first two sections aim to demonstrate the shifting nature of EU politics since the birth of the integration project and the changing need for legitimacy. The key argument is that output legitimacy via efficiency and performance dominated the EU integration project in the early years. It was not until a gradual transition occurred around the late 1970s and early 1980s, culminating in the Single European Act in 1986 and the 1992-3 crisis provoked by the Maastricht Treaty's ratification process and the Danes' rejection of it, that the issue of direct political or input legitimacy reached the top of the agenda. Part three explores the way in which CEC Advisory Committees were initially created and developed to provide gains in efficiency and effectiveness to the EU system. It argues that various features ensure that structures like the AAGs are well suited to enhance performance. However, a problem has arisen as a result of the new legitimacy burdens placed on the CEC, which have led it to promote the participation of organized civil society in its major functions and activities, as a means to acquire greater public acceptance and support and thus stronger input legitimacy. Consequently, the final section of this chapter questions whether the AAGs constitute an arena for the real and meaningful participation of organized civil society and whether they can actually deliver what is increasingly expected of them, namely, to provide a source of public consent and act as a generator of input legitimacy. It is posited here that they cannot fulfil this legitimation role as long as they suffer their own striking legitimacy deficits on the input side.

2. Negative integration and the marginality of legitimacy questions

During the first few decades of the EU's existence a period of negative integration was pursued, which left the autonomy of Member States (MSs) largely unaffected. At this time, the European institutional framework's political legitimacy was at best sidelined and at worst ignored, to the extent that as long as everybody benefited from the integration project, legitimacy was not considered an issue. Overall, there was largely thought to be no pressing need to address legitimacy, or that the latter was sufficiently ensured via the EU's outputs and outcomes. Indeed, it was assumed that its weak democratic nature or distance from popular identification was irrelevant. Instead it would be accepted on solely instrumental or technocratic grounds, because the creation of effective administrative government in discrete policy areas would provide economic welfare, which would in turn generate public support provided there were no conflicts of (re)distribution. It was equally assumed that indirect legitimacy would be conferred on the EU via its MSs who themselves possessed legitimate governments. Finally, Jean Monnet, and later those who continued to support a technocratic strategy, believed that the problem of popular consent or legitimacy could be deferred. Thus, although the EU was initially reliant on a combination of technocratic and indirect legitimation, issues of democratisation and identity formation could be dealt with later once people gained practical experience with the very institutions in need of legitimation. Indeed, it was initially considered that there was no room for the direct involvement of uninformed publics in such technocratic administrative affairs (Lord 2000: 4; Wallace and Smith 1995).

When the EU integration project began, there were two primary strategy options available; the pursuance of a future federalist entity and the pursuance of the 'Monnet method'. It is the latter that triumphed and became the preferred approach, particularly of the advocates of an 'elite-led gradualism' or the 'pragmatists' who underlined the immediate need for effective and efficient policy-making and prioritised the problem-solving capacity of European governance (Rhinard 2002: 187; Wallace and Smith 1995: 140). This approach's overall purpose was to skim over 'high' political issues in favour of splitting decisions along functional and administrative lines to ensure efficiency and performance. Indeed, Monnet was himself an elitist and pragmatist (Dinan 2006: 302) and favoured functional economic integration, whereby close economic cooperation would occur between countries in strictly defined economic sectors. Accordingly, popular consent or legitimacy would logically if slowly occur as a natural evolution to this elite-led gradualism.

This central focus on and quest for efficiency and performance certainly propelled the early European integration agenda. Its prioritisation is clearly evident, for example, in the Schuman Plan, which was 'a response to the contradictory requirements of reviving the West German economy and of containing a reviving German state: an elite enterprise, not a response to any popular pressure' (Wallace and Smith 1995: 141). Furthermore, the Treaty of Rome was clearly about 'enlightened administration on behalf of uninformed publics, in cooperation with affected interests and subject to the approval of national governments' (ibid.: 143). Efficiency then was clearly the key theme throughout the early Treaties. As Helen Wallace argued, the initial bargain was elite-led, as have been all subsequent partial bargains (Wallace 1990).

The prioritisation of efficiency was similarly at the root of the emergence of the neo-functionalist integration theory, which reigned long into the 1960s. The basis of this logic was an incremental strategy promoting elite-level group interaction as a means of enhancing sentiments of a 'common interest' via the education of groups, in order to impress upon them the benefits of working together. This strategy would be complemented by wider public-level transborder interactions, and would in time engender public support and thus a wider political community where groups and individuals would transfer loyalties, expectations and political activities to a supranational centre (Haas 1989).

In its early years, the CEC was also relatively disinterested in direct legitimacy and focused primarily on efficiency gains. Established by the Treaty of Paris (1951), the EC's predecessor, the High Authority (HA) of the European Coal and Steel Community (ECSC) was originally presided over by Jean Monnet and intended as an expert and authoritative body (Wallace and Smith 1995: 142). The Treaty invested the HA with independent powers to impartially manage and regulate coal and steel markets; it was thus primarily created as a small and informal entity aimed at enhancing efficiency. Monnet's aspiration to mould a slick, high performing regulatory mechanism are clear in his comment to a fellow HA member: 'If one day there are more than two hundred of us, we shall have failed' (Monnet 1987: 405 cited by Hooghe and Nugent 2006: 148).

Monnet's vision for the HA was actually a European level recreation of the *Commissariat du Plan* (Planning Commission) he had headed in his native France during the post-WWII period. It was to be supported by the advice of a Consultative Committee, which constituted a form of functional representation assisting technical experts comprised as it was of equal numbers of producers, workers, consumers and dealers nominated from lists of 'representational organisations' (Articles 18-19). Indeed, composed of a small team of high-ranking civil servants and experts, the Commissariat's main job was to produce five-year economic plans. Monnet certainly aspired to an HA composed of 'a small, organizationally flexible and adaptable multi-national nucleus of individuals' (Hooghe and Nugent 2006: 150) whose assigned role would involve the development of ideas as well as some advocacy and persuasion, whereas implementation would be left to national administrations. In reality, it gradually came to reflect national bureaucracies shaped by Weberian-type principles and modes of operation such as hierarchy, formality and impartiality.

In sum, in the early integration years, technocracy – or the increased role of experts and civil servants – was championed by Monnet and his supporters as a way to overcome the inefficiencies associated with the 'instability of the parliamentary regime, the importance of rhetoric' and 'politicians' dependence on electoral cycles' (Magnette 2005: 15). Monnet was in fact convinced of the need 'to correct the defects of the political game by using the virtues of technocracy' by relying on the 'continuity of the public service' (ibid.) and the technical knowledge of economists and engineers. This gave the HA and subsequent CEC a largely technical profile.

3. Positive integration and the need for new sources of legitimacy

The discussion so far has demonstrated that output legitimacy via efficiency and performance dominated the EU integration project in the early years. However, a gradual transition occurred around the late 1970s and early 1980s, which culminated in the Single European Act in 1986 and the 1992-3 crisis provoked by the Maastricht Treaty's ratification process and the Danes' rejection of it. These events made a significant contribution to propelling the issue of direct political or input legitimacy to the top of the agenda. Indeed, Wolton (1993) argues that Maastricht 'symbolized the beginning of democratic Europe'. At this time the EU began to make the transition from negative towards more positive integration, a process which gradually affected the MSs' autonomy. The Treaty reforms and events surrounding them certainly demonstrated two things: a) that the EU could no longer rely on or take for granted the existence of a passive permissive consensus or public consent by default and b) that the EU was in the process of developing into a political system in its own right. Consequently, it could no longer escape allegations that it harboured a 'democratic deficit'; the latter being defined by a European Parliamentary committee as:

> The combination of two phenomena: (i) the transfer of powers from the MSs to the EC; (ii) the exercise of these powers at Community level by institutions other than the European Parliament, even though, before the transfer, the national parliaments held power to pass laws in the areas concerned (1988).

Lord (2000) argues that the reason for the change of focus regarding legitimacy was essentially two-fold. Firstly, majority voting and the greater autonomy enjoyed by supranational institutions undercut the argument that indirect legitimation was ensured by the parallel consent of all EU MSs on each decision taken. Secondly, EU institutions became increasingly involved in areas where it was unable to claim legitimacy solely on the grounds of performance or efficiency (Lord 2000: 4) including employment and social issues, economic and monetary union (EMU), justice and home affairs and Common Foreign and Security Policy (CFSP). As a consequence the need for a new kind of legitimacy on the input side became ever more apparent.

For the CEC's part, although its instrumental and technocratic focus on efficiency and performance had long endured, the 1990s led to fundamental internal reform of its services and a consequent rethink of its political legitimacy basis. The Danish 'no' and narrow French 'yes' to the Maastricht Treaty marked the end of the so-called permissive consensus. European integration became a more politically contentious process, with citizens increasingly desirous to have their say. This politicisation resulted in increased pressure on the CEC to justify its role and activities. Moreover, responsible as it is for decisions by unelected officials, it has increasingly dawned on the CEC that it needs to exploit alternative sources of public consent.

Charges of internal bad practice provoked an institutional crisis in 1999 and created further pressure on the CEC to rethink its legitimacy. Faced with the now infamous allegations of 'fraud, nepotism and mismanagement', and as a direct result of the publication of a report by the Committee of Independent Experts (CIE), the Santer Commission resigned in March 1999. Mediatised aspects of the report focused on favouritism by certain Commissioners. However, 'the real message' was the 'numerous performance problems in the Commission services' (Hooghe and Nugent 2006: 155) and a second September 1999 CIE report exposed a detailed account of internal financial mismanagement.

The result of the events discussed thus far is that today 'there is a consensus among analysts[3] and policy-makers that the EU generally suffers a democratic deficit' (Eriksen and Fossum 2000: 5), and that this shortfall in democratic credentials, one of which is legitimacy, has been the subject of debates for a number of years and is well documented in the literature[4]. In response to criticisms addressing this issue made by scholars, policy-makers and citizens, the EU as a whole has had to undergo a substantial rethink in order to reinforce its legitimacy basis. Whereas 'European integration started as an elite process, in which popular consent was largely assumed' (Wallace

3 Although it should be noted that there are some scholars who insist that there is no democratic deficit: see for example Moravscik 2002, 2003, 2004; Majone 1993, 1998, 1999, 2000.

4 See recent debates by Zweifel 2002, 2006; Føllesdal and Hix 2006; Hix 2008; Føllesdal 2004; Moravscik 2002, 2003, 2004; Majone 1993, 1998, 1999, 2000.

and Smith 1995: 151) and whereby indirect legitimacy was thought sufficient, the 'Monnet method', 'despite succeeding in moving the integration process along (…) has caused some tensions, namely between technocracy and democratic accountability' (Wallace and Smith 1995 cited by Christiansen and Kirchner 2000: 10). Today, in a context of the end of the permissive consensus, the birth of the democratic deficit debate and a feeling that as the EU evolves into a supranational polity in its own right it must reflect some of the same democratic characteristics associated with national polities, the EU has had to redefine its stance on legitimacy so much that it has become a central internal preoccupation. In sum, if technocratic policy-making based on indirect legitimacy has ever been enough, today it certainly is not and the EU has been confronted with the task of exploring other sources.

To respond to the challenges it has increasingly faced, the CEC has had a particularly difficult time rethinking its political legitimacy. One avenue it has sought to pursue in order to re-validate and bolster its institutional role and activities is the sourcing of consent in alternative locations. One that it increasingly exploits is the participation of organised civil society in its major functions of policy preparation, formulation and proposal. With a view to winning public acceptance and support within the broader European institutional framework, gradually the CEC has developed an official discourse based on the concepts of 'civil society' and 'civil dialogue', and increasingly calls on organised civil society to actively contribute to its activities.

It currently attributes paramount importance to notions of participation, consultation and institutionalised interactions with intermediary civil society organisations (CSOs). This is particularly evident from the CEC's various official publications, especially from 1992 onwards. In 2001, the CEC noted that organised civil society offers 'valuable support for a democratic system of government' and constitutes an additional route for civic participation (EC 2000a: 4). Moreover, it asserts that certain elements of civil society can help foster 'participatory democracy' (EC 2000a: 4), which the CEC argues should complement the concept of representative democracy (EC 1997, 2000a). The 2001 White Paper on European Governance was published with the specific aim of legitimising CEC policy-making in the public eye via enhanced consultation and participation processes. Here, the EC suggested that 'democracy depends on people being able to take part in public debate' while today legitimacy 'depends on involvement and participation (…) from policy creation to implementation' (EC 2001: 11). 'The organizations that make up civil society' it notes, 'mobilise people and support' (ibid.). Indeed, participation, fulfils several roles; it is considered a response to Union citizens' expectations (ibid.: 35), can 'connect Europe' with these (ibid.: 3), can facilitate the adoption of a 'less top-down approach' (ibid.: 4), and prompt policy making to be more 'inclusive and accountable' (ibid.: 8). In sum, this added value should augment 'the quality, relevance and effectiveness of EU policies', 'create more confidence in the end-result and in the institutions which deliver policies' (ibid.: 10) and further still produce 'a sense of belonging to Europe' (ibid.: 11). Later in 2002, the CEC reaffirmed its commitment to an 'inclusive approach' during policy development and to 'consulting as widely as possible on major policy initiatives' (EC 2002: 16). In short, the CEC has for some time clearly been pursuing a discourse in which organised civil society participation in its core activities is being offered as an additional means by which to strengthen its public consent and therefore its own political legitimacy.

4. The European Commission and its Advisory Committees

As highlighted above, the CEC is represented on three main types of committee: 'management', 'regulatory' and 'advisory'. While the former two comprise mainly Member State (MS) civil servants and operate principally during the implementation phase of decision-making, the latter type is composed of representatives of relevant socio-economic interest groups,[5] which we can broadly label CSOs, and operate primarily during the preparatory or policy formulation phase of the EU decision-making process.

Committees were initially created and developed to increase output legitimacy via the provision of efficiency, performance and effectiveness gains. As Vos confirms, committees' 'ad hoc institutional evolution' is linked to 'the need to achieve effective and efficient decision making' (1999: 19). CAP related CEC committees were first created in the early 1960s, as the expansion of this first 'common' European public policy led the Council to delegate certain implementation or executive tasks to the CEC in an effort to reduce its own workload. According to Joerges, 'it was not a coincidence that the committee system was first developed under the auspices of the most intensively regulated sector of the European economy: agriculture' (1999: 8f) since committees were perceived to be a means of facilitating MS consent to and implementation of regulations. In sum, in broad terms CEC committees were initially created with an efficiency/effectiveness agenda in mind.

Arguably, committees like the AAGs continue to enhance efficiency and performance and thus provide a source of output-legitimacy to the European integration project in certain key ways. For example, the AAGs:

5 Agricultural producers and cooperatives, the agricultural and food manufacturing industries, the agricultural products and foodstuffs trade, farm and food industry workers, consumers, environmentalists and animal welfare groups.

1. ensure organised interest consultation and participation. Indeed, the AAGs were set up under the auspices of DG Agriculture as a result of the 1972 Paris Summit, which called for the increased participation of economic and social interests in the Community policy-making process. In response, the CEC created committees like the AAGs composed of interested representatives. This is significant and clearly indicates the contribution initially intended for such committees. Consultation has long been perceived by the CEC as a way of enhancing the effectiveness, efficiency and overall quality of policy outcomes since proposals are more likely to be 'technically viable, practically workable and based on a bottom-up approach' (EC 2002: 5).
2. function on the basis of the institutionalisation of collective rule and are thus 'an expression of, and a catalyst for, decision-making based on consensus and consultation' in the EU (Christiansen and Kirchner 2000: 9). This is one of the 'hallmark[s] of European integration' (ibid.) respecting the multiplicity and diversity of views and positions and the variety of vantage points and opinions within the policy community.
3. provide an institutionalised access point to DG Agriculture and thus overcome many of the problems and weaknesses associated with informal direct lobbying in the European agricultural policy sector.
4. are 'resorted to by the Commission in an attempt to satisfy its demand for technical and scientific information' (Vos 1999: 21) which committee members can supply.
5. facilitate processes of transnational socialization and mutual learning. The AAGs are a form of international social interaction and thus help in the process of constructing the identities and interests of actors involved in them. This is particularly important where access countries send representatives with observer status. Cultural learning is promoted by organised civil society members familiarising themselves with the nature of the CEC's processes and procedures.
6. provide a venue for transnational networking. The diversity of interests and nationalities represented creates a supranational, multi-interest arena that can be likened to an epistemic community.
7. facilitate multi-level governance by providing a context for linkage between actors at different levels.

While the above features attest that the AAGs are very well suited to the enhancement of performance and efficiency and thus the provision of output legitimacy, a problem has arisen as a result of the new legitimacy burdens placed on the CEC since the 1990s. As a result of these demands, the Commission has begun to promote the participation of organised civil society in its major functions and activities as a way to win greater public acceptance and support. Accordingly, the advisory committees have emerged via its participatory discourse as a key location for organised civil society participation and thus the provision of input legitimacy.

The aforementioned participatory discourse began to emerge in the early 1990s. It was at this time that the CEC first noted that advisory committees like the AAGs 'which assist the CEC in the exercise of its competences' are one of 'two forms of dialogue between the Commission and special interest groups' (EC 1992: 1). Similarly, the Governance White Paper notes 'the Commission already consults interested parties through different instruments such as (…) advisory committees' (2001: 15). Such institutionalised participatory mechanisms are thus advanced as a means to promote participation; one of the five principles of governance put forward by the Paper to enhance democracy within the EU. In addition, its website notes: 'Putting in place a committee' is about the EC opting for 'dialogue' and laying down rules for 'a formal consultation'. In a further document, the AAGs are advanced as means to 'improve the dialogue with the Community-scale socio-economic organizations'. Moreover, in the 1998 Commission Decision (CD) instigating the AAGs, their aim was noted as being threefold:

- for the CEC to 'seek the views of the economic sectors and consumers on matters arising in connection with the operation of the various common organizations of the market and other areas covered by the common agricultural policy';
- to provide the economic sectors directly involved in the operation of the market organizations and affected by agricultural policy decisions, as well as consumers with an opportunity to participate in drafting the opinions requested by the Commission;
- to enable relevant economic federations and consumer groups in the MSs, which have set up organizations at European Union level, to represent those concerned in all the MSs.

These aims confirm that the AAGs are envisaged as a formal, institutionalized, consultative and participatory forum for Common Agricultural Policy (CAP) and rural development (RD) affected organized interests representing civil society. Given that the CEC increasingly perceives such participation as an additional source of legitimacy, the AAGs naturally form part of its input legitimation strategy: to attract greater public consent and reinforce its status within the European institutional framework.

A core question emerges in the context of the expansion and transformation of EU policy, which as we have seen has created new legitimacy needs for the integration project as a whole, but more particularly for the CEC. Can its advisory committees actually constitute an arena for the real and meaningful participation of organised civil society, and can they also deliver what is increasingly expected of them, namely to form an additional source of public consent and thereby generate input legitimacy? Indeed, is the CEC right to promote them as such? In response, it is posited here that the AAGs cannot fulfil a legitimation role since they possess their own striking legitimacy deficits on the input side. This assertion can be supported by exploring, from the perspective of normative theory, the criteria which need to be fulfilled for an institution to function as a source of input legitimacy. An examination of Scharpf's input/output legitimacy dichotomy (2003) usefully reveals key conditions required for input legitimacy against which the AAGs can be assessed.

5. Commission Advisory Committees and the delivery of input legitimacy

Given that earlier chapters in this volume have explored the concepts, distinctions and relationship between input legitimacy and output legitimacy in some detail, it suffices here to note that the input-legitimacy of a structure of functional representation refers to legitimacy derived from the democratic process.

Here, following Scharpf (1999, 2003), input legitimacy specifically relates to political choices which derive legitimacy from reflecting *the will of the people*; that is, the authentic preferences of European Community citizens. The input-orientated legitimacy tradition is shaped by the ideals of participatory democracy in the Greek Polis and of the French Revolution. The starting point is Rousseau's equation of the common good with the *general will* of the people. Under this equation, legitimacy is guaranteed when political choices reflect the will of the people and is ensured by institutions maximizing either the direct participation of the governed in policy choices or the responsiveness of governors to the (collective) preferences of the governed. It is therefore about involving either European citizens or interest groups through direct participation as much as possible. We will call this representativeness. However, Scharpf posits that because not every aggregate of persons constitutes an electorate and because it is not certain that members of the electorate or their representatives will be orientated toward the common good, input-legitimacy in its modern sense also has an emphasis on 'government by discussion' (Habermas, 1962 cited by Scharpf 2003: 4) or deliberation.[6] In sum, based on Scharpf's analysis an institution's input-legitimacy

6 The output legitimacy of a structure of functional representation refers to legitimacy related to the performance and efficiency of decision-making. It necessitates institutional norms and incentives mechanisms that must serve two potentially conflicting purposes: the hindrance of the abuse of public power and the facilitation of effective problem solving (Scharpf 1999: 13). To assess the latter, the performance of a structure in fulfilling its as-

cannot only be judged by its representative character, but also by its deliberative nature (Smismans 2003: 8). The following discussion assesses balanced representation and deliberation.

Balanced representation

Research carried out in the context of other advisory institutions has advanced that the criterion of representativeness should actually refer 'to the degree to which' they 'incorporate diverse social, political, and disciplinary perspectives' (Brown et al. 2005: 84). It is also interesting to compare advisory committees in the EU context with their trans-Atlantic namesakes, whereby the US Federal Advisory Committee Act of 1972 requires that advisory committees be 'fairly balanced in terms of points of view represented and functions performed' (ibid.). This discussion adopts a perspective which conceives balanced institutional composition, rather than a literal mirroring between the composition of institutions and society, as being the paramount element of representativeness.

Drawing on and developing Schmitter's work, it is posited that the achievement of the first requirement of input legitimacy within institutions like CEC Advisory Committees, representativeness or internal balanced composition as we choose to entitle it here, is contingent on the presence of five key elements:

1. The institution should adopt a *minimum threshold principle* i.e. a composition that is not cumbersome but streamlined. In this way, there should be no other active members than those necessary to fulfil the institution's mandate or judged capable of contributing to its designated core task. In other words, all participants must possess some type or degree of *asset specificity*, i.e. they must demonstrably have material, intellectual or political resources that are relevant to the tasks to be accomplished.
2. The institution should conform to a *stake-holding principle* whereby it is solely composed of relevant stakeholders. The relevancy of stakeholders can be understood in two ways. First, those who possess knowledge or expertise, which renders them specialised in dealing with the task. That participants should be experts is important since 'average citizens are not capable of making decisions on complex public policy matters' (Crosby et al. 1986: 171). Second, those who are affected by the issues which the

---

signed role and the influence of a structure on the decision-making process may be examined. To assess the former, the presence of effective checks and balances within the structure can be evaluated. These should ensure accountability and transparency and that policy tracks public opinion.

institution's mandate conceivably allows it to address. 'For true representativeness to be achieved, members of all affected communities (...) should be canvassed' (Rowe and Frewer 2000: 12). After all, the possession of expertise is one of the critical motivations of the CEC consulting large CSOs: it has to select from all the demands (directed at it from various interested parties) and it does so 'on the basis of their ability to solicit substantial policy input' (Obradovic 2005: 5).

3. The institution should conform to the *principle of European privilege* and thus comprise CSOs that represent European-wide constituencies. This principle is based on the assumption that CSOs with broader constituencies are representative of a greater proportion of affected interests.
4. The institution should respect the *adversarial principle* and therefore not be composed of 'a preponderance of representatives who are known to have a similar position or who have already formed an alliance for a common purpose' (Schmitter 2001: 8). Participants should therefore be selected to represent constituencies that are known to have diverse and, especially, opposing interests.
5. Linked to the fourth aspect of balanced composition outlined above, an institution should lastly respect the criterion of *putative equality*. Accordingly, all participants in political institutions should be considered equal:

> Even when they represent constituencies of greatly differing size, resources, public or private status, and 'political clout' at national level, no EGA should have second and third class participants, even though it is necessary to distinguish unambiguously between those who participate and those who are just consulted (Schmitter 2001: 8).

While the limitations of this chapter do not permit a full exploration of the above five elements of balanced composition[7], as an illustration of this phenomenon it is possible to identify central concerns relating to the criteria of putative quality and the adversarial principle.

Firstly, equal consideration and therefore balanced representation is arguably undermined by an unequal distribution of AAG seats. This is all the more significant given that the CEC stresses that it composes AAGs 'with an eye to a fair balance of the different interests involved' (EC 2006). However, this claim is contentious. As Figure 9.1 demonstrates, over 50 per cent of seats are allocated to farmers and agricultural cooperatives, that is, for the most part to COPA-COGECA[8]. A third are accorded to trade and industry

7 For a full discussion of balanced composition in the context of Commission advisory structures see Heard-Lauréote 2009.

8 COPA (Comité des Organisations Professionnelle Agricoles de l'Union Européenne) and COGECA (Comité Général de la Coopération Agricole de l'Union Européenne) are umbrella Euro groups that represent a large proportion of the EU's farmers and many of its

interests. The AAG seat distribution thus ensures that the combined seats of farmers and agricultural cooperatives (plus, in some cases, those of trade and industry) are sufficient to give them a two-thirds majority in the AAGs highlighted.

This position of dominance is even more significant when the procedure for electing the AAG Chair is considered. This is done via a two-thirds majority of seats in the first round and a simple majority in subsequent ballots. The seat distribution outlined thus effectively allows the dominant European umbrella groups to dominate this function[9] and profit from the benefits this role accords: a substantial say in agenda setting, the compilation of minutes and control of the floor during meetings.

While they are composed of varied and sometimes divergent interests, balanced representation is further compromised because in certain AAGs, representatives prevail who are recognized as sharing similar views or who already have a close association. COGECA carries out its 'lobbying work (...) as a complement to' COPA (Cojeca 2005). Indeed, these sister organisations' secretariats merged in 1962 and approximately 50 joint working groups and 300 other meetings are held between them each year. COPA has an equally strong relationship with the CEJA: the President of the latter participates in COPA Presidium meetings and the two groups share policy positions on numerous issues.

---

agricultural cooperatives. Formed jointly in 1958, COPA is today made up of 59 organisations from the 27 countries of the European Union, one associated organisation from Romania and 28 partner organisations from Europe, Iceland, Norway, Switzerland and Turkey. COGECA has over 30 members representing 30,000 farm co-operatives across Europe. COPA has a highly developed organisational structure. The Presidency of COPA and COGECA together form a Coordination Committee, which tries to reach an agreement as far as the activities and positions of COPA and COGECA are concerned. COPA has more than 50 Working Parties, sub-Groups and Specialist Sections, either from specific commodity sectors or for general questions (structural, social, environmental etc.). Most of these Working Parties and Specialist Sections are constituted jointly with COGECA, but both COPA and COGECA also have separate Working Parties of their own. (Source: http://www.COPA-COGECA.be/en/).

9 A term of office for a Chairperson and VC was introduced in 2004 and now stands at two years renewable. The Chair may not serve more than two consecutive terms. Moreover, a new chair may not originate from the same socio-economic sector as his/her predecessor. The primary aim of this adjustment was to overcome substantial criticism emanating from various participating socio-economic organisations. Due to seat allocation and the majority voting method of electing a chair, COPA-COGECA almost always assumed this role. Despite these formal changes, empirical evidence demonstrates that most participants are unaware of this change to the statutes. This is perhaps largely due to the fact that, at the point of writing, only a period of three years has elapsed since 2004, meaning that the two-year renewable period is still operating in most cases. In short, COPA-COGECA continues to hold the majority of AAG chairs today and significant change is unlikely to occur until well into 2008.

Figure 9.1: Composition of Agricultural Advisory Groups 1998 and 2004

Interests represented	Seats 1998	Interests represented	Seats 2004
on Common Agricultural Policy (CAP)			
Farmers	22	Farmers & Agricultural	30
Agricultural cooperatives	8	cooperatives	
Traders	8	Traders	8
Industry	8	Industry	8
Workers	5	Workers	5
Consumers	5	Consumers	5
Other	4	Environmentalists	3
		Others	2
TOTAL	**60**		**61**
on Forestry & Cork (F&C)			
Producers (farmers managing woodland, private and public woodland owners)	23	Producers	28
Traders	1	Traders	2
Industry	8	Industry	11
Workers	3	Workers	3
Consumers	1	Consumers	1
Other	4	Environmentalists	4
TOTAL	40		49
on Rural Development (RD)			
Producers	22	Farmers & Agricultural	27
Agricultural cooperatives	4	cooperatives	
Traders	5	Traders	5
Industry	5	Industry	5
Workers	5	Workers	4
Consumers	3	Consumers	3
Other	16	Environmentalists	6
		Others	10
TOTAL	60		60
on Agriculture and the Environment (A&E)			
Producers	14	Farmers & Agricultural	21
Agricultural cooperatives	3	cooperatives	
Traders	3	Traders	4
Industry	3	Industry	4
Workers	2	Workers	2
Consumers	2	Consumers	2
Other	7	Environmentalists	8
TOTAL	34		41

Deliberation

It is not only the representative character of AAGs which is compromised via their inability to achieve balanced composition; their deliberative capacity is also questionable. Deliberation generally refers to *talk-centric* processes or discussion. More specifically for our purposes, deliberation in a democratic context infers a process in which reason, not power coercion, predominates (Trénel 2004: 2). It is posited that when seeking to assess the AAGs' deliberative nature, this could be done against six deliberative norms:

1. Deliberation is a process that addresses or seeks to resolve conflict and (moral) disagreement, or builds coordination. To do this it must take views from *across the political spectrum* into consideration.
2. *Rationality*: Deliberators must reason with each other, that is, be willing to reasonably justify their opinions and positions. This is based on the assumption that discussion is more deliberative if it incorporates accurate knowledge of relevant information. In short, the provision of evidence, the process of substantiating claims and the advancement of technical arguments necessitate expertise.
3. *Universality*: This element ensures that the reasons offered are understood by, attempt to appeal to, and can thus be accepted by, everyone. Accordingly, reasons have to be framed in terms of the common good by ensuring that the interests of those to be convinced are included. Participants can demonstrate such a consideration for the common good via a sense of empathy, which could manifest itself in the demonstration of an understanding of different stakeholders' interests as well as an appreciation of the impact of different policy options and collective problem solutions on other actors.
4. Deliberation requires that deliberators act according to the principles of *openness* (in terms of the availability of information), *intelligibility* (in terms of clear communication and the absence of jargon) and *equality* (in terms of inclusiveness and fairness) – everyone should have an equal opportunity to participate and an equal opportunity to be heard during deliberation. Participants must actually have five equal opportunities for action. They must be able to a) be present, b) speak, i.e. have their say, c) participate equally in the discussion, d) participate in decision-making, and e) influence the agenda.
5. Mutual respect or the principle of *universal respect*: In democratic deliberation this element is required to establish a social context in which participants are willing to put forth arguments, particularly those that constitute dissent, i.e. counter arguments (Fishkin 1991; Gastil 1993 cited by Burkhalter et al. 2002: 407). This respect must be upheld even if the positions of others seem wrong or contradict one's own conclusion (Gut-

mann and Thompson 1996 cited by Muhlberger 2006: 43). Mutual respect equally infers a willingness to listen to others and to the reasons they advance as well as a need to learn to respect the points of view of traditional adversaries. Repeated interaction of participating groups over a period of time, rather than just once, to solve a single common problem, may help them build a relationship of trust and mutual respect to facilitate deliberation (Schmitter 2001: 5). Neuhold (2001: 7) found that regular meetings between committee members over a number of years can 'partly enable them to come to a consensus rather quickly'.
6. *Accountability*: A willingness to respond to the objections of others and a readiness to be convinced by others. The latter is translated by a willingness to shift to new positions including that of opposing parties when they cannot respond to objections (Bohman 1996).

Again, the limitations of this chapter do not permit a full exploration of the above six aspects of deliberation.[10] To illustrate the way in which the AAGs possess a limited deliberative capacity, it is however possible to identify central concerns relating to the nature of discussions and the lack of mutual respect demonstrated by participants.

It is argued that AAG meeting formats are not conducive to verbal deliberation: Opening exposés by the CEC, a Chair-instigated roundtable of comments and reactions based on pre-prepared interest organization statements of official policy lines, followed by direct communications between individual committee members and CEC officials rather than broad discussion, does not equate to deliberation. A 'Muppet Show', 'predictable piece of theatre' and 'dialogue of the deaf' where traditional policy lines are 'dusted off' and wheeled out again as a way to justify the reimbursement received for expenses (personal communications, environment and consumer group members and Commission official, September 11th; October 2nd; and December 10th 2003), are a selection of member comments describing proceedings.

The side-lining of often-controversial or sensitive issues from AAG agendas also cultivates little mutual respect. Members perceive that obstacles exist which prevent them from influencing committee agenda-setting processes. Whilst officially the advisory groups are expected to discuss the matters on which the Commission has requested an opinion, the latter is accused of only discussing 'bits of legislation', which a) it is vaguely considering proposing, b) have already been proposed or c) have already been decided up-stream of the AAGs and are no longer susceptible to amendments. 'Strategic debate' of mid or long-term policy or discussions of matters under internal consideration are rare. 'Such hot potatoes as the GMO[11] one', are

10 For a full discussion of deliberative capacity in the context of Commission advisory structures see Heard-Lauréote 2009.

11 Genetically Modified Organism.

avoided despite numerous attempts to insert it on the Agriculture and Environment Group agenda. When it finally came up, 'the Commission (…) said that it didn't agree with that point on the agenda and therefore would be making no comment' (personal communication, socio-economic group committee member, 24 September 2003).

Finally, AAG meetings are generally infrequent: approximately once and twice per year for the CAP and Agriculture and Environment Advisory Groups respectively. AAGs also suffer from postponements and/or cancellations by DG Agriculture. Indeed, 50 per cent of Rural Development Group meetings scheduled between April 2001 and November 2003, and one of three Agriculture and Environment Group meetings scheduled between February 2001 and May 2003, were postponed. Regular and iterative interaction between committee members and thus the AAGs' deliberative capacity are accordingly compromised.

6. Conclusions

Although the AAGs obviously constitute formal institutionalised consultative mechanisms for the participation of organised civil society, this paper has sought to demonstrate the extent to which these structures also represent a viable source of additional CEC legitimacy. The possession of certain key features arguably renders them well suited for enhancing effectiveness and efficiency, and thus output legitimacy. Problems have nevertheless arisen since the CEC has been forced, as a result of its difficulties securing public consent, to link advisory committees to a different type of legitimation strategy. In short, in the context of the democratic deficit debate, the CEC has come under increasing pressure to demand a new type of legitimacy from structures like the AAGs: input legitimacy. As the discussion has sought to demonstrate, however, they are not at all suited as providers of legitimacy in the sense that is increasingly demanded of them. This mismatch between on the one hand the official narrative, that is, what the CEC expects and even demands of the AAGs; and on the other hand, what they can factually deliver, arguably adds to the functioning problems from which the AAGs currently suffer. To address these, the CEC may be advantaged by acknowledging the historical role of committees like the AAGs in the wider European integration project as providers of output legitimacy via the enhancement of efficiency and performance; a role they continue to perform effectively. Disassociating AAGs from the institution's more recent strategy to strengthen public consent in its role and functions via organised civil society participation may be worthwhile, given their clear weaknesses as a source of input legitimacy.

Each successive treaty reform since the Treaty of Rome has improved the Union's democratic functioning and has sought to reduce so-called democratic and legitimacy deficits. The Lisbon Treaty signed in December 2007 is no exception; indeed, there are a number of significant changes affecting such deficits. Firstly, the Lisbon Treaty suggests that the European Council should elect a Chair by QMV for a 2.5-year term, thus providing greater leadership and a longer-term legislative view. Secondly, more policy areas are supposed to come under co-decision so that the EP gets even more influence over legislation, even the CAP. Thirdly, national parliaments are to be brought into the legislative process, as they are accorded the right to object to draft legislation on the grounds of subsidiarity and proportionality and can ask the Commission to rethink proposals. Fourth, the Council will meet in public when considering legislation. This will give the Commission a stronger political mandate, thus strengthening its legitimacy credentials. Finally, and perhaps most noteworthy in the context of this discussion, the European Council will be obliged to take European Parliament (EP) elections into account when nominating the Commission President. In fact the Treaty provides scope for European political parties to each nominate candidates to fulfil this function and the EP elections could thus serve as a platform for a competitive election between them. This modification would give the EP more influence over the Commission, and European citizens would have a greater influence in choosing the Commission President. All of this could significantly strengthen the Commission's political mandate and its legitimacy credentials, which in turn bears the potential to lead this institution away from its current pursuit of organised civil society participation as a source of input legitimacy via ill-adapted structures such as the AAGs.

References

Bohman, J. (1996): *Public Deliberation. Pluralism, Complexity, and Democracy*, Cambridge, Mass.: The MIT Press.

Brown, M.B./Lentsch, J./Weingart, P. (2005): 'Representation, Expertise, and the German Parliament: A Comparison of Three Advisory Institutions', in: Maasen, S./Weingart, P. (eds) *Democratization of Expertise? Exploring Novel Forms of Scientific Advice in Political Decision-Making*, Dodrecht: Springer, pp. 81-100.

Burkhalter, S./Gastil, J./Kelshaw, T. (2002): 'A Conceptual Definition and Theoretical Model of Public Deliberation in Small Face-to-Face Groups', in: *Communication Theory* 12/4, pp. 398-422.

Christiansen, T./Kirchner, E. (2000): *Committee Governance in the European Union*, Manchester: Manchester University Press.

Cojeca (2005): 'Cojeca Objectives', at: http://www.copa-cogeca.be/en/cogeca_objectifs.asp (accessed: 10 March 2006).

Crosby, N./Kelly, J.M./Schaefer, P. (1986): 'Citizen Panels: A New Approach to Citizen Participation', in: *Public Administration Review* 46/2l, pp. 170-78.

Dinan, D. (2006): *Origins and Evolution of the European Union*, Oxford: Oxford University Press.

EC (1992): 'An Open and Structured Dialogue between the Commission and Special Interest Groups', OJ C 63 of 5/3/1993, at: http://www.europa.eu.int/comm/secretariat_general/index_en.htm (accessed: 2 September 2004).

EC (1997): 'Promoting the Role of Voluntary Organizations and Foundations in Europe', COM(97) 241 final, at: http://europa.eu.int/comm/enterprise/library/lib-social_economy/orgfd_en.pdf (accessed: 2 September 2004).

EC (2000a): 'The Commission and NGOs: Building a Stronger Partnership', COM(2001) 11, at: http://www.europa.eu.int/comm/secretariat_general/index_en.htm (accessed: 2 September 2004).

EC (2000b): *Agricultural Committees*, Brussels: European Commission Directorate General for Agriculture.

EC (2001): 'European Governance: A White Paper', COM(2001) 428 of 25.7.2001, at: http://www.europa.eu.int/comm/governance/white_paper/index_en.htm (accessed: 2 September 2004).

EC (2002): 'Communication from the Commission: 'Towards a Reinforced Culture of Consultation and Dialogue – General Principles and Minimum Standards for Consultation of Interested Parties by the Commission'', COM(2002) 704 final 11.12.2002.

EC Decision (1998): 'Of 11 March 1998 on the Advisory Committees Dealing with Matters Covered by the Common Agricultural Policy', CD 98/235/EC. Official Journal, L88/59, 24/03/98.

Eriksen, E.O./Fossum, J.E. (2000): *Democracy in the European Union: Integration through Deliberation?*, London: Routledge.

European Parliament (1988): 'Rapport fait au nom de la Commission institutionnelle sur le déficit démocratique des Communautés européennes', par Michel Toussaint, PE DOC A 2276/87 of 1 February 1988.

Fishkin, J.S. (1991): *Democracy and Deliberation: New Directions for Democratic Reform*, New Haven, CT: Yale University Press.

Føllesdal, A. (2004): 'Legitimacy Theories of the European Union', Arena Working-Papers 04/15, Oslo: University of Oslo.

Føllesdal, A./Hix, S. (2006): 'Why There is a Democratic Deficit in the EU: A Response to Majone and Moravcsik', in: *Journal of Common Market Studies* 44/3, pp. 533-62.

Haas, E.B. (1989): *The Uniting of Europe: Political, Social and Economic Forces, 1950-57*, London: Stevens.

Heard-Lauréote, K. (2009): *Efficiency and Legitimacy in European Commission Advisory Committees*, London: Routledge.

Hix, S. (2008): *What's Wrong with the European Union and How to Fix it*, Cambridge: Polity.

Hooghe, L./Nugent, N. (2006): 'The Commission's Services', in: Peterson, J./Shackleton, M. (eds) *The Institutions of the European Union*, Oxford: Oxford University Press, pp. 147-69.

Joerges, C. (1999). 'Good Governance through Comitology?', in: Joerges, C./Vos, E. (eds) *EU Committees: Social Regulation, Law and Politics*, Oxford: Hart Publishing, pp. 311-38.

Lord, C. (2000): 'Legitimacy, Democracy and the EU: When Abstract Questions Become Practical Policy Problems', Policy paper 03/00 for the One Europe or Several? Programme, at: http://www.one-europe.ac.uk/cgi-bin/esrc/world/db.cgi/publications.htm (accessed: 8 March 2006).

Magnette, P. (2005): *What is the European Union? Nature and Prospects*, Basingstoke: Palgrave Macmillan.

Majone, G. (1993): 'The European Community: An 'Independent Fourth Branch of Government'', EUI Working Paper 94/17, Florence: EUI.

Majone, G. (1998): 'Europe's Democratic Deficit', in: *European Law Journal* 4/1, pp. 5-28.

Majone, G. (1999): 'The Regulatory State and its Legitimacy Problems', in: *West European Politics* 22/1, pp. 1-13.

Majone, G. (2000): 'The Credibility Crisis of Community Regulation', in: *Journal of Common Market Studies* 38/2, pp. 273-302.

Moravcsik, A. (2002): 'In Defence of the 'Democratic Deficit': Reassessing Legitimacy in the European Union', in: *Journal of Common Market Studies* 40/4, pp. 603-24.

Moravcsik, A. (2003): 'The EU ain't broke', in: *Prospect* March, pp. 38-45.

Moravcsik, A. (2004): 'Is there a 'Democratic Deficit' in World Politics? A Framework for Analysis', in: *Government and Opposition* 39/2, pp. 336-63.

Muhlberger, P. (2006): 'Report to the Deliberative Democracy Consortium: Building a Deliberation Measurement Toolbox', Texas: Texas Tech University.

Neuhold, C. (2001): 'Much Ado About Nothing? Comitology as a Feature of EU Policy Implementation and its Effects on the Democratic Arena', ECPR Workshop Paper, Colchester: ECPR.

Obradovic, A. (2005): 'Participatory Democracy and the Open Access Policy for Interest Groups in the European Union', Paper presented at the EUSA Ninth Biennal International Conference, Austin, Texas, 31.03-2.4.2005.

Rhinard, M. (2002): 'The Democratic Legitimacy of the European Union Committee System', in: *Governance* 15/2, pp. 185-210.

Rowe, G./Frewer, L.J. (2000): 'Public Participation Methods: A Framework for Evaluation', in: *Science, Technology and Human Values* 25/1, pp. 3-29.

Scharpf, F. W. (1999): *Governing in Europe. Effective and Democratic?*, Oxford: Oxford University Press.

Scharpf, F.W. (2003): 'Problem Solving Effectiveness and Democratic Accountability in the EU', Max-Planck-Institut für Gesellschaftsforschung (MPIFG) Working Paper 03/1, Köln: MPIFG.

Schmitter, P.C. (2001): 'What Is There to Legitimize in the European Union and How Might This be Accomplished?', Jean Monnet Working Paper No. 6/01, New York: Jean Monnet Programme.

Smismans, S. (2003): 'Representation through Interest Committees: The Case of the Tripartite Advisory Committee for Safety, Hygiene and Health Protection at Work', in: Saurugger, S. (ed.) *Les modes de représentation dans l'Union européenne*, Paris: L'Harmattan, pp. 249-78.

Trénel, M. (2004): 'Measuring the Deliberativeness of Online Discussions', at: http://www.wz-berlin.de/~trenel.

Vos, E. (1997): 'The Rise of Committees', in: *European Law Journal* 3/3, pp. 210-29.

Vos, E. (1999): 'EU Committees: The Evolution of Unforeseen Institutional Actors in European Product Regulation', in: Joerges, C./Vos, E. (eds) *EU Committees: Social Regulation, Law and Politics*, Oxford: Hart Publishing, pp. 19-51.

Wallace, H. (1990): 'Making Multi-lateral Relations Work', in: Wallace, W. (ed.) *The Dynamics of European Integration*, London: Pinter.

Wallace, W./Smith, J. (1995): 'Democracy or Technocracy? European Integration and the Problem of Popular Consent', in: *West European Politics* 18/3, pp. 137-57.

Wolton, D. (1993): *La dernière utopie: naissance de l'Europe démocratique*, Paris: Flammarion.

Zweifel, T. (2002): '. . . Who Is Innocent Cast the First Stone: The EU's Democratic Deficit in Comparison', in: *Journal of European Public Policy* 9/5, pp. 812-40.

Zweifel, T. (2006): *International Organizations and Democracy: Accountability, Politics, and Power*, Boulder, Colo.: Lynne Rienner.

Chapter 10
More Input – Better Output: Does Citizen Involvement Improve Environmental Governance?

Jens Newig and *Oliver Fritsch*

1. Introduction

As earlier chapters have argued and demonstrated in some detail, contemporary politics is experiencing a crisis of legitimacy, and this is most prominently the case with regard to European Union policy. A lack of democratic legitimacy, transparency and accountability in the face of complex multi-level governance has long been evident, not only since the failure of the Constitution (Hansen and Williams 1999; Schmitter 2003). But the intricacies of modern society, the complex interlinkages of technological, environmental and societal factors as well as the multiplicity of actors and interests involved have also undermined the legitimacy of policy-making at the levels of nation states and below (Blühdorn and Jun 2007; also see Blühdorn in the first chapter of this volume). The legitimacy crisis affects both input and output aspect of legitimacy (Scharpf 1997): While the continuing implementation deficits of (European) policy reflect the virtual impossibility of effective policy delivery, the apparent public disenchantment with politics expresses the lack of transparency and the remoteness of policy-making from the constituency. A harsh example illustrating this is environmental policy. Over the past decades, the spatial and functional scope of human environmental impacts has intensified considerably, contributing to an increase in complexity for modern environmental governance (Young et al. 2006; Newig et al. 2008). It is thus probably not surprising that policy delivery in this field has remained exceptionally low (CEC 1999; Jordan 2002; Newig et al. 2008).

In an attempt to respond to the challenges brought about by increasing socio-ecological complexities (Funtowicz and Ravetz 1993) as well as growing normative and factual uncertainties (Pellizzoni 2003; Newig et al. 2005), participation is being touted as an effective remedy (Heinelt 2002). International and EU environmental policy in particular have been fervently promoting a shift from central state, top-down regulation to more transparent, local decision-making structures involving private companies, non-governmental organisations, citizens and interest groups. These participatory forms of governance have been institutionalised in documents such as the Århus Convention, the Commission's White Paper on European Governance (CEC 2001) or various recent European Union directives.

In section two, we examine more closely the rationales attached to participation in current international and European Union policy, drawing on a text analysis of several policy documents. We show that rationales for public participation, having become an 'official' and integral element of EU rhetoric, appear to have changed. As basic democratic deficits of EU *policy formulation* cannot be resolved from within the EU institutions, the latter seek to compensate for this deficit by enhancing legitimacy through the participation of non-state actors in the phase of policy *implementation* (Kaika and Page 2003). More specifically, this legitimacy is sought through an increased effectiveness of policy by advancing cooperation and participation. In other words, *output* legitimacy (policy effectiveness) is to be enhanced by means of improved *input* legitimacy (inclusion, procedural legitimacy) – albeit input at the implementation rather than the policy formulation stage. The crucial question becomes whether this claim actually holds, i.e. to what extent participation not only increases input legitimacy but also improves policy outputs and outcomes (Beierle and Cayford 2002; Koontz and Thomas 2006).

In section three, we expound how, in theory, participation is expected to enhance the legitimacy and effectiveness of governance. We outline a number of causal mechanisms relating to how participatory processes are expected to improve the quality of decisions as well as their implementation. Particular attention is being paid to the context conditions, including the complexity of the governance situation or the number of governance levels involved.

Section four presents results of a meta-analysis of 40 published case studies of environmental decision-making, drawing on the case-survey method (Lucas 1974; Larsson 1993). This approach is highly suitable to integrate findings from a large number of cases lacking a rigorous design. Based on the above conceptual reflections, we developed a detailed coding scheme comprising several dozen context, process and output/outcome variables that were mostly coded on a semi-quantitative, 0 to 4 point scale by the two authors, proving a high inter-coder reliability. The results of our qualitative and quantitative analysis underscore that participatory environmental decision processes in the majority of cases improve legitimacy of decisions based on input and throughput criteria. However, advances in output-oriented legitimacy are only achieved in certain constellations, while in others, participation contributes to a decrease in environmental standards. This chapter closes with a comparative analysis of how the different dimensions of legitimacy are to be achieved through participatory governance in the face of growing complexity.

2. Managing the legitimacy crisis through participatory governance

The participation of non-state actors in public decisions – beyond democratic elections and referenda – has of course a long tradition. From the 1960s, when the environmental movement and grass-root actors began to demand a say in political matters, an emancipatory motive had been prevalent in the societal discourse that became most highly developed in Habermas' concept of deliberative democracy (Habermas 1991 [1962]). While this has continued to play a role (Renn et al. 1995; Dryzek 1997), the current emphasis on participation is rather one 'from above' in that state and supranational organisations have discovered participation as a means to secure legitimacy for their policies, and thus also for their polity.

This can be demonstrated by an analysis of recent European policy documents. The Aarhus Convention on Access to Information, Public Participation in Decision-Making and Access to Justice in Environmental Matters of 1998 has been legally implemented in the EU by the Public Participation Directive 2003/35/EC. In this spirit, three further EU directives were passed that explicitly demand public participation in environmental decisions. Of these, we analyse the Water Framework Directive (2000/60/EC; WFD)[1], which combines substantive requirements ('good water status') with procedural obligations, including information and consultation of the public as well as its 'active involvement' in the implementation process (Art. 14 WFD).

Rationales that stress *outcome-oriented legitimacy (effectiveness)* can be found in the Århus Convention as well as in the WFD (see Figure 10.1). Both documents mention the importance of better informed *decisions* through the inclusion of lay (local) knowledge. In particular, the documents accompanying the WFD point to the relevance of information regarding the possible acceptance of decisions by the addressees. Furthermore, *policy implementation* is expected to be improved through participation. According to preamble 14 WFD, 'the success of this Directive relies on close cooperation and coherent action at Community, Member State and local level as well as on information, consultation and involvement of the public, including users'. More specifically, the WFD guidance document on public participation[2] states that 'public participation is not an end in itself but a tool to achieve the environmental objectives of the Water Framework Directive' (EU 2002: 6). All three

1 The other two, purely procedural, ones are the Directive 2001/42/EC on the Strategic Environmental Assessment and the new Environmental Information Directive (2003/4/EC).

2 The CIS – an unprecedented institution for fostering and ensuring the coherent implementation of an EU directive – has produced 14 thematic guidance documents which were agreed by representatives ('water directors') of all 15 Member States (at that time) and the Commission.

documents assume that participation improves the environmental awareness of non-state actors. Very importantly, participation is expected to improve the acceptance of and identification with decisions on the part of the involved actors and, therefore, facilitate implementation. Notably, the WFD guidance document believes that participatory processes will mediate conflicting interests in the forefront of a decision and thereby reduce the potential of future litigation and thus the involved costs. Moreover, improved mutual trust both among the non-state actors and between them and the authorities is expected, which in the long run is likewise supposed to lead to an improved acceptance and implementation of decisions.

Figure 10.1: Rationales for Public Participation in the Århus Convention and the WFD Guidance Document

Rationale for public participation			Århus Convention	WFD (GD)
Output-legitimacy	Improving environmental quality, reach environmental goals		preambles 5, 6, 7, 9	pp. 7, 26
Output-legitimacy	quality of decision	Making available of lay local knowledge to public decision-makers	preamble 16	pp. 24, 26, 41
Output-legitimacy	quality of decision	Making available of knowledge regarding attitudes and acceptance on the part of civil society actors to the public decision-makers		p. 24
Output-legitimacy	quality of implementation	Increasing environmental awareness, education, information on the part of civil society actors	preambles 9, 14	p. 4, 26
Output-legitimacy	quality of implementation	Increasing acceptance of and identification with a decision on the part of civil society actors	preamble 10	pp. 4, 26, 41
Output-legitimacy	quality of implementation	Building trust among civil society actors and between them and public authorities		p. 26, 41
Output-legitimacy	quality of implementation	Alleviating conflicts by mediation of interests		pp. 26, 41
Input-legitimacy	Increasing transparency of decision-making and control of state policy and governmental decision-makers		preambles 10, 11	p. 26
Input-legitimacy	Pursuit of legitimate self-interests on the part of the non-state actors (with respect to access to courts)		preamble 18	
Input-legitimacy	Strengthening democracy		preamble 21	

Rationales of *input-oriented legitimacy* are on the whole less important in the analysed documents, although they figure quite prominently in the Århus Convention. The main argument here is the transparency of decision-making, in the sense of a control of state decision-makers. This, however, also touches upon an aspect of increased effectiveness. Perhaps the most important argument of legitimacy, namely the 'strengthening of democracy', is only mentioned in the Århus Convention.

As summarised in Figure 10.1, public participation in environmental decisions in the European policy context is expected to increase legitimacy, predominantly on the part of improved policy outputs. Specifically, *output-oriented legitimacy* (policy effectiveness) is to be enhanced by means of improved *input-oriented legitimacy* (inclusion, procedural legitimacy).

3. Conceptual framework: How participation can enhance governance

If we are to understand whether and how public participation enhances the legitimacy of public decisions – predominantly in terms of their effectiveness – we need hypotheses on causal mechanisms against which we can compare empirical findings. This section attempts to integrate existing hypotheses and causal assumptions from the literature on public participation and policy implementation. The guiding hypothesis can be borrowed from an EU-funded research project, namely 'that participation leads to a higher degree of sustainable and innovative outcomes' (Heinelt 2002: 17). Or, as has been formulated in the US-context: 'The value of public participation will ultimately be judged by its ability to enhance implementation and show demonstrable benefits for environmental quality' (Beierle and Cayford 2002: 76) – which is to be put to the test.

By participation we understand 'all forms of influence on the design of collectively binding agreements by persons and organisations that are not routinely in charge of these tasks' (Renn 2005: 227), thus excluding all those forms of civic engagement that do not aim at collective decisions, such as Agenda 21 processes, as well as participation in elections or referenda. Public participation thus ranges from public consultation by competent authorities to cooperative decision-making, including different forms such as public hearings, consensus conferences, regional forums, councils, citizens' juries or stakeholder platforms, to name but a few.

How can these forms of participation contribute to an improved *input-oriented legitimacy* of public decisions? As opposed to classical top-down oriented administrative decision-making (which in parliamentary democracies is typically indirectly legitimised through democratic elections), participatory governance involves a wide variety of societal groups. Input-oriented legitimacy derives from a legitimate representation of these groups. According to Schmitter (2002), different types of 'holders' can be distinguished, indicating different criteria (such as rights, spatial location, knowledge, interest or status) of who should be involved in order to maintain legitimacy. Furthermore, the design and realisation of the – participatory – decision process have an impact on legitimacy. This involves open communication and information flows among participants (Rowe and Frewer 2005), opportunities for free deliberation in face-to-face settings as well as an overall 'fair' process that does not discriminate any party and in which civil society actors are actually granted a degree of influence on decisions (Webler and Tuler 2000). Last but not least, the acceptance of a decision by participants as well as non-participants is an indicator of legitimacy.

Looking at the way in which participation can enhance *output-oriented legitimacy,* we analyse – in line with the dimensions of Figure 10.1 – how the quality of decision outputs as well as their implementation can be improved through participation. Important variables to be taken into account are summarised in Figure 10.2 and will be elaborated below.

It is claimed that participation enhances the quality of decisions. The main mechanism that can be assumed is that, in the course of the participatory process, information is generated or made available that would not have been so otherwise, and that, further, this information is indeed incorporated into the decision. Thus, it seems plausible that environmental decisions can benefit from the factual knowledge of actors about their (local) conditions (Pellizzoni 2003), assuming that those who are closest to a problem develop the best understanding of it. Moreover, there may be information that 'emerges' from the close interaction of actors in a group process. Many authors stress the positive effects of social learning, the plurality of perspectives and thus the more creative decision-making as characteristics of participatory decision-making (e.g. Pahl-Wostl and Hare 2004). Another type of information from which decisions could benefit is information regarding the extent to which planned measures will be accepted by the addressees. In this respect, participation becomes an 'instrument for the anticipation of resistance to planning and implementation' (Linder and Vatter 1996: 181). Finally, participation of civil society actors can serve to break up established networks between public authorities and business or development advocates, allowing the inclusion of more environmental concerns in decision-making. It is thus assumed that participatory decisions involving civil society actors will be more favourable to ecological concerns than command-and-control decisions. However, in societal contexts characterised by a highly committed environmental administration and a less environmentally friendly citizen body, participatory decision-making can also lead to watered-down environmental standards.

Figure 10.2: Important variables in analysing the relationship between participation and legitimacy

Context	Process	Results
– Problem structure	– Process design	– Direct results of the participation process
– Problem complexity (expertise and time required for understanding)	– Opportunities for civil society actors to participate	– Information gain
– Spatial scale	– Representation of actor groups	– Conflict resolution
– Number of governance levels	– Degree of formalisation	– Acceptance and identification of participants (and non-participants) with the decision
– Possible solutions (technical and other)	– Process realisation	– Strengthening of trust relationships among civil society and governmental actors
– Actors	– Information flows	– Substantive output and outcome
– Interest, concern	– Fairness	– Result of decision (suitability of measures; implementability)
– Power/resources	– Face-to-face communication	– Implementation and compliance by the addressees
– Constellations, e.g. NIMBY, degree of conflict	– Facilitation or mediation	
– Social structure	– Actual participation and influence on the part of the civil society actors	
– Public attention to the issue		
– Collective social capital		
– Social norms		

Secondly, participation is expected to improve the implementation of decisions. Quite plausibly, the addressees of a decision must know of it in order to comply with requirements. By being involved in decision-making, addressees can take the necessary steps of reorganisation and adaptation to new (regulatory) conditions at an early stage. Furthermore, compliance with a decision is expected to depend positively on the degree of acceptance, or even identification, on the part of the addressees (e.g. Renn et al. 1995; Bulkeley and Mol 2003). Acceptance can be supported by providing the interested actors with early and comprehensive information. This may prevent actors from feeling left out or ignored and create a sense of involvement and belonging. Also, certain educational effects can play a role, e.g. in the sense of an improved environmental awareness. Moreover, intensive involvement of the concerned actors in a decision process that is perceived as fair and based on mutual communication is expected to enhance the acceptance of the decision. This even holds when the result does not correspond to the actors' expectations, as procedural justice research has shown (Lind and Tyler 1988). Furthermore, a decision involving conflicting interests is more likely to be accepted by the different parties if it is based on either a consensus, or at least a compromise to which most of the parties agree. This in turn most likely requires an intensive participatory process that allows the concerned actors to effectively claim their stakes, but also a spectrum of interests that does not fundamentally rule out any consensual solutions. Finally, in the medium and long term, the building of trust relationships both among the non-state actors involved and between non-state and state actors through participation can lead to an increased regional collective social capital, and can thus influence the context of future decision processes. In particular, the building of trust can improve acceptance of and thus the willingness to comply with measures (Bulkeley and Mol 2003).

Research has suggested that the societal and environmental *context* of decision processes plays a decisive role for what can be considered legitimate decision processes and outcomes. First and foremost, the characteristics of actors and their constellations have to be considered. Particular importance lies with social dilemma situations, which regularly arise in environmental conflicts (Ostrom 1990). Here, legitimacy (both input and output oriented) can only be ensured by internalising all externalities or regional spill-overs, and thus overcoming spatial misfits between the scale of decision-making and that of the environmental problem (Young 2002). Scales of decision-making are also important with respect to multi-level governance aspects. The more governance levels involved (and therefore, the more complex the decision process becomes), the less likely it appears that citizens and environmental groups are effectively involved. Power positions are another important factor (Lee and Abbot 2003). The more powerful the involved actors, the more likely it is that decisions will actually be implemented. High power asymmetries among actors, however, tend to involve biased decisions scoring low on input legitimacy. Finally, the structure of a problem can have a decisive influence on the success of a participatory decision process. The more complex and intricate a governance issue, the more difficult it is for all actors, but especially the non-experts, to comprehend (Diduck and Sinclair 2002). In these cases, deliberative and inclusive decision-making can open up possibilities for win-win situations and more creative – and ultimately more effective – solutions.

To sum up, there are many factors which plausibly suggest that the design of participation processes and the representation of societal actors are likely to have significant effects both on input-oriented as well as output-oriented legitimacy. Decision-making situations characterised by high complexity and uncertainty in particular lend themselves to highly inclusive and deliberative processes.

All this, however, is not to say that participation is universally expected to deliver in the ways mentioned, for numerous are its critics. Scholars have pointed out multiple dangers and trade-offs which Dahl (1994) has termed a 'democratic dilemma' between effectiveness and participation. Recently, more and more authors have been asking whether participatory modes of implementation actually improve substantive policy outcomes. Or, more specifically, to what extent and under what circumstances they do so. Even if one does not embrace the notion of participation as the 'new tyranny' (Cooke and Kothari 2001), 'there is something of a dilemma if participation turns out, empirically, not to improve outcomes' (Lee and Abbot 2003: 87f).

4. Evidence from empirical cases of public environmental decision-making

In this section we present the results of a meta-analysis of 40 case studies on – more or less participatory – environmental decision-making. The aim is to put the approaches previously discussed to an initial empirical test. Based on a broad, but surely not exhaustive, literature review, we have built up a database of some 200 case studies on environmental decision-making in late-modern democracies carried out within the last three decades. The most important selection criterion has been the completeness of provided information. Even though these do not constitute a population in a statistical sense and are presumably not representative of all actually carried out environmental decision-making processes in late-modern democracies, they do represent a broad variety of policy issues, political scales, decision contexts and forms of participation. Figure 10.3 gives an overview of the analysed case studies.

Approximately 80 per cent of the cases stem from North America, reflecting the popularity of public participation approaches, mediation and negotiated rule-making in the United States and Canada. The remaining cases are from Europe, mostly Germany. Although we are primarily interested in the European context, we found the inclusion of North American cases highly instructive for three major reasons: First, the rationales attached to participation as well as the processes employed have developed quite similarly on both sides of the Atlantic. Second, the literature on participation itself is highly interlinked among European and American scholars. And third, a statistical analysis has shown virtually no significant correlations between the continent of the case study and other variables, which means that both structural and process characteristics are highly comparable across the Atlantic.

In the following, we will discuss in what respect (and to what extent) participation enhances legitimacy. The relevant dimensions we analyse comprise (1) input in terms of process characteristics, (2) output in terms of environmental standards of decisions, (3) implementability of decisions, and (4) the importance of the context of decision-making for these latter three dimensions.

Figure 10.3: Analysed case studies for environmental decision-making

Policy field	Place	Issue	Source
Land use planning	Belmont, Massachusetts, USA	Salc of area of environmental value heats up public concern	Layzer 2002
	Chiwaukee Prairee, Wisconsin, USA	Development of a land use plan between ecological and economic interests	Haygood 1995
Forest manage-ment	San Juan National Forest, Colorado, USA	Logging in a national forest violates environmental and economic inter-ests	Tableman 1990
Air policy	Brayton Point, Massachusetts, USA	Air quality affected by conversion of oil-based power plant to coal-based	Burgess and Smith 1983
	Colstrip, Montana, USA	Air quality affected by extension of existing power plant	Sullivan 1983
Natural resources manage-ment	Everglades National Park, Florida, USA	Increased water use in residential areas endangers protected natural resources in a national park	Abrams et al. 1995
	Cold Lake, Alberta, Canada	Authorisation of oil drilling in a pro-tected area	Elder 1981
	Spreewald, Germany	Riparian Land Project	Baranek and Günther 2005
	Portage Island, Washington, USA	Dispute over the public recreational use of a protected area	Talbot 1984
	Saguache County, Colorado, USA	Uranium mining in a protected area	Kartez and Bow-man 1993
	Sand Lake Quiet Area, Michigan, USA	Oil drilling in a protected area	Nelson 1990
	Münchehagen, Germany	Clean up of a hazardous waste site	Striegnitz 1997
	Yukon territory, Canada	Management of wolf population between animal protection and ecosystem perspective	Todd 2002
	Wilfield Locks, West Virginia, USA	Clean up of a hazardous site	Langton 1996
	Albermarle-Pamlico, North Carolina, USA	Development of a large estuary management plan	Koontz et al. 2004
Transportation policy	Berlin and Brandenburg, Germany	Airport extension with additional runway	Barbian et al. 1998
	Frankfurt, Germany	Airport extension with additional runway	Geis 2005
	Seattle, Washington, USA	Highway extension and develop-ment of a public transport concept	Talbot 1984
Waste pol-icy	Aargau, Switzerland	Siting of a hazardous waste fa-cility	Renn et al. 1998
	Jackson, Wyoming, USA	Siting of a sewage treatment plant	Hill 1983

Policy field	Place	Issue	Source
	Lübeck, Germany	Development of a municipal waste management plan	Wiedemann et al. 1995
	Maine, USA	Siting of a nuclear waste facility	Clary and Horn-ney 1995
	Neuss, Germany	Development of a regional waste management plan	Fietkau and Weidner 1998
Water policy	Animas River, Colorado, USA	Development of a water man-agement plan	Koontz et al. 2004
Water policy	Ashtabula, Ohio, USA	Development of a water man-agement plan	Letterhos 1992
	Bay of Quinte, Ontario, Canada	Development of a water man-agement plan	Stride et al. 1992
	Collingwood, Ontario, Canada	Development of a water man-agement plan	Krantzberg 2003
	Denver, Colorado, USA	Construction of a dam to adapt to increased water use	Burgess 1983
	Grand Canyon National Park, Colorado, USA	Development of a river manage-ment plan	Orton 2005
	Hudson River, New York, USA	Extension of power plant endan-gers fish populations and water quality of river	Talbot 1984
	Kingsport, Tennessee, USA	Effluent regulation for a chemical factory	Jaegerman 1983
	Milwaukee, Wisconsin, USA	Development of a water man-agement plan	Kaemmerer et al. 1992
	Richmond County, California, USA	Installation of flood protection measures	Mazmanian 1979
	Sandspit Harbour, British Columbia, Can-ada	Construction of harbour endan-gers several marine species	Sigurdson 1998
	Snoqualmie River, Washington, USA	Installation of flood protection measures	Cormick 1976
	Sugarbush	Withdrawal of water for ski slopes to the concern of environmental-ists	Fitzhugh and Dozier 1996
	Swan Lake, Maine, USA	Construction of new power plant impacts on water resources	Talbot 1984
	Umatilla, Oregon, USA	Water management between fishing, agricultural and environ-mental interests	Neuman 1996
	Upper Narragansett Bay, Rhode Island, USA	Deliberation on combined sewer overflows	Burroughs 1999
	Wisconsin, USA	Drafting a new state groundwater legislation	Edgar 1990
	Spey River, Scotland, UK	Development of a river basin management plan	Blackstock and Richards 2007

(1) Does participation improve the *input-oriented legitimacy* of environmental decisions? In a way, the question is wrongly posed. That is, most indicators of the degree of participation are either identical with those of input-

oriented legitimacy (e.g. fairness, representation) or they relate to process characteristics (such as intensity of information flows, process facilitation or face-to-face-communication) which cannot be temporally separated from the other criteria. In the 40 cases analysed, these indicators range from very low to very high values. That many of these variables are correlated thus does not indicate causality but rather conceptual relatedness. However, we also measured acceptance of participants and non-participants (the latter only, as far as the data allowed us to). Here, we find a high correlation with fairness ($r = .5$ with $p < .01$)[3], but not with representation or communication-related variables. On the contrary, variables that measure the formalisation of a participation process (controlled participant selection, facilitation of information elicitation, structured information aggregation according to Rowe and Frewer 2005) correlate negatively with participant acceptance.

(2) In most of the 40 cases, new and useful information was generated. The variable 'information gain' received an average score of 2.2 points[4] (with a standard deviation of 1.0), but is only positively correlated with process variables that relate to the degree of formalisation, yet negatively correlated with the degree of citizen involvement. Indeed, in many of the cases in which much useful information was generated, issues were very technical, leaving little room for citizens to contribute. In the *Lübeck* and *Neuss* waste management cases, for instance, much useful information was generated, but mainly through the involvement of experts. On the other hand, environmental groups and engaged citizens succeeded in the *Albemarle-Pamlico* estuarine process to work closely with experts and generate an immensely improved scientific basis for an estuarine conservation and management plan. All things considered, although there is a considerable gain of useful information in the cases analysed, our findings suggests that – contrary to theory – private citizens have (at least on average) little specific knowledge to offer compared to governmental agencies.

In terms of finding new and creative solutions ('collective learning'), participation does seem to make a difference. The variable obtains an average score of 2.1 (with a standard deviation of 1.0) and is positively correlated with many process-related variables such as the degree of stakeholder interaction and the intensity of communication and information flows, and also aspects of process fairness and legitimate representation of stakeholders. This suggests that an effective information flow presupposes deliberation, reflection and the development of creative solutions. Variables related to input-oriented legitimacy (e.g. representation, fairness), consistent with theory, appear to influence the willingness of stakeholders to actually cooperate and

3 Correlation coefficients according to Spearman. Full correlation tables can be obtained from the authors.

4 Unless otherwise noted, we used a 0 to 4 point semi-quantitative scale.

thus learn collectively. A positive example is the *Aargau* case, in which four citizens' fora, composed of citizen representatives of nine Swiss communities proposed as potential waste sites, successfully (and consensually) developed an ecologically rational ranking of waste sites. Conversely, the insufficient involvement of citizens and open-space proponents in the *Belmont* hospital case contributed to the fact that, although an enormous amount of information was generated, hardly any innovative solutions could be developed.

Comparison of the results regarding 'collective learning' with those of 'information gain', leads us to conclude that collective learning, to a much larger extent than information gain, appears to depend on the way the process is conducted. Information and technical data, it seems, can be generated without having to rely on participation; creative new solutions and the use of win-win potentials, on the other hand, appear to presuppose high degrees of participation.

Ultimately, we are interested to see whether participation not only improves the knowledge base of the decisions but actually leads to more ecological decisions. Measured on a scale from -4 to 4, the ecological standard of decisions averages at .4 (standard deviation: 1.9). In some cases, environmental programmes were enacted, while in others, large development projects, harmful to the environment, were decided upon. The highest correlation by far is with the variable 'mean actor environmental preferences' (.86, $p < .001$). Clearly, the interests of participants determine the output more than any other factor. The *Colstrip* mediation might serve as an example here. This case reports how a tribe of Indians opposed the upgrading of a power plant close to their homelands and achieved additional measures of air pollution control as a precondition for the upgrading. Conversely, in the *Spreewald* riparian land project, local actors from agriculture, forestry, fishery and tourism opposed strict measures, fearing expropriation and loss of incomes. One of the few notable exceptions is the *Yukon* wolf management case in which the well-designed participation process led to ecological outputs far superior than the original preferences of the participants.

Contrary to theory, the learning-related variables 'information gain' and 'collective learning' are not significantly correlated with either of the environmental output variables. This suggests that both are really two different matters. Improved ecological standards do not require an improved knowledge base; conversely, learning effects need not lead to ecologically better decisions.

(3) As regards the implementation of decisions, we can first note that intermediary variables such as conflict resolution, acceptance and trust-building are highly positively correlated with variables related to input-legitimacy (representation, fairness, communication). Remarkably and unexpectedly, methods of facilitated and structured information elicitation, although they contribute to an education of stakeholders, seem to impede acceptance and

trust-building. The *Snoqualmie* river mediation may serve to illustrate a case of a highly participatory process with a well-accepted decision. The mediated process served both to resolve a year-old conflict and to produce a solution that was accepted by stakeholders and government. In contrast, the decision made in the *Albemarle-Pamlico* process, highly participatory as well – although not mediated – was accepted to a lesser degree, largely due to the voluntary non-participation of one particular actor group.

While the examined cases generally provided thorough material on decision outputs, much less information was given on their implementation. This is mainly due to the fact that the case descriptions typically end with a successfully completed decision, partly because case studies were published before implementation could even have taken place. For those eleven cases in which we could code environmental outcomes, this variable shows few significant correlations with process variables. Only face-to-face communication appears to improve environmental outcomes. Trust building, contrary to theory, is negatively correlated with environmental outcomes. The *Holston* river case presents a clear example of an improved implementation through a negotiated settlement. If we follow the reasoning of the author, an environmentally less stringent agreement was negotiated, but has a much better chance of implementation as compared to a hypothetical top-down case because of the substantially reduced risk of long court trials with an uncertain conclusion and delayed implementation. Similarly, without the participatory agreement in the *Spreewald* case, federal funds for the large nature conservation project would not even have been granted; given the local opposition to the project, the participatory agreement constituted virtually a prerequisite for implementation.

(4) Finally, the context of the decision process played an important role in the analysed cases in a twofold way. First, context variables such as the degree of conflict, agenda-setting by governmental (as opposed to civil society) actors or the degree of problem complexity show more significant correlations with environmental outputs and outcomes than do process variables. This clearly puts into perspective the claim of participation research that it is mainly the process that matters. Moreover, context characteristics appear to influence processes. One of the most 'influential' factors appears to be the degree of problem complexity. It is positively correlated with a structured participation process designed to maximise information inputs and aggregation, but negatively correlated with variables characterising input-oriented legitimacy (fairness, communication, face-to-face-communication). Second, context variables also influence the way process affects output and outcome. Acting as 'third variables', they affect the correlations between other variables. For instance, in cases with high problem complexity, outputs positively correlate with factors such as win-win, formalisation, but negatively with information flows, process facilitation and the degree of conflict. In cases with low prob-

lem complexity, on the other hand, we find positive correlations of outputs with fairness and face-to-face communication.

5. Conclusions

Current European policy-making faces a twofold challenge of legitimacy: On the input side of the policy process, European policies lack democratic legitimacy, transparency and accountability. On the output side, implementation deficits prevail, quite prominently so in the field of environmental policy. Against this background, EU policies seek to reconfigure democracy in that they promote, following recent international developments, the participation of civil society in the *implementation* of European policies. This is expected to enhance both input-oriented legitimacy – albeit at a later stage in the policy cycle – as well as output-oriented legitimacy, particularly in the face of increasingly complex socio-ecological interactions. Our meta-analysis of 40 cases of environmental decision-making from North America and Europe processes reveals a mixed picture with regard to these expectations.

First, carefully designed participatory decision processes, ensuring the representation of all affected societal actors and maintaining a fair process, clearly improve acceptance of participants (and non-participants). This can be taken as a measure of enhanced legitimacy. Second, while participation – contrary to theory – does not significantly account for the generation of information, it does seem to foster social learning and thus more creative solutions, the latter being another indicator of improved legitimacy. However, both an improved information base, as well as more creative solutions, on average do not contribute to more 'ecological' outputs, let alone outcomes. Third, we found participation to clearly foster the resolution of conflicts and the building of trust among participants – which is perhaps also a measure of legitimacy. Yet this again does not contribute – at least not substantially – to improved environmental outputs or outcomes. Fourth, the fact that participation does increase environmental standards of outputs and outcomes, if only to a small degree, can largely be attributed to the preferences of the involved actors which are on average slightly in favour of stronger environmental standards, actor preferences being the single most important factor influencing environmental outputs and outcomes. Finally, the context of (environmental) decision-making appears to be crucial for both the process, its outputs/outcomes *and* for the way process affects outputs and outcomes. A notable example is problem complexity. In cases where it is high, environmental outputs/outcomes depend on structured decision processes, allowing the maximisation of information input and aggregation, while aspects of (input-oriented) legitimacy such as fairness and representation do not play a role. Conversely, cases with low problem complexity appear to provide an environment in which input-oriented legitimacy fosters substantive outputs/outcomes.

To conclude, civil society participation in environmental decisions brings about all kinds of merits, several of which very likely enhance legitimacy in one way or another. Yet whether substantive policy outputs can be improved through participation – this being the main expectation of current European policies – is highly contingent upon the respective context. Whether participation not only increases legitimacy and effectiveness, but is also an *efficient* means, has been left aside and remains to be studied. Given its strong instrumental focus on participation, European policy-making will be well-advised to carefully consider the conditions under which it promotes – or even mandates – participation, if this is to substantially bring about more than merely symbolic legitimacy.

References

Abrams, K.S./Gladwin, H./Matthews, M.J./McCabe, B.C. (1995): 'The East Everglades Planning Study', in: Porter, D.R/Salvesen, D.A (eds) *Collaborative Planning for Wetlands and Wildlife*, Washington, D.C., Covelo: Island Press: pp. 225-56.

Baranek, E./Günther, B (2005): 'Erfolgsfaktoren von Partizipation in Naturschutzgroßprojekten – Das Beispiel: Moderationsverfahren im Gewässerrandstreifenprojekt Spreewald', in: Feindt, P.H./Newig, J. (eds) *Partizipation, Öffentlichkeitsbeteiligung, Nachhaltigkeit. Perspektiven der Politischen Ökonomie*, Marburg: Metropolis-Verlag, pp. 299-319.

Barbian, T./Jeglitza, M./Troja, M. (1998): 'Das Beispiel „Bürgerdialog Flughafen Berlin Brandenburg International" ', in: Zilleßen, H. (ed.) *Mediation. Kooperatives Konfliktmanagement in der Umweltpolitik*, Opladen: Westdeutscher Verlag, pp. 108-36.

Beierle, T.C./Cayford, J. (2002): *Democracy in Practice. Public Participation in Environmental Decisions*, Washington, DC: Resources for the Future.

Blackstock, K.L./Richards, C. (2007): 'Evaluating Stakeholder Involvement in River Basin Planning: A Scottish Case Study', in: *Water Policy* 9, pp. 493-512.

Blühdorn, I./Jun, U. (eds) (2007): *Economic Efficiency – Democratic Empowerment. Contested Modernisation in Britain and Germany*, Lanham, Maryland: Rowman & Littlefield (Lexington).

Bulkeley, H./Mol, A.P.J. (2003): 'Participation and Environmental Governance: Consensus, Ambivalence and Debate', in: *Environmental Values* 12/2, pp. 143-54.

Burgess, H. (1983): 'Environmental Mediation (The Foothills Case)', in: Susskind, L./Bacow, L./Wheeler, M. (eds) *Resolving Environmental Regulatory Disputes*, Cambridge: Schenkman Publishing Company, pp. 156-221.

Burgess, H./Smith, D. (1983): 'The Uses of Mediation (The Brayton Point Coal Conversion Case)', in: Susskind, L./Bacow, L./Wheeler, M. (eds) *Resolving Environmental Regulatory Disputes*, Cambridge: Schenkman Publishing Company, pp. 122-55.

Burroughs, R. (1999): 'When Stakeholders Choose: Process, Knowledge, and Motivation in Water Quality Decisions', in: *Society & Natural Resources* 12/8, pp. 797-809.

CEC (1999): 'Commission of the European Communities: Sixteenth Annual Report to the European Parliament on Commission Monitoring of the Application of Community Law', COM(99) 301 (final), Brussels.

CEC (2001): 'European Governance: A White Paper', Commission of the European Communities, Brussels.

Clary, B.B./Hornney, R. (1995): 'Evaluating ADR as an Approach to Citizen Participation in Siting a Low-Level Nuclear Waste Facility', in: Blackburn; J.W./Bruce, W.M. (eds) *Mediating Environmental Conflicts. Theory and Practice*, Westport, London: Quorum Books, pp. 121-37.

Cooke, B./Kothari, U. (eds) (2001): *Participation: The New Tyranny?*, London, New York: Zed Books.

Cormick, G.W. (1976): 'Mediating Environmental Controversies: Perspectives and First Experience', in: *Earth Law Journal* 2, pp. 215-24.

Dahl, R.A. (1994): 'A Democratic Dilemma: System Effectiveness versus Citizen Participation', in: *Political Science Quarterly* 109/1, pp. 23-34.

Diduck, A./Sinclair, A.J. (2002): 'Public Involvement in Environmental Assessment: The Case of the Nonparticipant', in: *Environmental Management* 29/4, pp. 578-88.

Dryzek, J.S. (1997): 'The Politics of the Earth. Environmental Discourses', New York: Oxford University Press.

Edgar, S.L. (1990): 'Wisconsin Groundwater Legislation Negotiations', in: Crowfoot, J.E./Wondolleck, J.M. (eds) *Environmental Disputes: Community Involvement in Conflict Resolution*, Washington, D.C., Covelo: Island Press, pp. 226-53.

Elder, P.S. (1981): 'Heating Up Cold Lake. Public Participation and Esso Resources' Heavy Oil Project' in: Ross, W.A (ed.) *Occasional Papers*, Calgary.

EU (2002): 'Common Implementation Strategy for the Water Framework Directive' *(2000/60/EC). Guidance Document No. 8 on Public Participation in Relation to the Water Framework Directive*, Luxemburg: European Union.

Fietkau, H.-J./Weidner, H. (1998): *Umweltverhandeln: Konzepte, Praxis und Analysen alternativer Konfliktregelungsverfahren – ein erweiterter Projektbericht*, Berlin: Ed. Sigma.

Fitzhugh, J.H./Dozier, D.P. (1996): 'Finding the Common Good, Sugarbush Water Withdrawal', Montpelier.

Funtowicz, S.O./Ravetz, J.R (1993): 'Science for the Post-Normal Age', in: *Futures* 25/7, pp. 739-55.

Geis, A. (2005): 'Regieren mit Mediation. Das Beteiligungsverfahren zur zukünftigen Entwicklung des Frankfurter Flughafens', in: Greven, M. T. (ed.), *Studien zur politischen Gesellschaft Vol. 6*, Wiesbaden: VS Verlag für Sozialwissenschaften.

Habermas, J. (1991 [1962]): *The Structural Transformation of the Public Sphere: An Inquiry into a Category of Bourgeois Society*, Cambridge, Mass.: MIT Press.

Hansen, L./Williams, M.C. (1999): 'The Myths of Europe: Legitimacy, Community and the 'Crisis' of the EU', in: *Journal of Common Market Studies* 37/2, pp. 233-49.

Haygood, L.V. (1995): 'Balancing Conservation and Development in Chiwaukee Prairie, Wisconsin', in: Porter, D.R./Salvesen, D.A (eds) *Collaborative Planning for Wetlands and Wildlife*, Washington, D.C., Covelo: Island Press, pp. 157-80.

Heinelt, H. (2002): 'Achieving Sustainable and Innovative Policies through Participatory Governance in a Multi-Level Context: Theoretical Issues', in: Heinelt, H./Getimis, P./Kafkalas, G./Smith, R./Swyngedouw, E. *Participatory Govern-*

ance in Multi-Level Context. Concepts and Experience, Opladen: Leske + Budrich, pp. 17-32.

Hill, S. (1983): 'Intergovernmental Grant Negotiation (The Jackson Case)', in: Susskind, L./Bacow, L./Wheeler, M. (eds) *Resolving Environmental Regulatory Disputes*, Cambridge: Schenkman Publishing Company, pp. 86-121.

Jaegerman, A. (1983): 'Behind-the-Scenes Negotiation in the NPDES Permit Process (The Hoslton River Case)', in: Susskind, L./Bacow, L./Wheeler, M. (eds) *Resolving Environmental Regulatory Disputes*, Cambridge: Schenkman Publishing Company, pp. 30-55.

Jordan, A. (2002): 'The Implementation of EU Environmental Policy: A Policy Problem without a Political Solution?', in: Jordan, A. (ed.) *Environmental Policy in the European Union: Actors, Institutions and Processes*, London: Earthscan Publications, pp. 301-28.

Kaemmerer, D./O'Brien, A./Sheffy, T./Skavroneck, S. (1992): 'The Quest for Clean Water: The Milwaukee Estuary Remedial Action Plan', in: Hartig, J.H./Zarull, M.A. (eds) *Under RAPs. Toward Grassroots Ecological Democracy in the Great Lakes Basin*, Ann Arbor: University of Michigan Press, pp. 139-60.

Kaika, M./Page, B. (2003): 'The EU Water Framework Directive: Part 1. European Policy-Making and the Changing Topography of Lobbying', in: *European Environment* 13, pp. 314-27.

Kartez, J.D./Bowman, P. (1993): 'Quick Deals and Raw Deals: A Perspective on Abuses of Public ADR Principles in Texas Resource Conflicts', in: *Environmental Impact Assessment Review* 13, pp. 319-30.

Koontz, T.M./Steelman, T.A./Carmin, J./Smith Korfmacher, K./Moseley, C./Thomas, C.W. (2004): *Collaborative Environmental Management. What Roles for Government?*, Washington, D.C.: Resources for the Future.

Koontz, T.M./Thomas, C.W. (2006): 'What Do We Know and Need to Know about the Environmental Outcomes of Collaborative Management?', in: *Public Administration Review* 66, pp. 111-21.

Krantzberg, G. (2003): 'Keeping Remedial Actions Plans On Target: Lessons Learned from Collingwood Harbour', in: *Journal of Great Lakes Research* 29/4, pp. 641-51.

Langton, S. (1996): *An Organizational Assessment of the U.S. Army Corps of Engineers in Regard to Public Involvement Practices and Challenges*, Reston, VA: U.S. Army Corps of Engineers, Institute for Water Resources.

Larsson, R. (1993): 'Case Survey Methodology: Quantitative Analysis of Patterns across Case Studies', in: *The Academy of Management Journal* 36/6, pp. 1515-46.

Layzer, J.A. (2002): 'Citizen Participation and Government Choice in Local Environmental Controversies', in: *Policy Studies Journal* 30/2, pp. 193-207.

Lee, M./Abbot, C. (2003): 'Legislation: The Usual Suspects? Public Participation Under the Aarhus Convention', in: *The Modern Law Review* 66/1, pp. 80-108.

Letterhos, J.A. (1992): 'Dredging Up the Past: The Challenge of the Ashtabula River Remedial Action Plan', in: Hartig, J.H./Zarull, M.A. (eds) *Under RAPs. Toward Grassroots Ecological Democracy in the Great Lakes Basin*, Ann Arbor: University of Michigan Press, pp. 121-38.

Lind, E.A./Tyler, T.R. (1988): *The Social Psychology of Procedural Justice*, New York, London: Springer.

Linder, W./Vatter, A. (1996): 'Kriterien zur Evaluation von Partizipationsverfahren', in: Selle, K. (ed.) *Planung und Kommunikation*, Wiesbaden, Berlin: Bauverlag, pp. 181-88.

Lucas, W.A. (1974): 'The Case Survey Method: Aggregating Case Experience', Santa Monica: RAND.

Mazmanian, D.A. (1979): *Can Organizations Change? Environmental Protection, Citizen Participation, and the Corps of Engineers*, Washington, D.C.: The Brookings Institution.

Nelson, K.C. (1990): 'Sand Lakes Quiet Area Issue-Based Negotiation', in: Crowfoot, J.E./Wondolleck, J.M. (eds) *Environmental Disputes: Community Involvement in Conflict Resolution*, Washington, D.C., Covelo: Island Press, pp. 183-208.

Neuman, J.C. (1996): 'Run, River, Run: Mediation of a Water-Rights Dispute Keeps Fish and Farmers Happy – for a Time', in: *University of Colorado Law Review* 67/2, pp. 259-340.

Newig, J. (2007): 'Does Public Participation in Environmental Decisions Lead to Improved Environmental Quality? Towards an Analytical Framework', in: *Communication, Cooperation, Participation. Research and Practice for a Sustainable Future* 1/1, pp. 51-71.

Newig, J./Pahl-Wostl, C./Sigel, K. (2005): 'The Role of Public Participation in Managing Uncertainty in the Implementation of the Water Framework Directive', in: *European Environment* 15/6, pp. 333-43.

Newig, J./Voß, J.-P./Monstadt, J. (eds) (2008): *Governance for Sustainable Development: Steering in Contexts of Ambivalence, Uncertainty and Distributed Power*, London: Routledge.

Orton, M. (2005): 'The Colorado River through the Grand Canyon: Applying Alternative Dispute Resolution Methods to Public Participation', in: Bruch, C./Jansky, L./Nakayama, M./Salewicz, K.A. (eds) *Public Participation in the Governance of International Freshwater Resources*, Tokyo, New York, Paris: United Nations University Press, pp. 403-32.

Ostrom, E. (1990): *Governing the Commons. The Evolution of Institutions for Collective Action, Political Economy of Institutions and Decisions,* Cambridge et al.: Cambridge University Press.

Pahl-Wostl, C./Hare, M. (2004): 'Processes of Social Learning in Integrated Resources Management', in: *Journal of Community & Applied Social Psychology* 14/3, pp. 193-206.

Pellizzoni, L. (2003): 'Uncertainty and Participatory Democracy', in: *Environmental Values* 12/2, pp. 195-224.

Renn, O. (2005): 'Partizipation – ein schillernder Begriff', in: *GAIA* 14/3, pp. 227-28.

Renn, O./Webler, T./Wiedemann, P. (1995): 'The Pursuit of Fair and Competent Citizen Participation', in: Renn, O./Webler, T./Wiedemann, P (eds) *Fairness and Competence in Citizen Participation: Evaluating Models for Environmental Discourse*, Dordrecht: Kluwer Academic Publisher, pp. 339-68.

Renn, O./Kastenholz, H./Schild, P./Wilhelm, U. (eds) (1998): *Abfallpolitik im kooperativen Diskurs. Bürgerbeteiligung bei der Standortsuche für eine Deponie im Kanton Aargau*, Polyprojekt Risiko und Sicherheit, Zürich: vdf Hochschulverlag AG an der ETH Zürich, Vol 19.

Rowe, G./Frewer, L.J. (2005): 'A Typology of Public Engagement Mechanisms', in: *Science, Technology, & Human Values* 30/2, pp. 251-90.

Scharpf, F.W. (1997): *Games Real Actors Play. Actor-Centered Institutionalism in Policy Research*, Boulder, CO: Westview Press.

Schmitter, P.C. (2002): 'Participation in Governance Arrangements: Is There Any Reason to Expect It Will Achieve Sustainable and Innovative Policies in a Multi-Level Context?', in: Grote, J.R./Gbikpi, B. (eds) *Participatory Governance. Political and Societal Implications*, Opladen: Leske + Budrich, pp. 51-69.

Schmitter, P.C. (2003): 'Making Sense of the EU. Democracy in Europe and Europe's Democratization', in: *Journal of Democracy* 14/4, pp. 71-85.

Sigurdson, S.G. (1998): 'The Sandspit Harbour Mediation Process', in: Weidner, H. (ed.) *Alternative Dispute Resolution in Environmental Conflicts. Experiences in 12 Countries*, Berlin: Edition Sigma, pp. 33-62.

Stride, F./German, M./Hurley, D/Millard, S./Minns, K./Nicholls, K./Owen, G./Poulton, D./de Geus, N. (1992): 'An Overview of the Modeling and Public Consultation Processes Used to Develop the Bay of Quinte Remedial Action Plan', in: Hartig, J.H./Zarul, M.A. (eds) *Under RAPs. Toward Grassroots Ecological Democracy in the Great Lakes Basin*, Ann Arbor: University of Michigan Press, pp. 161-83.

Striegnitz, M. (1997): 'Das Mediationsverfahren Münchehagen-Ausschuß', in: Köberle, S./Glöde, F./Hennen, L. (eds) *Diskursive Verständigung? Mediation und Partizipation in Technikkontroversen'*, Baden-Baden: Nomos, pp. 27-46.

Sullivan, T.J. (1983): 'The Difficulties of Mandatory Negotiation (The Colstrip Power Plant Case)', in: Susskind, L./Bacow, L./Wheeler, M. (eds) *Resolving Environmental Regulatory Disputes*, Cambridge: Schenkman Publishing Company, pp. 56-85.

Tableman, M.A. (1990): 'San Juan National Forest Mediation', in: Crowfoot, J.E./Wondolleck, J.M. (eds) *Environmental Disputes: Community Involvement in Conflict Resolution*, Washington, D.C., Covelo: Island Press, pp. 32-65.

Talbot, A.R. (1984): *Settling Things. Six Case Studies in Environmental Mediation*, Washington, D.C.: The Conservation Foundation.

Todd, S. (2002): 'Building Consensus on Divisive Issues: A Case Study of the Yukon Wolf Management Team', in: *Environmental Impact Assessment Review* 22, pp. 655-84.

Webler, T./Tuler, S. (2000): 'Fairness and Competence in Citizen Participation', in: *Administration & Society* 32/5, pp. 566-95.

Wiedemann, P.M./Claus, F./Gremler, D. (1995): 'Ergebnisse des Forums Abfallwirtschaft Lübeck', in: *Arbeiten zur Risiko-Kommunikation* Heft 15, Programmgruppe Mensch, Technik Jülich Forschungszentrum.

Young, O.R. (2002): 'The Institutional Dimensions of Environmental Change: Fit, Interplay, and Scale, Global Environmental Accord', Cambridge, Mass. et al.: MIT Press.

Young, O.R./Berkhout, F./Gallopin, G.C./Janssen, M.A./Ostrom, E./Van der Leeuw, S. (2006): 'The Globalization of Socio-Ecological Systems: An Agenda for Scientific Research', in: *Global Environmental Change* 16, pp. 304-16.

Chapter 11
Towards Horizontalisation and Politicisation: Challenging the Governance Rationale of Finnish Technology Policy

Soile Kuitunen and *Kaisa Lähteenmäki-Smith*

1. Introduction

It is claimed that technology policy is currently being transformed, both in Finland and elsewhere, with its closed, highly hierarchical decision-making structure developing into a more open and flexible system, with horizontal networks blurring the boundaries between public and private spheres and re-structuring the interaction between them (e.g. Caracostas and Muldur 1998; Edler et al. 2003).

Within the emerging system, technology issues no longer remain under the control of a closed and internally cohesive technology-elite. This can be seen as part of a broader development, encapsulated in the notion of the move from government to governance (Tiihonen 2004; Kjær 2004) and in particular as a move towards broadening the basis of policy legitimation. The new governance system, as opposed to traditional systems of government, implies that decisions concerning technology and innovation are initiated, prepared and decided upon by a larger group of actors representing a broad array of socio-political sectors, incorporating even the political sphere with popularly elected politicians at its core. Societal questions are becoming increasingly complex, while more integrated and coherent policies are called for to meet stakeholder needs, to strengthen competitiveness, and to ensure innovativeness.

In addition to the re-structuring of the traditional forms of power and political competence, the transition towards horizontal public policy action in general and innovation policy in particular, implies a change in the rationales and objectives of these policies. With particular reference to innovation policy, the goals of economic growth and prosperity are coupled with the broader aims of producing well-being and quality of life. The economic-growth-driven paradigm is, however, now widely claimed to have been replaced by much richer accounts which entail such broad concerns as health, social cohesion, sustainable development and security. These aims are sought through policy processes that meet the criteria of good governance. Good governance usually incorporates the three basic aspects of democracy, namely participation, accountability, and efficiency (CEC 2001; Tiihonen 2004; World Bank 2001). Horizontalisation links these different aspects, as it is based on an emerging policy paradigm stressing the horizontal links between policy and much larger societal aims, as well as incorporating the need for the empowerment and deliberation of stakeholders and citizens alike. Thus, measures and procedures through which people can become more widely involved, their opinions heard and taken into account in the policy process, are called for (e.g. Pelkonen 2006; also see other policy-related contributions in this volume).

In this article, our aim is to shed light on the assumed shift from a sector-based technology policy to a more broadly based, cross-sectoral, or horizontal innovation policy.[1] In the first two sections, we explore in a more theoretical fashion the features of two 'mega-trends' affecting and potentially transforming traditional technology policy; namely, horizontalisation and politicisation. Our aim here is to differentiate between the factors posing a challenge to the current governance modes and rationales of technology policy, by drawing upon issues raised in the ongoing debate and on empirical findings gathered in the context of previous studies. The fourth and fifth sections are devoted to investigating empirically the process of Finnish technology policy, by focussing on the dialogue between technology policy and other policy domains, as well as on the ways in which power and political responsibility are delegated and shared in relation to technology issues. The final section summarises our findings while highlighting their implications.

The target group in our study was a select sample of representatives from the Finnish technology 'elite' and key societal interest groups. These actors were divided into five groups: public sector, research, politics, 'third' sector, and business. The selection of individuals was based on the assessment of their formal position in the technology decision-making process, which in turn was perceived as being highly dependent on their ability to affect the allocation of Research, Development and Innovation (RDI) funding. Bearing this in mind, we chose key individuals from Parliament (MPs), financing bodies and ministries, but also from research and business communities and the third sector. Representatives of various voluntary groups were also included, such as actors within the environmental movement. All of the individuals selected for our sample either held an executive position in their organisation or were senior specialists.

---

1 The research project this paper draws upon was undertaken, as a collaborative effort, by VTT Technology Studies and Nordregio (Nordic Centre for Spatial Development), from 2004 to 2006. It is part of a broader research programme on science and technology, 'ProAct', financed by the Ministry of Trade and Industry and TEKES, the Finnish Funding Agency for Technology and Innovation.

Data collection was undertaken in three stages. Firstly, a limited number of elite in-depth interviews were conducted in order to draft the questionnaire and specify our research questions. In this phase, five interviews were carried out with persons representing the above-mentioned sectors. Secondly, a survey was undertaken with a randomly selected sample of potential respondents representing the five key sectors.[2] Despite a low response rate, the data gathered nevertheless illustrate the perceptions of Finnish technology decision-making as a process and as a governance mode. It should however be acknowledged that the conclusions drawn from the survey data cannot be generalised in statistical terms across all the societal groups in question.

To justify and further test the survey observations, a second round of interviews was then conducted after the survey results had been analysed. What is more, this round of interviews was intended as a way to further disseminate its findings. Altogether, five interviews were carried out, with most of the interviewees having significant experience of technology and innovation issues but not belonging to the core group of technology decision-makers as defined by their access to financial resources. We were able to gather interesting information on the factors triggering the horizontalisation process as well as more general information on the horizontalisation process itself, by being involved in the preparation of the Finnish innovation strategy during autumn 2007 and spring 2008. We employ these experiences and first-hand observations in the article, especially in order to shed light on the challenges attached to the endeavour of transforming the traditional sector-based technology policy.

Throughout the article, we also employ data gathered in the research project OECD Monit carried out in 2004-2005. The project dealt with the development of Finnish information society, and six interviews were conducted within its sub-project on *e*-Democracy. The interviewees were mostly public officials in charge of implementing the information society strategy at the local level, as well as researchers focusing on *e*-Democracy issues. The interview data illustrate not only the challenges information society is faced with, but also the development needs of technology policy.

---

2 Altogether, some 914 survey questionnaires were sent out. The returned questionnaires of two groups of actors originally included in the study, namely, the media and others categories, were not included in the final data due to the internal heterogeneity of these groups and their low return rates. The number of questionnaires sent and returned were as follows: public sector (205/46), research (195/37), politics (213/11), 'third' sector (116/19), business (100/21). The majority of the respondents were male (77%) and highly educated with 90% holding a university degree.

2. Societal trends and other factors triggering 'horizontalisation'

Recent discussions on the challenges facing the public sector are anchored in the contrasts between concepts such as 'government' and 'governance'. Government is perceived as representing the old, stagnant system in which the boundaries between the public and private spheres on the one hand, and between the various public sector authorities on the other, are well established and not easy to cross (Kazancigil 2000; Stoker 1998). Within this system, policies are designed, implemented, and evaluated mostly by closed elites composed of members with similar backgrounds and perceptions, thus forming cohesive and coherent entities. Within these elites, the substantive understandings, interests, discourse, language etc., are not only shared by the members of the elite groups in question, but also reproduced and maintained within the networks (similarly to the notion of 'epistemic communities' as introduced by Peter Haas (1992). The shared understandings gradually lead to the perpetuation of a consensual understanding of the future options open to decision-makers and of the activities required in order to achieve them (e.g. Olsson 2003: 287).

In contrast to government, 'governance' implies an inclusive and flexible decision-making system, with more open access to various societal actors coming not only from the public but also from the private sector, and civil society. The success of this move from government to governance is based mostly on the fact that Western societies are becoming increasingly differentiated, complicating public decision-making and its preparation (Kazancigil 2000; Stoker 1998; Tiihonen 2004). Governing in such an environment calls for horizontal networks in which the competencies and information sources of multiple actors can be merged, and solutions for highly multi-dimensional societal problems sought through open dialogue and collaboration. Societal problems are becoming increasingly complex, thus calling for action in which sector boundaries are crossed and reflexive rationality predominates, as opposed to the traditionally predominant mode of 'substantial rationality' which remains dominant in the sphere of the regulative state.

Demands for a more horizontal mode of public action in the field of technology policy have been made by both policy-makers and researchers (Caracostas and Muldur 1998; Chamberlin and De la Mothe 2004; Edler et al. 2003; Häyrinen-Alestalo et al. 2005; OECD 2002). For example, the European Commission has taken note of the horizontalisation concept in its Lisbon strategy. In an attempt to make the EU the most competitive and dynamic economy, innovation and support for it are set at the core of the adopted strategy. This strategy has not been very successful thus far, particularly as the agenda has in recent years been dominated by other, rather traditional intergovernmental issues of relevance, while 'governance' issues have often been relegated to the backburner. Innovation is thought to be too important and too all-encompassing in our new information societies as to be confined to the realm of technology policy alone. Innovation is thus sometimes presented as a panacea, an answer to almost all our societal problems, even those that for political reasons are currently less amenable to reform (see Blühdorn's and Blatter's discussion of the issue in earlier chapters of this volume).

Another factor paving the way for a more horizontal mode of governance is to be found in the changing meanings of the core concepts of technology and innovation. Individuals in their isolated laboratories no longer conduct Research and Development (R&D) leading to technological advancement and innovation. Rather, this takes place in heterogeneous networks encompassing developers and users of technology, as well as organisations acting as intermediaries and financiers. These actors not only strive to achieve a common goal, but they are also highly dependent on each other's actions (e.g. Edler et al. 2003; Lemola and Honkanen 2004; OECD 2002, Boekholt et al. 2005). The new perception presupposes horizontal collaboration and co-ordination between formerly isolated policies. As such, traditional sector-based decision-making should be replaced with a system that is better able to come to grips with the complex problem of promoting innovation.

As a whole, the evolution from a one-dimensional, hierarchical and unipolar technology policy to a multidimensional, horizontal and multipolar innovation policy implies changes at all levels, from the rationales and drivers of these policies to the role played by politics in technology decision-making. We have summarised these features in Figure 11.1 (also see Kuitunen 2004) which illustrates that horizontalisation also necessarily implies changes in the way politics is presented and exercised in public action. In technology policy, politics is ubiquitous and yet to an extent hidden, meaning that technology issues are not dealt with openly in democratic political institutions and processes. However, it should be pointed out that the neutrality of technology policy is in itself a *political* decision. Indeed, it is as a result of the current nature of the political process that technology issues are left outside the realm of the political arena. The prevailing situation highlights the clear division of labour between politicians and policy-makers, in which the former are charged with the task of determining the overall financial preconditions and budgetary schemes for RDI, while the latter are tasked with establishing the operational guidelines for RDI.

Despite the multitude of potential benefits brought by horizontal innovation policy as an approach, it is nevertheless highly problematic. While technology policy as an approach provides an overly self-limiting perspective on innovation and is unable to capture all of the relevant aspects of technological advancement, the innovation policy approach in turn suffers from potentially serious drawbacks relating to its all-embracing character, leading in the worst case to a conceptually void and empirically indefinable entity.

Figure 11.1: Key features of traditional technology and modern innovation policy

	Traditional technology policy	Modern innovation policy
rationales and drivers	economic growth and prosperity	overall welfare or common good to society and its subgroups; promotion of security, well-being and sustainable development
values	efficiency (in monetary terms)	democratic values (transparency, equality, equity), efficiency (both in monetary and more qualitative terms)
key players	'technology-elite' composed of technology experts/bureaucrats (representing the public sector to a large extent)	actors represent a wide variety of socio-political sectors, from social and cultural policies to defence; also encompasses the political spheres
sources of power	access to financial resources; ability to take part in the allocation process; discursive power (power to produce and reproduce the concept of technology and innovation)	capability to enter the governance networks and get one's voice heard in them
features of governance system	closed; inflexible; hierarchical; vertical decision-making structures predominate	open; flexible; non-hierarchical; horizontal networks predominate
presence of politics	immanent but hidden; neutrality predominates which however is in itself a result of a political decision-making	immanent and explicit; politicians actively take part in designing and launching innovation policy
key problems associated with the approach/policy	too limited a perspective on technology and innovation; too few players; distance from the most acute and important societal problems and challenges	too broad a perspective on technology and innovation (covering everything but becoming too broad, with too many meanings melted into one and too many players, making coordinating them difficult or even impossible; horizontality becomes an overarching concept, encompassing almost everything, though without strong enough linkages to 'real world' practices and procedures

If taken literally, innovation policy effectively becomes a super-policy, and the criteria attached to innovation or innovation capacity become omnipresent, against which each and every aspect or issue should be assessed and valued in our society. This type of tendency towards an overly generalised societal policy is by no means desirable from the viewpoint of innovation policy or societal development. Ultimately, in becoming too all-encompassing, there is a risk that innovation policy becomes blurred and loses much of its distinctness, one of the main historical and comparative success factors of Finnish innovation policy and competitiveness.

Politics has become the unspoken 'elephant in the room' with regard to supposedly technocratic technology policy discussions – everyone knows it is there but nobody utters its name. In the innovation policy domain, the demand for politics can often be strong and political opinions are usually explicitly articulated. At least in the most idealistic form of innovation policy politicians are involved at all stages of the political and policy processes; they debate the pros and cons of each action, bring forth alternative future scenarios for innovation, and criticise those views that are in conflict with their own by relying on both personal and ideological reasoning.

Undoubtedly, however, this move of politics into the technology decision-making process has both positive and negative effects. Figure 11.2 identifies some of the most evident drawbacks and benefits associated with this process of *politicisation* from the technology/innovation decision-making point of view.[3]

We may conclude, on the basis of the observations made above, that while the overall efficiency of the decision-making process may suffer from politicisation, a system in which politics plays a more prominent role will be better equipped to meet the challenges that modern societies are now encountering. In saying this, we are mostly thinking of the debate on democratic values, which calls for more open, transparent and flexible modes of both public and private action.

Good governance, according to the definition put forward by the World Bank and adopted by several authorities and researchers worldwide, necessitates managing public affairs in a transparent, accountable, participatory, and equitable manner, safeguarding also the efficient and economical use of a nation's resources. Modern governance is defined as operating under the auspices of the political system, and it strives to encourage bottom-up participation and mutual networking, as well as the autonomy of markets and citizens (Tiihonen 2004; World Bank 2001).

Despite the tensions between the elements which constitute the good governance concept, the notion itself serves as a particularly useful heuristic tool to illustrate and identify pertinent tendencies transforming the rationales and structures of public intervention, such as technology policy. It is also valu-

3 Compare the discussion of *depoliticisation* by Blühdorn, Maggetti and Landwehr in this volume.

able in elucidating the linkages and interdependencies between various realms, especially in relation to politics and democracy. In the next section, we place these issues under closer scrutiny and elaborate on them empirically.

Figure 11.2: Benefits and drawbacks associated with the politicisation of technology/innovation policy decision-making

	Drawbacks	**Benefits**
actorness	The group of actors involved is expanded at the expense of the expertise of participating actors. This may undermine the quality, and especially the efficiency, of decision-making.	The number of involved actors increases, potentially bringing new voices into the decision-making process.
features of the decision-making process	Decision-making becomes non-consecutive and difficult to forecast.	Debate on policy alternatives and long-term implications of current policies and other options is encouraged.
	Short-term gains may easily override long-term ones, putting into question the coherence of the policy.	Decision-making across the various stages of the policy cycle process becomes more transparent.
	There is more room for opportunism, which is not sanctioned but is rather encouraged through the election mechanism (those incumbents who are able to articulate the interests of their voters and have a proven record of their ability to pursue them in the policy process are rewarded).	Despite the possible tendency for opportunism, the functionality of the system is not eroded or endangered, thanks to its ability to process and pick up the most felicitous and top-rated views.
characteristics of power	Due to the low rate of success and the incoherence in the system, both decision-making initiative and power seep beyond the confines of the formal decision-making arenas, which are conceived of as being inefficient.	Power is exercised and delegated within the boundaries of the system.
consequences for responsiveness and for the overall legitimacy of policy	The overall legitimacy of the system is being endangered as policy proves to be inefficient and is not capable of meeting the demands of societal groups and of society at large.	By diversifying policy options and the long-term implications of prevailing policies, decision-making becomes more responsive to the needs of society and its sub-groups. The overall legitimacy of the governance system is strengthened, thanks to the diminished distance between decision-makers and societal groups as well as better ensuring the inclusion of relevant stakeholders.

3. Horizontal links and the dialogue between technology and other policy domains: some empirical observations concerning Finland

In this section our aim is to shed light on the (assumed) horizontalisation of technology policy, relying on interview and survey data gathered during the period 2004 to 2006. Besides these data sets, we are able to draw upon our experiences with the preparatory process of drafting the national innovation strategy. In order to test the hypothesis concerning horizontalisation, we will focus on three major questions: To what extent are technology and innovation issues perceived as being raised in other policy sectors? Should technology issues be dealt with in other policy domains in the future? How should a modern innovation policy be implemented? The third question elaborates on the means and procedures employed in respect to the preparation and implementation of a modern innovation policy, which we suggest should clearly differ from traditional technology policy making.

As our survey interview databases and our experiences of the innovation strategy project indicate, the horizontal links, at least when examined on the basis of personal perceptions, are not very strong, even though contacts with certain policy sectors and issues are firm and well-established. There is nonetheless a strong tendency towards horizontalisation, as well as the perceived need to achieve more 'joined-up' policies, i.e. making the policy process more integrated across various policy sectors.

According to our empirical analysis technology issues, perhaps unsurprisingly, are first and foremost viewed as issues of technology and science, while the linkages between technology and cultural issues are seen as being extremely weak. The latter observation is reflected in our survey results, according to which only eleven per cent of the respondents regarded technology issues as being dealt with extensively in the cultural policy domain.

By relying on the survey analysis, as well as on the expert interviews, we can divide the linkages between technology policy and the other policy domains into four main types: very close linkages (issues related to science and education, technology, trade and industrial development policies, as well as energy, the environment and competition), relatively close linkages (regional policy issues, defence and transportation issues), relatively weak linkages (monetary, labour and health issues) and extremely weak linkages (social, taxation and cultural issues).

Interestingly enough, the overall picture drawn of horizontalisation becomes somewhat different when the focus is placed on the prospective linkages between technology and other policy domains. The survey results indicate that there is a relatively strong need to strengthen the dialogue between, in particular, such areas as health and environmental policies.[4] The policy domains for which horizontalisation is considered least important are taxation and defence. This result is striking given the fact that these issues are highly relevant to decisions concerning technology and innovation.

Figure 11.3: Current and prospective issues of technology decision-making (% of respondents considering the issue central; N=120-134)

	What issues are currently most central to technology decision-making?	What issues will or should become, more central in the future?
Science and research issues	83	57
Trade and industry policy	76	54
Education	70	61
Energy	70	63
Environment	65	70
Competition	65	53
Regional development	61	53
Defence	51	34
Security	46	46
Transport	45	59
Finance	37	45
Labour and employment	33	49
Health	40	71
Social issues	16	55
Taxation	13	33
Culture	11	41

In innovation terms, the emerging relevance of the health and environment sectors is however less surprising. In the health and welfare sectors, rhetoric and discursive practice have been identified as particular challenges for the established understandings of politics and technology (and politics *in* technology) (e.g. Tarkiainen 2004). Concepts such as *social* and *societal* innovation have been launched as a means to bring the often rather distant spheres of innovation and welfare policy closer together, though the ambiguity of these concepts remains a problem (ibid: 276f). Yet this very ambiguity may also be a means of promoting debate across the sectors: discursive practices may be opened up for re-interpretation and reflection.[5]

Despite its ambiguity, social or societal innovation is a useful concept, which can contribute to bridging the rigidity of the sector-based logic of intervention and innovation in the public sector. Finland, as most European

4 Compare the chapters by Landwehr and Newig and Fritsch in this volume.

5 For similar comments in the context of the welfare cluster see Tarkiainen 2005: 87.

countries, is increasingly faced with the challenge of creating welfare and wealth and providing services in an environment undergoing major demographic and societal change. Innovation throughout society, rather than traditional public sector led re-distribution, is thus increasingly now seen as the major political challenge. Indeed, even in the Nordic welfare systems the debate over other models of service provision (both public and private, and a mix thereof) is being actively pursued.

It is often argued that social innovation is now required simply to maintain the welfare system and its key services, let alone to promote more innovative practices within this area. This is an area where consensus prevails, though the ways in which this challenge is dealt with, and the ways in which the roles of different sectors, organisations, and actors within these processes are defined, are often widely divergent. This observation is further confirmed by the experiences gathered in relation to the preparation of the Finnish innovation strategy, in which the renewal of the public sector by means of the more active utilisation of innovation, as well as the promotion of public sector innovation, were the object of lively discussion. As yet, however, few concrete suggestions have emerged with respect to future policy initiatives. Efforts to promote innovation activities beyond the traditional technology sphere (i.e. within the service sector or procurement), as well as the renewal of public sector processes overall, emerge as particularly central in this debate, though without any general agreement on who is to take the lead in promoting them or what the concrete contents should be.

In our interviews, we also elaborated further upon the reasons for the relatively low level of horizontalisation suggested by our survey data. It seems plausible to argue that it is the Finnish sector-based system, with closed decision-making arenas and selective responsibilities, which creates the principal hindrances to more horizontal modes of action. The tendency is discernible even within the various sectors; as for instance, the barriers between different sections within a particular ministry are high enough to prevent horizontal collaboration and negotiation. The political will to transform and not just redefine the system is however generally lacking, due in the main to its perceived success in producing high-level technologies and successful innovations. Nonetheless, Finland is currently experiencing a significant wave of transformation, particularly when it comes to the governance of innovation issues with the introduction, in January 2008, of the new Ministry of Employment and the Economy. The integration of two formerly separate ministries designates the strengthening inter-linkages between employment, industrial and innovation issues. We will now turn to the question of how technology and innovation issues are governed and administered in Finland.

4. The governance of technology and innovation issues in Finland

In the previous sections, we briefly referred to some of the governance characteristics of technology and innovation decision-making. The examples given and the features described were mostly drawn from the available literature, with the exception of the observations summarised in the preceding section. We will now discuss, in the light of our survey and interview data, the issues of *who* decides on technology and upon what principles decisions are taken.

Who has the power?

As highlighted in Figure 11.4, there is a clear and distinct division of labour in Finland in the field of technology decision-making. Some of the actors and policy domains are viewed as being highly influential throughout all stages of the policy cycle, whereas others lack the power to influence or even meaningfully participate in the process. The most powerful actors are the Ministry of Trade and Industry (since January 2008 called Ministry of Employment and the Economy), *Tekes* and the *Academy of Finland*, while other sector Ministries, in particular the Ministry of Health and Social affairs and the Ministry for Foreign Affairs, together with ordinary citizens, were seen as being actors with considerably less power on these issues. Figure 11.4 categorises the type of influence as follows: A= general influence; B= agenda-setting influence; C= introducing new issues or approaches on the agenda; D= influencing opinions; E= communicating and informing about technology decision-making in the media; F= bringing the issue of risks into the debate.

Our survey also reveals that power in technology issues is most strongly associated with the power to decide on financial resources, though other factors, particularly relating to expertise and the maintenance of good relationships with the most important decision-makers, are also considered important. This is illustrated in Figure 11.5. Although personal charisma was not ranked as highly as the other characteristics, it is by no means unimportant. Almost 50 per cent of our survey respondents saw it as being an important factor in relation to technology decision-making.

In general, as one of our interviewees stated, the position and power of a body in technology and innovation decision-making is perhaps not as dependent on the body's formal position in the governance system, as on its capabilities to foresee future developments and provide relevant stakeholders with innovative and exciting views on technological and innovation development. Substantial knowledge of RDI issues, expertise, and the ability to disentangle oneself from the prevailing reality in order to more accurately perceive future demands, may thus be some of the most crucial assets in gaining power in the innovation policy domain. The ability to assess societal issues in a comprehensive manner is considered an asset, though in reality it is very difficult for experts and professional groups to distance themselves from their professional positions. This has also been apparent in the process of preparing the national innovation strategy. A genuinely horizontal process in this regard would also seem to suggest much more personal and professional risk-taking and a move away from professional roles and 'comfort zones'.

Figure 11.4: The role of different players in technology decision-making (% of respondents considering the particular actor as significant; N=124-134)

	A	B	C	D	E	F
Parliament	67	49	18	45	23	48
Interest associations	71	75	67	85	77	64
Public research institutions	74	84	88	78	73	79
NGOs	20	46	59	74	55	78
Ministry of Trade and Industry	95	90	65	66	70	46
Consumers/citizens	25	19	36	51	22	70
Local politicians/local administration	32	20	12	31	22	20
Ministry of Transport and Communications	79	76	59	57	65	44
Regional and provincial admin	33	26	17	23	19	14
Micro-businesses	29	35	64	34	27	34
Ministry of Education and Culture	60	52	44	56	43	31
SMEs	55	52	75	49	46	40
Prime Minister	69	64	31	59	36	24
Sitra (The Finnish National Fund for Research and Development)	79	85	85	79	77	63
Ministry of Social Affairs and Health	28	26	31	29	27	50
Finnish Academy	76	81	81	58	56	66
Big businesses	93	93	81	89	84	41
Tekes	96	93	91	86	88	63
Ministry of Foreign Affairs	15	15	11	9	14	10
The Science and Technology Policy Council of Finland	80	87	76	65	52	53
Ministry of Finance	77	52	23	26	19	15
Private research institutes	63	66	77	55	55	56
Universities	71	80	87	75	67	77
Ministry of the Environment	52	57	53	52	42	67

A= general influence; B= agenda-setting influence; C= introducing new issues or approaches on the agenda; D= influencing opinions; E= communicating and informing about technology decision-making in the media; F= bringing the issue of risks into the debate.

Figure 11.5: The significance of various factors in determining the distribution of power in technology decision-making (N=140)

Factor affecting the distribution of power	% of respondents considering the factor important
Power to decide on the allocation of financial resources	97
Expertise	81
Good relationships with the most important decision-makers	79
Formal position	76
Networks	71
Charisma/personal attributes	49

In the next section, we will look in more detail at the principles and norms directing technology and innovation decision-making.

The principles involved in technology and innovation decision-making

What then are the principles upon which technology and innovation decision-making is constructed? In our survey, we listed a wide variety of the principles that decision-making should adhere to. The importance of these principles among survey respondents is illustrated in Figure 11.6. The results reveal that the most important principles or norms to be followed in decision-making emanate more from the legal than the political realm. This is in line with the results obtained in other studies, regarding the predominance of legality principles in Finnish decision-making when it comes to the central issues relevant to technology (e.g. energy) (Säynässalo 2005). The commitment to legalism is reflected, for example, in the fact that it is highly favourable for decisions to be based on laws and regulations. Besides legalism, expertise was highly valued by our survey respondents in contrast to the relatively low level of support shown for the mode of action particular to politics. Approximately 90 per cent of the survey respondents agreed that expertise is a highly or somewhat important principle in technology decision-making, whereas only 40 per cent characterised political reasoning as being imperative.

Figure 11.6: The importance of various principles in technology decision-making (N=134)

Decision-making principle	**very or quite important (% of respondents)**
decisions are based on the broadest expertise available	94
decisions are communicated as openly as possible	90
experts are in charge of preparing policy	85
decisions include the consideration of their societal impacts to the greatest extent possible	84
decisions include the consideration of their environmental impacts to the greatest extent possible	82
decisions are based on laws and regulations	79
business representatives are involved in the decision-making	78
those with the best expertise available are in charge of the decisions	76
decisions are prepared in the public sphere	74
decisions are not predominately political	57
decisions take into account the different interest groups	51
those accountable to the electorate are responsible for decisions	49
representatives of organised business interests have a strong position in decision-making	48
decisions are politically justified	40
decisions emerge as unanimous agreements from negotiations	15

Besides the significance of various norms, we also investigated, as summarised in Figure 11.7, the effects of a wide array of principles on technology and innovation decision-making. Our survey data reveal that the principles mostly associated with democratic governance ranked highest in contrast to the norms inherent in political action, which garnered the least support among our respondents. The difference is indeed a striking one. Democratic principles such as transparency and debate on the targets and means of decision-making were considered to have a positive impact by one-tenth to one third of the surveyed respondents, while only two per cent considered the effects of disagreements concerning goals to be positive. Notwithstanding this, politicisation and increased participation/transparency may also be mutually reinforcing: politicisation may produce democratic effects in several ways, for example, it can provide political representation and an infrastructure for political claim-making, which in turn may strengthen the institutional conditions for democracy, or it may contribute to the formation of citizenship identities.

Figure 11.7: The effects of various principles on technology decision-making (% of respondents; N=130-132)

	Would significantly improve	Would make significantly worse
Increasing scientific knowledge on societal and environmental effects	42	1
Debate on the goals and means of decision-making	30	1
Increased information on decisions	26	0
Improving transparency in decision-making	21	1
Paying attention to cultural and/or social points of view, together with the financial ones	23	3
Paying more attention to business interests	19	1
The inclusion of new types of actors in decision-making	11	1
Unanimity regarding goals	20	3
Increasing citizens' opportunities to influence decision-making	11	5
Allowing as varied a group of actors as possible to take part in decision-making	11	9
Paying more attention to third sector organisations' interests	9	7
Goal-conflicts	2	24

It is, therefore, interesting to note that the inclusion of new actors, which in principle is integrally linked to the transformation of traditional technology policy towards a more horizontal mode of public governance, was assessed as having a positive impact on decision-making by only a small minority (11 per cent). Taking this and the other observations summarised in Figure 11.7 into account, we argue that the prospects for building up a more diversified decision-making system appear relatively bleak. To sum up, and to emphasise the most relevant findings from our data, the positions of key actors as well as the factors affecting their position in the technology decision-making realm are captured in Figure 11.8.

We were able to chart the principles followed in the innovation policy-making sphere at close range, while consulting on the drafting of the new national innovation strategy. It is argued that the new horizontal innovation policy calls for such procedures which enable the active involvement of a large array of actors, representing not only the traditional technology elites but other groups, such as the third sector, ordinary citizens, and actors from sectors to which technology policy links have traditionally been weak. Horizontal innovation policy requires methods for both gathering and utilising the views of these diverse groups; of making them count, rather than just making them heard. The methods used are deliberative in their nature, more broadly referring to the accommodation of a wide array of opinions and subsequently creating a mutual understanding of the phenomena under scrutiny.

Figure 11.8: Key actors in technology and innovation decision-making and the determinants of their position

	Citizens	Politicians	Technology experts (mostly researchers)	Technology elite	Civil society
interest in technological and innovation issues	low in technolo-gy but high in innovation	low in technology but should be high in innovation	high	high in technology and should be high in innovation	low; higher in some questions; high in innovation issues
confidence in technology	high	high	high	high	high
understanding of technology	predominantly technical understanding	predominantly technical understanding	predominantly technical understanding but broader than other actors	predominantly technical understanding	predominantly technical understanding but broader than others
perceived expertise in technology issues	low	low	high	high	low
support for the technology establishment	indirect support	indirect support	indirect support	part of the establish-ment	indirect support
distance from technology decision-making	long	long	rather long, some at the edges of the establishment, but position unstable	short	long
ability/willing-ness to challenge prevailing understanding of technology and decision-making	low	low	ability to challenge exists, but incentives missing	ability exists, no willingness	ability may exist, but no incentives

In the preparation of the new Finnish innovation strategy, the deliberative approach was employed through the adoption of workshops and open consultancy methods. These methods have rarely been used in the area of technology policy prior to this process, and few examples exist of creating interactive and deliberative fora between citizens, policy-makers, academic experts, business representatives and the third sector. Though horizontalisation has been seen as a necessity for technology and innovation policy, less acknowledgement has been given of the need for deliberative processes in policy development. Only recently has a broader acceptance emerged that horizontalisation is essentially a process of interdependence between expert- and evidence-based policies and public acceptance. The method by which the deliberative drafting of the innovation strategy was taken forward involved a series of interactive workshops and open consultation by the general public.

But is the public interested in responding to such calls for open web-based consultation and deliberation? Within the public consultation process, a total of 565 respondents put their comments forward. Considering how novel this approach was in the Finnish administrative and policy deliberation context, the number can be considered quite satisfactory. The piloting of this approach can be viewed as participatory and positive for the strengthening of public commitment and empowerment, while also contributing to the renewal of democratic processes at the national level. In addition, it can be seen as contributing to the quality of innovation and technology policy, making this policy area more inclusive and more broadly based. The benefits achieved through this first step should not however be over-estimated, as too few new target groups, ranging from the third sector to consumers and citizens, were reached through this process. In order to improve on this in future, the need clearly remains to further develop the substance and language used, i.e. making the policy more understandable to the broader public and ordinary citizens. On the other hand, the business sector was reached quite well in the process, which has traditionally been a concern or a weak point in developing Finnish innovation policy.

5. Conclusions

Horizontalisation is currently a lively topic for both researchers and policy makers on technology and innovation issues. As our research has shown, the tendency towards a more horizontal mode of action implies changes at all levels of technology and innovation decision-making, starting from the delegation of power and public responsibilities up to the dominant values and rationales of the policy. Even if the empirical observations made in the study mostly concern Finland, we argue that many can be generalised and thus potentially hold true for other western countries as well.

In the context of the traditional form of hierarchical and sector-based government, technology policy includes a limited number of actors forming a cohesive and essentially closed technology elite, while modern innovation policy implies a larger and more heterogeneous group of players drawn from a wide and crosscutting array of policy sectors. The need for a more widespread base of policy-making remains, since the policy issues dealt with increasingly require the expression of interest, views and opinions of the wider citizenry, as well as their approval. Horizontal innovation policy is expected to increasingly encompass issues closer to the lives of individuals as consumers, citizens and stakeholders. Besides promoting economic growth, the new horizontal innovation policy is expected to deal with broad concerns, such as health, security and sustainable development. Not only are responsibilities spread more widely within the innovation policy realm, but the rationales and goals of the policy are more extensive, even encompassing the aim of producing a common good and overall well-being. Moreover, in striving for these aims, the need for innovation should be prioritised in every sector of society, from social policy to cultural and even taxation policy.

In Finland, as our study shows, the horizontalisation of the traditional form of technology policy can best be attributed to a change in discourse and rhetoric rather than to a physical transformation taking place in, for example, its governance structures. While most observers of the technology policy field admit that horizontalisation is a pre-requisite to ensure that future technology policy can meet the post-industrial challenges now faced, there is nevertheless little empirical evidence available to confirm that this kind of development is actually under way. The prevailing mode in technology decision-making is far from being truly horizontal. It includes an extremely limited number of key players who have strong and unquestioned autonomy in producing the dominant understanding of technology and innovation. These actors are also highly independent when it comes to decisions on such issues as the kinds of technologies to be supported by public funding, or what the prospective development trends in technology and innovation are likely to be.

What is perhaps most striking in our study is the observation that the legitimacy of key actors is founded on support from all relevant societal subgroups, from ordinary citizens to politicians, not to mention technology and innovation experts (e.g. researchers). Clearly, critics are for the most part excluded from the process. Few voices are heard which seek to challenge the current modes of operation in the technology decision-making realm.

It is worth highlighting, however, that the latter observation does not mean that politics is lacking in the technology decision-making realm. Quite the contrary, the current governance (or government) system was set up as a result of a political process establishing the key players and their positions, as well as the 'rules of the game', such as the principles of decision-making.

When it comes to the possibility of the system transforming itself from being sector-based and closed into a more horizontal mode of action, our conclusions suggest that a high degree of scepticism should be in order. The conditions for such a transformation are relatively unfavourable, and it is highly questionable whether the technology decision-making system will be capable of transforming itself into a horizontal innovation policy on its own. Moreover, the question also remains as to whether the mindset which places innovation at the forefront of all facets of society will be rooted strongly enough to force the agencies concerned to include highly sectoral interests for the sake of pursuing the 'common good'. Perhaps a major transformation or crisis is needed, such as a recession as dramatic as that of the early 1990s, to unbundle the current system for handling technology issues. However, as our observations demonstrate, there is a clear demand for policy transformation and the rationales behind this shift are recognised and already relatively well-known.

The principles involved in the development and implementation of Finnish innovation policy once again reflect the tensions within this policy area. Lurking in the background is the question of the need to strike a balance between democratic values and efficiency. It could be argued that the traditional sector-based technology policy is more efficiency-based than the emerging and more broad-based innovation policy. Without doubt, limiting the group of actors involved in the policy elaboration process has improved the ability for steering and control. However, horizontalisation seeks to question this control and order. The field is becoming more complex, more inclusive and less predictable. The boundaries between those involved in policy deliberation and implementation is becoming increasingly blurred and less clearly defined. The re-articulation and re-definition of the policy arena and its actors is broadening the group of actors involved, and in so doing also potentially slows the process of policy deliberation and implementation. The question of who participates, and under which conditions, thus emerges here as an important concern.

Democracy questions and deliberative concerns have remained surprisingly absent from the Finnish debate in connection with innovation policy. It is desirable that in the future this important topic will re-emerge with more vigour, and in so doing benefit the quality of governance and democracy, as well as policy substance. On the other hand, the democratisation tendency attached to innovation policy development also has its drawbacks. Despite involving a multitude of actors in the decision-making process, some groups may still lack the capacity or resources necessary to participate effectively. Furthermore, even when disadvantaged groups have the requisite skills and resources to take part, their views may be dismissed, as they may not have an established position within the governance (or government) system. Additionally, managing the divergent opinions in the decision-making process is a problem. Some sort of co-ordinating authority is required to oversee the expression of opinions and attitudes on technology and innovation issues, highlighting venues in which opinions can be processed and debated.

One of the ways in which many European countries, including Finland, have sought to come to terms with the challenge on governance is through programme-based policy intervention. Performance management within the public sector has in recent years also been developed in ways that allow for cross-sectoral goal-setting and performance-steering of societal impacts, which are highly dependent on interaction and co-operation across sector- and organisational boundaries (e.g. Ministry of Finance 2005). It is evident that new horizontal programmes are required to concretise and promote the horizontalisation of policy. Experience gathered from large cross-sectional programmes such as those promoting the renewal of Finland's public health care services show that it is difficult but still possible to co-ordinate the activities of various policy-actors in a satisfactory manner, and to establish a common vision for these actors. Positive examples of policy integration should be made explicit to cultivate the efforts made thus far, as well as to facilitate a better understanding of the interactions and linkages between social, health-care and innovation policies.

Although there is an evident bias towards discourse and less substance in terms of the political realities of every-day activities in respect of the modes and governance of technology decision-making, the concept of *horizontal innovation policy* may still prove useful for researchers and policy-makers by providing them with a heuristic tool, enabling them to get to grips with the dynamics of the technology decision-making process. Similarly, if elaborated and developed further, it may be of great value to the groups involved by exhibiting those alterations which are indispensable in order for the system as a whole to survive.

References

Boekholt, P./den Hertog, P./Remøe, S.O. (2005): *Governance of Innovation Systems: Case Studies In Innovation Policy, Executive Summary*, Paris: OECD.

Caracostas, P./Muldur, U. (1998): *Society, the Endless Frontier: A European Vision of Research and Innovation Policies for the 21st Century*, Luxembourg, Brussels: Office for Official Publications of the European Communities.

CEC (2001): 'European Governance: A White Paper', Brussels, 25.7.2001, COM (2001) 428 final.

Chamberlin, T./De la Mothe, J. (2004): 'The Integration of Innovation Policies: The Case of Canada', in: *Prometheus* 22/11, pp. 3-20.

Edler, J./Kuhlmann, S./Smits, R. (2003): 'New Governance for Innovation. The Need for Horizontal and Systemic Policy Co-ordination', *Fraunhofer ISI Discussion Papers* 2/2003, Karlruhe: ISI.

Häyrinen-Alestalo, M./Pelkonen, A./Teräväinen, T./Villanen, S. (2005): 'Changing Governance for Innovation Policy Integration in Finland', Monit WP1 Final Report, Case Finland, Paris: OECD.

Haas, P.M. (1992): 'Introduction: Epistemic Communities and International Policy Coordination', in: *International Organization* 46/1, pp. 1-35.

Independent Expert Group on R&D and Innovation (2006): 'Creating an Innovative Europe', Report of the Independent Expert Group on R&D and Innovation appointed following the Hampton Court Summit, Luxembourg: Office for Official Publications of the European Communities.

Kazancigil, A. (2000): 'Governance and Science: Market-like Modes of Managing Society and Producing Knowledge', in: *International Social Science Journal* 50/155, pp. 69-79.

Kjær, A.M. (2004): *Governance*, Cambridge: Polity Press.

Kuitunen, S. (2004): 'OECD Monit WP2A: Information Society Sub-study: E-Democracy', unpublished background report. VTT Technology Studies.

Lemola, T./Honkanen, P. (2004): *Innovaatiopolitiikka – keiden hyväksi, keiden enhdoilla?*, Helsinki: Gaudeamus.

Ministry of Finance (2005): *The Manual of Performance Guidance [Tulosohjauksen käsikirja]*, Helsinki: Ministry of Finance.

OECD (2002): 'Dynamising National Innovation Systems', Paris: OECD.

Olsson, J. (2003): 'Democracy Paradoxes in Multi-Level Governance', in: *Journal of European Policy* 10/2, pp. 283-300.

Pelkonen, A. (2006) 'The Problem of Integrated Innovation Policy – Analyzing the Governing Role of the Science and Technology Policy Council of Finland', in: *Science and Public Policy* 33/9, pp. 669-80.

Stoker, G. (1998): 'Governance as Theory: Five Propositions', in: *International Social Science Journal* 50/1, pp. 17-29.

Säynässalo, E. (2005): 'Between Politics and Law: Explaining the Failure of the Greens to Prevent the Further Building of Nuclear Energy in Finland', Paper presented at the YHYS Conference "*ISSUES IN GREEN DEMOCRACY*", Workshop: Revision of the nuclear energy policy? Turku, 24.-25.11.2005.

Tarkiainen, A. (2004): 'Innovaatioretoriikka ja hyvinvointiklusteripolitiikka teoksessa', in: Lemola, T./Honkanen, P. (eds) *Innovaatiopolitiikka: kenen hyväksi, keiden ehdoilla?*, Helsinki: Gaudeamus.

Tarkiainen, A. (2005): *Avaimia ja lukkoja vertailemassa: hyvinvointiklusterista uusi ovi innovaatiopolitiikkaan*, Helsinki: Kauppa-ja Teollisuusministeriö, Rahoitetut tutkimukset – sarja.

Tiihonen, S. (2004): *From Governing to Governance. A Process of Change*, Tampere: Tampere University Press.

World Bank (2001): *World Development Report 2002: Building Institutions for Markets*, Oxford: Oxford University Press.

Chapter 12
Legitimacy Problems in the Allocation of Health Care: Decision-Making Procedures in International Comparison

Claudia Landwehr and *Ann-Charlotte Nedlund*

1. Introduction

The debates about the future of European health care systems still widely assume that the distribution of services follows the principle of need alone: everyone gets what they need, neither more nor less. Remaining regulative challenges such as the appraisal of new pharmaceuticals and technologies are regarded as purely technocratic problems to be resolved by experts. Ever increasing costs for new drugs, demographic change and decreasing employment rates, however, have in most countries long made cost containment policies necessary. Their failure to effectively control expenses enhances the pressure for explicit priority-setting in health care and increases the probability of its politicisation. The challenge of fairly distributing health care raises the question of whether and how legitimate decisions are possible under conditions of uncertainty and complexity.

Health policy is traditionally closely connected with the nation state and modern welfare statehood (Steffen et al. 2005: 1). It can be seen as a 'specific state-building or state-stabilizing resource' (ibid.) that promotes trust in the state and the government. The opposite may be expected to apply for cost containment, and especially explicit rationing. Here, health policy is no longer about reducing risks and fears but about cutting back entitlements and removing securities. If the creation of health care services was state-stabilizing, the reverse could be true for cutbacks: they are potentially destabilizing and trust-erosive. Health policy decisions immediately affect citizens in their everyday life. Far from being a purely regulative task, the allocation of health care under conditions of budget constraints thus constitutes an essentially distributive conflict that gives rise to questions about justice and a democratic definition of its standards.

The analysis in this chapter proceeds in four steps: In section two, we outline the inevitability of rationing in health care and discuss advantages and disadvantages of implicit and explicit rationing strategies. In section three, we address issues of legitimacy. In particular, we look at concepts of internal and external legitimacy, the politicisation and depoliticisation of rationing decisions and discuss Daniels and Sabin's concept of 'accountability for reasonableness' as a possible escape from legitimacy dilemmas. Section four consists of three case studies from Germany, the UK and Sweden, showing how rationing decisions are taken in practice, followed by a discussion of the main results of the comparison. The conclusion seeks to define the possible and necessary role of different types of forums in decision-making processes and attempts an answer to questions about the limits of democratically legitimated decisions in highly complex matters with immediate consequences for citizens' welfare.

2. The rationing challenge

When the first public health insurance systems were created in the late 19th Century, their main task consisted in the coverage of loss of wages due to illness. Serious physical conditions could rarely be treated or cured. Since the end of World War II, by contrast, the potential of medical research and treatment has literally exploded. At the time of a general expansion of the welfare state, budgets for health care were simply raised to meet growing expenses. Since the 1970s, however, most developed countries have tried to limit increases in health care spending in proportion with the growth of their GNP. As there are no natural limits to medical and technological innovation nor to medical needs, wishes and hopes, societies need to decide what proportion of their resources they want to use for the provision of health care and what opportunity costs in other areas are acceptable.

While health itself is normally seen as an indispensable primary good, health care goods thus become scarce goods. Moreover, health care goods are heterogeneous goods: it matters who receives which treatment when and where, as the utility derived from it depends on the recipient and his condition (Elster 1995: 3-6). This is fundamental to the information problem their allocation constitutes: how do we find out under precisely what conditions an allocation generates utility or not? While this information aspect is central to decisions over the allocation of health care, the distributive aspect is equally important. Calabresi and Bobbit (Calabresi and Bobbit 1978: 20) distinguish 'first-order-determinations' of the total amount of resources to be used from 'second-order-determinations' of how these resources are to be used. As long as both types of decisions are directly linked, no serious conflicts are to be expected. This was the case where contributions to public insurances were directly determined by health care spending. The policy shift towards cost containment has decoupled first- from second-order-determinations, which, according to Calabresi and Bobbit, necessitates 'tragic choices'.

Given a limited total budget, decisions over the distribution of health care are, if not in every case tragic, always particularly difficult, as they require the comparative evaluation of entitlements to help. To the patient, the rejection of claims means avoidable suffering or even premature death, and seems to be connected with the message that the needs of some patients count less than those of others (Fleck 1992: 1604f). Accordingly, it is little surprising that politicians as well as many experts recommend increasing efficiency instead of cutting back services in order to contain costs. They claim that enhanced competition on both the supply and the demand side will activate efficiency reserves that make rationing unnecessary (Aaron and Schwartz 1990). However, the anonymous, neutral and non-political character of enhancing efficiency conceals the fact that what it is really about is often only implicit instead of explicit rationing (Fleck 1992: 1606).

Implicit rationing takes place by means of limited budgets for specified domains, which shifts distributive decisions from the macro- to the meso- or micro-level (single doctors). Explicit rationing decisions, by contrast, specify groups of patients, conditions or treatments for which funding is denied or which receive lower priority in the allocation of resources. If one accepts the judgment that efficiency reserves are limited, implicit rationing is likely to become more and more visible and will enhance the pressure for reforms. The most significant increases are found in expenses for intensive care and pharmaceutical products. In both areas, cost containment by means of budgets is comparatively difficult. If new technologies and treatments are available, they will be demanded by patients. This leaves the choice of either uncritically funding new technologies at the expense of more efficient ones with less lobby-group support or explicitly denying funding for specific drugs and treatments.

Over the last 10-15 years many countries have tried different approaches and models to deal with the rationing challenge. Some approaches are more systematic and well-structured than others, and there are clearly no simple solutions to handle this dilemma. What the approaches and models have in common is the ambition to move from implicit to explicit in the decision-making processes of priorities and resource allocation. Before we take a closer look at how rationing decisions are taken in practice and in different countries, we have to deal with the legitimacy problems they confront.

3. Legitimacy

In a comprehensive public system, where different needs compete, elements of fairness are crucial. Consequently, it is of vital interest that the setting of priorities and the allocation of resources should be perceived as fair and legitimate as possible. Fairness concerns the question of whether and when patients and clinicians have sufficient reason to accept a particular priority setting decision as right and fair. Legitimacy concerns the conditions under which authority over priority setting should be placed in the hands of a particular organization, group or person (Singer et al. 2006). These issues, fairness and legitimacy, can be seen as being at the heart of the rationing challenge, they are distinct but related issues. Distinct in the way that a decision-maker can have legitimacy and at the same time take unfair decisions, and related in the way that a legitimate decision-maker who deviates from the routine of fair procedure can lose its legitimacy (Daniels and Sabin 1997).

Input and output legitimacy

As outlined in the introductory chapter of this volume, Fritz Scharpf has distinguished two ways in which a political system can gain legitimacy: through its input or through its output (Scharpf 1970). The most important input in democratic systems consists in free and equal elections. Political debates in the media or smaller deliberative forums, political activism and a vivid public sphere with functioning associations also make up part of the input side of a political system. In practice, however, input legitimacy usually boils down to the question of whether decisions are taken by a democratically elected body and whether they are taken in an explicit and transparent way.

The concept of output legitimacy is somewhat more difficult to grasp. Scharpf points out that a political system can claim legitimacy not only by virtue of governments being democratically elected, but also, and in some cases first and foremost, by virtue of the output it produces. This output consists in laws, directives and regulations and their implementation. For the case of health care rationing, policy outputs can claim legitimacy in so far as they are perceived as fair, efficient and expedient. In some cases, however, out*comes* are more important than the output itself. Even where the output, i.e. explicit decisions, is well-justified and perceived as fair, outcomes can be dissatisfactory and illegitimate. Deficiencies in outcomes can be unexpected side-effects of a legitimate policy output, or they can be due to external and uncontrollable factors. For example, a decision to fund a new therapy can lead to difficulties in service provision, or a new drug may be found to have severe side-effects even though it was conscientiously tested. In both cases, authorities are likely to be held accountable even if the results were not foreseeable and they are strictly speaking not responsible.

Internal and external legitimacy

A public health care system is a professionally governed organization with professional power. At the same time, the system is divided between politicians and mangers/administrators. The complex decision form that characterises health care systems leads to problems of legitimacy and often a deficiency of trust, as the assignment of responsibility between elected representatives and providers (officials and medical staff) is difficult. To citizens, it is difficult to know where the power and the influence on decisions are and who is to be held accountable for them. The lack of trust and problems of legitimacy can be addressed both internally and externally (Garpenby 2003a; Garpenby 2004). Internal legitimacy relates to input and output legitimacy within the organization of a public health care system, i.e. between different functions and between politicians, officials and professionals. External legitimacy relates to input and output legitimacy between the health care organization and the citizens, patients or users.[1]

Attempts to strengthen the internal legitimacy (when setting priorities) can be based on four components: (a) collaboration methods, used for the selection of stakeholders, to achieve well-balanced standpoints, gain different types of information, collect and evaluate decision data, make decisions and find ways to strengthen trust in the priority setting process; (b) decision data, which are the facts and knowledge needed when balancing and making standpoints, (c) a value platform, which consists of goals and essential definitions that determine the information and decision data collected and how these are to be interpreted, and (d) institutions that create trust, which are meeting arenas and dialogue methods that are important for the priority setting process. The collaboration methods consist of several phases, an initiating phase, a problem definition phase, a decision-making phase and, finally, an implementing phase, all of which are important for the priority setting process. While there will always be deficits in some of these components, the key to strengthening internal legitimacy is the ability among different stakeholders (politicians, researchers, officials, medical professionals) to find stable collaboration methods to handle and interpret information and act on it when setting priorities (Garpenby 2004).

With regard to external legitimacy, many theorists have pointed out the qualities of public deliberation as an important component of a responsive and responsible democracy (Delli Carpini et al. 2004). The idea is that through deliberation citizens gain information about their own and others' needs and develop skills to resolve deep conflicts, so that deliberation will lead to a 'healthier' civic life. Although a lot of time and resources have been

1 The distinction between internal and external legitimacy is more commonly used in the field of organizational management studies (see for example Kostova and Zaheer, 1999).

spent to strengthen citizen involvement through deliberative methods, the citizens' motivation to get involved in the decision-making process is controversial. One argument is that most people want to be involved in the planning of health services and that the authorities should listen to the public (Bowling 1996). Another argument is that there are only limited areas where public input actually might be in question since the average citizen lacks both interest and necessary skills (Lomas 1997). However, Abelson (2001) argues that the question discussed by policy-makers and researchers is mainly one of 'who should be involved, in what decision, how, and in what capacity'. The discussion should also be about how what kind of power and influence should be shared, and decision-makers welcome the public to share this difficult task.

Involvement of the public and the patients is recommended on two grounds: on democratic grounds with the intention to legitimise the decision process, and managerial grounds in order to improve public and patient involvement in health-care planning. However, external legitimacy is not just about the citizens and their perceptions but also about the patients' and the users' perception of how the priority-setting decisions are made. Patients and users apparently have different levels of trust in the health care system, with trust in the medical staff being higher than trust in representatives of the health plans (Fondacaro et al. 2005). This can imply that different approaches to strengthening external legitimacy are appropriate depending on where you are in the health-care organization.

A lot of effort, time and resources, especially for different public participation activities, have been devoted to strengthening the external legitimacy. Public consultation has been introduced with different results. McIver (1998) has evaluated citizen juries in health care contexts in Britain, coming to the conclusion that the citizen jury is a valuable form to increase the possibilities for the local community to participate in priority-setting processes. Experience from Canada indicates that citizens want to have a role as consultative part at both system and program level, but do not want to shoulder the responsibility for the final decision (Abelson and Eyles 2002). Against the background of increasing demands for accountability and transparency, citizens need to be assured that their resources are allocated in such a way that their interests are represented adequately. Openness is required both concerning the principles that are applied and concerning the evidence decisions are based on (ibid.).

Nevertheless, there are generally still problems of legitimacy for the health care system, in particular concerning the citizens' trust in some parts of the system. The crucial question, however, is if all the activities for strengthening external legitimacy are a successful and effective way to handle the legitimacy problems that occur when dealing with tough priority-setting decisions.

Politicisation and depoliticisation of rationing decisions

Where health care is publicly funded or publicly sanctioned, explicit rationing decisions must be generally binding and thus political decisions. Collective decisions qualify as genuinely political by virtue of being contingent (Greven 1999). Contingency of decisions means that they are neither predetermined by external forces nor clearly deducible from principles or evidence. Decisions are political because there exist alternatives over which citizens and politicians can, more or less autonomously, form preferences. Neither of the alternatives is evidently the 'correct' one, but typically, several are viable and supported by good reasons.

There exist two ways in which an issue may be politicised. The first is by demanding the replacement or regulation of decisions hitherto taken in the private sphere or on the market by generally binding law. The second is by pointing out the contingency of, and thus the alternatives to, political decisions that are otherwise regarded as inevitable or without alternatives. The latter presupposes the former in that it takes for granted the necessity of a decision on the political level. For government and administration, or the powerful in general, a strategy to mitigate opposition consists in highlighting both the necessity of a generally binding decision and the lack of alternatives to their preferred option. Such de-politicisation, it is suggested, allows for rational and efficient decisions by avoiding compromises and allowances. Opposition parties and groups excluded from power and influence can be expected to initiate politicisation by pointing out alternatives, mobilizing veto power and exacting concessions for their benefit. The degree to which depoliticisation is successfully countered in this way may be regarded as an indicator either for the distribution of power or for the prevalence of conflicts within a society.

What are the preconditions and consequences of politicisation or depoliticisation with regard to the allocation of health care? On the one hand, priority-setting definitely entails distributive conflicts. That is, certain groups of patients or potential patients are privileged over others and their claims and needs attended to with priority. Such distributive conflicts are to a large extent irreducible and cannot be solved in an expertocratic fashion. On the other hand, the matter is extremely complex and decisions obviously require a sound basis in expert information. As allocation decisions immediately affect the welfare of citizens, poorly informed, 'unreasonable' decisions are likely to result in a public outcry. In the face of cut-backs of entitlements, the expectation to achieve optimal results with limited means grows. It seems that where a government curtails entitlements, it must increase productivity and cannot afford watered down, inefficient policies. Seemingly sub-optimal outcomes that fail to meet expectations might undermine the acceptance and legitimacy of decisions more profoundly than a lack of transparency and participation on the input-side. In so far as depoliticising decisions increases welfare, it could thus not only be desirable under ethical aspects, but also be preferred by a majority of the population.

One strategy to depoliticise decisions over health care has been to derive them from an overarching and allegedly uncontroversial principle of efficiency. The allocation of health care is efficient, health economists would say, where services optimally meet requirements and neither too much or too little, nor the wrong kind of care is provided in any place. Where resources are finite and some requirements cannot be met, efficiency can only be plausibly measured in terms of the absolute utility produced. However, the problems of establishing such an interpersonally comparative measure for utility have long characterized utilitarian theorizing. Do we consider subjective wishes or objective needs? How do we determine or weigh either?

Accountability for reasonableness'

Rationing decisions in a public health care system with limited resources can thus obviously lead into legitimacy dilemmas. The call for more explicit rationing and transparency challenges legitimacy even more, especially if the explicit decisions are not perceived as fair by those affected. Even though well-established distributive principles exist, it seems like we can never come to an agreement about how they should be interpreted and specified in different situations. Therefore, the only viable strategy to escape legitimacy dilemmas in health care rationing must be to provide and develop procedures that can be perceived as fair and legitimate.

Dimensions that can be seen to characterise procedural justice are (not in order of importance) the following: voice, neutrality, consistency, accuracy, reversibility and transparency (Dolan et al. 2005). However, it is essential to keep in mind that procedural dimensions can have different degrees of importance depending on context and the circumstances that are present in that actual situation and context. The importance of one dimension can relate to the present alternative dimensions (ibid.). Procedures that individuals value as fair in one context can be valued less in another context. The different condition can also have different weights depending on the desired effect, for example if the aim is to strengthen external or internal legitimacy. Combinations of procedures that are well suited for a particular situation may not be suitable for another. Procedures that are regarded as just can improve trust in decision-making authorities, but may also have intrinsic values, e.g. the perception of respect and dignity. Several studies have come to the conclusion that the experience of procedural justice has effects not only at the individual

(Tyler 1994) and the group level (Lind et al. 1993), but also at the societal level (Grimes 2005; Gibson et al. 2005).

From this context, Daniels and Sabin (Daniels and Sabin 1997; Daniels and Sabin 2002) have proposed the framework 'accountability for reasonableness' for a fair and legitimate procedure for setting priorities in health care. They state that decisions concerning limit and priority setting are of a moral kind and since there is no consensus on how scarce resources should be allocated, a democratic procedure is the only acceptable and proper way to handle these moral questions. Daniels and Sabin propose four conditions for a fair decision-making process, which together make up the notion of 'accountability for reasonableness': (a) *publicity*, demanding that reasons for a decisions should be public, (b) *relevance*, demanding that those reasons should be relevant to 'fair-minded people', (c) *revision and appeals*, demanding that there should be possibilities and mechanisms for a reappraisal in the light of new evidence or arguments and (d) *regulation*, demanding that there should be a public regulation of the process to ensure that conditions (a) to (c) are met. Deliberation and revision are supposed to enable the adjustment of decisions to specific situations and circumstances, whereas purely theoretical distributive principles remain abstract and inflexible.

Daniels and Sabin's notion of 'accountability for reasonableness' has influenced the design of decision-making processes and organizational settings in several countries. However, it is essential to note that these conditions should be seen as guidelines rather than as a checklist since situations and the context never, or rarely, are the same or take place between the same levels within the organization.

4. Case studies

Germany

In the late 1970s, German health policy made the first moves from service expansion to cost containment. Since then, the Joint Committee, where health insurers and doctors negotiate services to be covered, has gained in importance. Committees of doctors, hospitals and insurers are part of a system of corporatist self-regulation in the German social insurance sector. Institutions and their competences are sanctioned by federal law, so that actors negotiate in the 'shadow of hierarchy' (Scharpf 1997: Ch. 9). Wherever they are charged with specific tasks, they are independent and their decisions are binding. This is a notable difference in comparison with the majority of other bodies charged with priority setting decisions, which issue only recommendations.

The move from expenditure-oriented revenue policy towards revenue-oriented expenditure policy that began with the first cost containment law in 1977 was accompanied by an instrumentalisation of the Joint Committee for the regulation of distributive conflicts (Döhler and Manow-Borgwaldt 1992: 584). In return for its commissioning for cost containment goals, the Committee received far-reaching instruments for its implementation (Urban 2001: 10). In 2004, a new Federal Joint Committee was set up which merges several existing committees and covers inpatient and outpatient medical and dental care. It issues legally binding decisions on the lists of services covered and thus possesses remarkably far-reaching competences for the allocation of health care. Interestingly, however, responsibility for assessment of naturopathic drugs, many of which fail efficiency tests, has remained with the ministry of health. Also, the ministry can object to committee decisions and it can issue regulations where the committee fails to act.[2] And, last but not least, the government could at any time choose to abolish or replace the committee, as it does not enjoy any constitutional protection.

The latest major health care reform has considerably restructured the committee's decision-making procedures. To begin with, the participation of patient representatives, albeit only with consultative influence and without voting rights, improves the publicity of meetings. Previously, the committee's role was hardly known in public and proceedings were entirely inaccessible to outsiders. The fact that each of the separate panels is now chaired by three experts not only increases pressures for justification but at the same time reduces decision costs. Whereas previously, each party at the bargaining table (insurers vs. doctors or hospitals) practically held veto powers, majority decisions are now possible. In case of a confrontation of interests, it is the experts who dispose of the deciding vote. As a minimal winning coalition requires either expert support or compromises with the opposite side, incentives for coordination nonetheless remain strong. In addition, an 'Institute for Quality and Efficiency in Health Care' was established to provide the Joint Committee with reports on specific technologies. Forums in the Joint Committee consider publicly available cost-benefit assessments of this expert forum as a basis for decisions.

Increasing institutionalisation and the reform of consultation and decision procedures have changed the Federal Joint Committee's structures in a way that it significantly deviates from its earlier character as a forum of distributive bargaining. Nevertheless, the fact that a forum that was originally set up for bargaining purposes was charged with allocation decisions is in itself remarkable, as its lack of legitimation and justificatory faculties is so obvious. The apprehension of insufficiently justified decisions at the expense of

---

2 This has happened in the case of the introduction of 'diagnosis related groups' (DRGs) in German hospitals, which the committee refused to develop.

third parties seems less warranted after the recent reforms. Yet, a lack of transparency remains problematic: forums remain inaccessible to citizens, media or researchers. With regard to the rationing principles applied in decisions, it is too early for an appraisal. A recent decision to deny funding for a new type of insulin, known to be effective but extremely expensive, indicates that cost-benefit assessments are likely to play an increasing role.

Concerning the issue of politicisation and depoliticisation, the involvement of major veto players reduces potential opposition and facilitates implementation. Given that the Federal Joint Committee still enjoys comparatively little public attention, the strategy of blame avoidance by means of delegation is apparently successful in Germany. However, the corporatist tradition, along with a still widely held belief that the German health care system is among the best in the world and an official rhetoric against rationing is an important factor here. Nevertheless, recent conflicts between the committee and the German Ministry of Health indicate a notable development. When the minister revoked one of the Committee's decisions, the Committee insisted on its legislative capacities and took steps to justify the ruling to a wider public. Remarkably, the minister typically objects to negative decisions and thus contributes to the politicisation of rationing decisions, which delegation to the Committee was probably supposed to prevent.

Looking into the future, it will be particularly interesting to see how the relationship between the newly founded institute and the committee develops. Already, corporatist structures are being increasingly replaced by expert assessment where more obvious rationing decisions become necessary. While corporatist decision-making structures are a likely threat to the external legitimacy of the system, moves towards expert assessment could put internal legitimacy at risk – i.e. corporatist actors could denounce their loyalty to the system. At the same time, a broader public debate about distributive principles and priorities in health care remains a desideratum. While decisions are explicit, thus fulfilling Daniels and Sabin's publicity condition, meeting the relevance condition would require a more inclusive and transparent decision-making process. Moreover, there exists no reliable appeals procedure that could meet the revision and appeals condition.

United Kingdom

In the UK, a National Institute of Clinical Excellence (NICE) was set up in 1999 as an expert commission, with the task of evaluating new and existing technologies to be funded by the National Health Service (NHS). The NHS charter requires that any person living in Britain is entitled to medical care and that no medically necessary and useful services may be denied to patients. Given its comparatively low budget, though, the NHS has a long tradition of implicit rationing that surfaces in waiting lists, shortages of hospital beds and overloaded medical staff. Most allocation decisions are in fact taken by local primary care trusts, which leads to regional inequalities and a lack of transparency. NICE was intended to improve transparency, participation and quality control and to provide explicit guidance to local trusts. Formally, trusts are still free not to follow NICE recommendations. However, the positive case (funding drugs not recommended) is usually prevented by cash shortages, while the negative case (not funding recommended drugs) is likely to result in public protests.

Within NICE, the 'technology appraisal committees' are of particular relevance in the present context. Authorized by the Department of Health, they evaluate drugs and technologies. Working with three independent chambers, the committee charges universities or research institutes with a report before it assesses a specific treatment. Besides academic experts, practicing nurses and physicians, patient representatives and representatives of the pharmaceutical industry are members in the committee's chambers. The committee aims at consensual decisions; however, the chairman can call a simple majority vote if consensus cannot be reached. Reports and decisions are published promptly in an expert and a lay version and justified extensively. In case of negative votes, patients can make use of an appeals procedure and explicitly challenge the reasons named for the decision – in this regard, NICE fulfils Daniels and Sabin's revision and appeals condition.

The fact that the committees are staffed not only with experts, but also with interest groups and patient representatives increases the impact of interests compared to medical and economic controversies. This seems to make compromises easier and accounts for NICE's high productivity. Willingness to compromise is also reflected in its decisions. So far, drugs and treatments were rarely denied funding categorically, but only for specific indications or groups of patients. However, an evaluation of NICE by the WHO criticizes that ethical and social aspects which affect decisions are, in contrast to economic and medical ones, not sufficiently articulated (Devlin et al. 2003). Others argue that under pressures from patient representatives and the pharmaceutical industry, NICE passes too many positive votes on new drugs, which leads to aggravated forms of implicit rationing elsewhere (Cookson et al. 2001).

NICE guidance is predominantly based on utilitarian cost-benefit assessment in the form of so-called "Quality Adjusted Life Years" (QALYs).[3] Although NICE does not aim to produce a ranking of services, the WHO report comes to the conclusion that it applies an implicit threshold of £ 30.000

3 A QUALY-calculus seeks to determine how much a quality adjusted life year a patient on average gains through a treatment costs.

per QALY (Devlin et al. 2003). The application of QALYs is also acknowledged and defended by its chairman, Michael Rawlins (Rawlins and Dillon 2005). On the whole, NICE deals primarily with the assessment of new pharmaceuticals and is less concerned with distributive decisions. Comparative evaluations for the justification of priority setting and 'tragic choices' do not take place.

Partly in response to criticism, NICE set up a 'Citizens' Council' in 2002 (see Davies et al. 2005; Rawlins 2005). The council is modelled on American citizen juries and meets twice a year. Its lay members are supposed to be representative of the population at large and are appointed for three years; doctors, nurses and interest group representatives are banned from taking part. NICE chairman Rawlins argues that the council provides NICE with 'social value judgments', which an expert body is not as qualified to make, and which receive due consideration in NICE guidelines (Rawlins 2005: 473). However, the Citizens' Council's reports do not deal with the appraisal of single treatments, but address more general topics such as clinical need or age (NICE 2003; NICE 2004). Moreover, it is unclear whether the citizens' recommendations have any real impact on decisions. Mike Stone of the Patients' Association has argued that the council is merely a 'tokenistic body', 'a tiger without teeth' (quoted in Gulland 2002: 406).

At first sight, NICE appears to be a classical example of blame-avoidance by means of delegation, covered up by an official rhetoric of quality control. Without ultimately giving up control (after all, the function of NICE is only advisory), political authorities thus seek to prevent the politicisation of the highly explosive rationing topic. Somewhat surprisingly, delegation of allocation decisions to NICE has failed to effectively depoliticise rationing in the UK. Given the centralized system and the low budget of the NHS, health care has always been more politicised in the UK than elsewhere. Decentralization through the introduction of primary care trusts not only led to more competition within the NHS but also helped to diffuse political accountability for rationing decisions and deny their political nature. As the recent debate about funding for the breast cancer drug Herceptin shows, however, NICE as a national expert forum is a likely target for protest whenever funding for services is denied.[4]

While the government thus escapes the immediate line of fire, rationing seems to be more politicised today than before the establishment of NICE. In addition, more genuinely distributive decisions would probably bring NICE to the limits of its democratic legitimacy. With its focus on cost-benefit analysis, decision-making apparently fails Daniels and Sabin's relevance

---

4 In the Herceptin case, NICE recommendations were not involved because the drug had not even been licensed for early stage breast cancer, so that there was no basis for NICE to assess it. Nonetheless, protests were directed at NICE.

condition. Despite recent improvements, the prevalence of implicit rationing challenges the output legitimacy of the NHS. Attempts to improve external legitimacy by means of citizen participation might play a role in the future, but so far remain at an experimental stage. Moreover, internal legitimacy and thus the loyalty of health care professionals with the system is of particular relevance within the NHS. The majority decision of an expert body will hardly suffice to guarantee the acceptance and implementation of decisions. Consequently, the question of how and by whom such decisions will be taken in the future remains open, although it is likely that respective procedures will be established within the existing institutional framework of NICE.

Sweden

In Sweden, too, the discussion about setting priorities in health care and explicit rationing has intensified in the 1990s. In accordance with Swedish tradition, a parliamentary commission was set up and charged with the development of a priority plan, i.e. to discuss the role of the health care system and clearly define a publicly funded basic health care package, and also to establish ethical principles and guidelines for setting priorities. In 1995, the commission presented a consensual report pointing out three guiding principles that together constitute an 'ethical platform', which was supposed to form the basis for priority setting in health care: the human dignity principle, the needs and solidarity principle and the cost-effectiveness principle (in order of importance).

In 1997, the ethical platform was, by a decision of the Swedish parliament, supplemented with a number of general statements concerning the application of the principles. The amendment to the Health and Medical Services Act e.g. confirms the ethical principles by law. This approach did not result in recommendations for the exclusion of specific services or categories but rather provided some guidance for decision-makers responsible for rationing decisions, i.e. abstract principles which are to be converted into concrete decisions by other governing bodies. Apparently, the parliamentary consensus was possible only at the price of factoring out controversial issues, while the far more explosive evaluation of specific treatments and services had to be relocated to a lower level.

The parliament thus ruled that the ethical platform was to be turned into a compulsory basis for concrete allocation decisions and stated that priorities are a necessary element in health care and must be discussed openly with citizens. In the decentralised Swedish health care system priority setting decisions are primarily taken at the level of County Councils. These 21 democratically elected local government bodies are providers of health care.

Therefore, priority-setting decisions in Sweden can be made on at least four different levels: at the national level, the county council level, the clinical management level and the clinical individual level. However, priorities are in practice almost always set through numerous, varying and blurry decisions, which make them difficult to grasp and to follow (Garpenby and Carlsson 2007).

Immediately after the parliament decision not much happened. Today there are some activities at several levels that may indicate a development towards greater transparency, but still explicit rationings tend to cause political disorder (Carlsson and Garpenby 2006). At the county council level two councils are at the frontline of explicit rationing: Östergötland and Västra Götaland Region. Östergötland uses ranking lists for broad disease groups in order to move towards greater transparency. With discussions involving medical representatives, officials and policy-makers preceding the decisions, the decision-making process entails some deliberative elements. These transparent decisions can definitely be a target for politicisation, as experienced in 2003 when a rationing list (limiting supply) was presented and received a lot of attention from media, general public and among central government politicians (Carlsson and Garpenby 2006; PrioriteringsCentrum 2008:2). This caused some disorder both concerning internal and external legitimacy.

In Västra Götaland Region, too, bodies representing medical specializations developed ranking lists (per medical specialty). This work was reported to county council politicians in spring 2004 and was also presented explicitly to the citizens. In the subsequent process, a special prioritization council was formed, where officials and medical representatives had the task to produce prioritization proposals and give recommendations concerning new technologies (including drugs). The prioritization council seems to be an example of successful depoliticisation, as it makes it difficult to hold politicians accountable for rationing decisions (Garpenby and Carlsson 2007; PrioriteringsCentrum 2008:2).

In other county councils cases where politicians initially denied funding for extremely expensive drugs received great media attention, resulting in councils eventually approving funding. It is important to note that these large unforeseen costs can have crucial consequences for all health services provided by a county council, especially for smaller, and therefore more vulnerable, ones. Several county councils also have citizen dialogues but still citizens are rarely involved in the work of setting priorities.

At the national level, the National Board of Health and Welfare has been commissioned with the development of guidelines to serve as a foundation for priority setting in health care. These guidelines include information on medical and health economical knowledge and rank interventions on the basis of collective decisions that consider the parliament's 1997 ethical platform (PrioriteringsCentrum 2008:2). At the beginning these guidelines were intended to serve as a dialogue with politicians at the county councils, but today they can be seen as a good example, and as a tool, for how the state affects rationing decisions made at the clinical level while avoiding their politicisation. These activities, where several professionals and experts are involved, have strengthened internal legitimacy both at the input and output side.

Another state activity is the Pharmaceutical Benefits Board (Läkemedelsförmånsnämnden, LFN), a government agency staffed with experts and with the task to decide which drugs should be subsidised by the county councils. The priorities made by LFN are based on the ethical platform and its assessment takes a broad societal view. Although LFN's explicit decisions thus seek to comply with Daniels and Sabin's conditions, a lack of transparency remains (Anell and Jansson 2005). Decisions made by the LFN have strengthened external output legitimacy, and few of them have been politicised. A recent decision to deny funding for several antihypertensive drugs has received little public attention, although it affects large numbers of citizens. There are also several promising pilot projects that were initiated and implemented by health care staff and professional associations, both locally and nationally, which can be seen as activities strengthening internal legitimacy. At this level decisions are not targets for politicisation.

Nevertheless, after the governmental decision to explicitly set priorities, discussions and activities have been more open and involved more stakeholders, thus to some extent fulfilling Daniels and Sabin's publicity criteria. In practice, however, priorities in health care are almost always set implicitly. In situations where available resources are scarce it is the health care staff that have to take the greatest responsibility to decide and carry out the rationing of health care (PrioriteringsCentrum 2008:2). This can be seen as a result of a deficiency in the regulation condition. From the national level, concrete priority setting decisions have been relocated to lower levels with the help of an ethical platform that should serve as a basis and guidance for tough priority setting decisions. At the lower levels the ethical platform is perceived as too indistinct and sometimes contradictory which results in the question how explicit priority settings should be made being pushed back to the national level.

However, a lot of effort is made to strengthen internal legitimacy, e.g. the work with guidelines at the National Board of Health and Welfare and the activities initiated by health care staff at clinical level. However, this effort concerns only one part of the organization, i.e. the medical professionals. A challenge is therefore to strengthen the internal legitimacy for the whole organization, where politicians, officials and professionals can agree how decisions should be made. This would probably also make it easier to confront the challenge of external legitimacy.

5. Conclusion

The learning process that has taken place in the rationing debate can be described as consisting of two phases (Holm 2000). The first phase was characterized by the search for an 'objectively' rational and just method of priority-setting. Allocation decisions taken on the basis of the correct principle would escape politicisation by virtue of being *ipso facto* legitimate. The second phase, which the debate in most countries has now reached abandons the search for simple solutions and acknowledges the complexity of the matter and contingency of decisions. Decisions have come to be regarded as gaining legitimacy through the use of the correct procedure rather than the choice of the correct principle (see also Goold 1996). But how are we to choose procedures where requirements of transparency and accountability run into conflict with demands for expert knowledge and efficiency?

Every public health-care system has different strategies for allocating resources. A literature review by Garpenby (Garpenby 2003b) finds at least six strategies that are applied in publicly financed systems: 'muddling through elegantly' (Hunter 1997; Mechanic 1997), 'rational decision-making' (Williams 1999), 'pluralistic bargaining' (Klein 1997), a 'community approach' (Callahan 1990), a 'model of health requirements' (Coast et al. 1996), and finally, 'explicit *and* implicit rationing' (Chinitz et al. 1998). Beyond the variety of strategies, we find a variety of forums involved in rationing decisions, with expert commissions, citizen conferences and hearings and pluralistic bargaining tables in addition to government agencies and the parliament itself. Moreover, decision-making takes place at different levels in more or less decentralized systems, thus rendering the assignment of accountability difficult if not impossible.

But not only strategies, actors and forums are numerous, multifaceted and often difficult to grasp, but so are requirements of legitimacy. As we pointed out in the first part of this chapter, input and output, external and internal legitimacy as well as politicisation and depoliticisation and 'accountability for reasonableness' of decisions are important aspects for the acceptance of priority-setting as fair. It is no coincidence that in each of the three countries we looked at, more than one body was charged with decision-making: in Germany, a pluralistic bargaining forum was complemented by an expert institute; in the UK, an expert forum was complemented by a citizen council; and in Sweden, the parliament's ruling was implemented by several interdependent bodies at national and county council levels. It seems that these different bodies address different aspects of legitimacy, such as requirements of information, participation, justification and democratic accountability.

Although we come to the conclusion that a 'correct procedure' is as illusionary as the 'correct method', the assessment and evaluation of different decision-making procedures is far from pointless. Daniels and Sabin's model of 'accountability for reasonableness' provides a valuable framework in this respect and can be applied both to single forums and to the decision-making process as a whole. While it seems unrealistic that a single democratically legitimated body can possibly fulfil all the requirements for decisions to be perceived as reasonable, fair, efficient and expedient, the ways in which authority and accountability are divided among them – as well as the reasons for this division – must clearly be rendered more transparent. Moreover, 'mediating institutions' could play an important role in improving internal legitimacy in public health care systems. These can be already existing bodies within the system such as NICE or the LFN that have opportunities to establish and develop procedures which can have great importance for the perception of fairness. Mediating institutions can have the capacity to handle different kinds of information, such as medical knowledge, ethical standpoints and citizens opinion, which should be used in the decision-making process and in the dialogue between different parts of the system and stakeholders.

As the acknowledgment of the necessity of cost containment by means of cut-backs in services is still fresh, the competences, design and composition of respective bodies remain contested in most countries. Regarding the distribution of health care, Western democracies are thus approaching a kind of 'constitutional moment', at which societies need to decide what distributive results they want to achieve by which type of procedure. While procedures themselves necessarily seem to require some degree of delegation and segmentation of authority, it is important that they are selected deliberately, democratically and transparently.

References

Aaron, H./Schwartz, W.B. (1990): 'Rationing Health-Care – The Choice Before Us', in: *Science* 247/4941, pp. 418-22.

Abelson, J. (2001): 'Understanding the Role of Contextual Influences on Local Health-Care Decision Making: Case Study Results from Ontario, Canada', in: *Social Science & Medicine* 53/6, pp. 777-93.

Abelson, J./Eyles, J. (2002): 'Public Participation and Citizen Governance in the Canadian Health System', Discussion Paper 7, Commission on the Future of Health Care in Canada.

Anell, A./Jansson, S. (2005): *Subventionering av läkemedel – förutsättningar för öppna och legitima beslutsprocesser i Läkemedelsförmånsnämnden,* PrioriteringsCentrum Rapport 2005:1, Linköping: PrioriteringsCentrum, National Centre for Priority Setting in Health Care.

Bowling, A. (1996): 'Health Care Rationing: The Public's Debate', in: *British Medical Journal* 312, pp. 670-74.

Calabresi, G./Bobbit, P. (1978): *Tragic Choices*, New York: Norton.

Callahan, D. (1990): *What Kind of Life. The Limits of Medical Progress*, New York: Simon and Schuster.

Carlsson, P./Garpenby, P. (2006): 'Democracy', in: Marinker, M. (ed.) *Constructive Conversations about Health – Policy and Values*, Oxford: Radcliffe Publishing, pp. 63-74.

Chinitz, D./Shalev, C./Galai, N./Israeli, A. (1998): 'Israel's Basic Basket of Health Services: The Importance of Being Explicitly Implicit', in: *British Medical Journal* 317, pp. 1005-07.

Coast, J./Donovan, J./Frankel, S. (eds) (1996): *Priority Setting. The Health Care Debate*, Chichester: John Wiley & Sons.

Cookson, R./McDaid, D./Maynard, A. (2001) 'Wrong SIGN, NICE Mess: Is National Guidance Distorting Allocation of Resources?', in: *British Medical Journal* 323, pp. 743-45.

Daniels, N./Sabin, J.E. (1997): 'Limits to Health Care: Fair Procedures, Democratic Deliberation, and the Legitimacy Problem for Insures', in: *Philosophy and Public Affairs* 26/4, pp. 303-50.

Daniels, N./Sabin, J.E. (2002): *Setting Limits Fairly. Can We Learn to Share Medical Resources?*, Oxford: Oxford University Press.

Davies, C./Wetherell, M./Barnett, E./Seymour-Smith, S. (2005): *Opening the Box: Evaluating the Citizens' Council of NICE*, Milton Keynes: Open University.

Delli Carpini, M.X.,/Cook, F.L./Jacobs, L.R. (2004): 'Public Deliberation, Discursive Participation, and Citizen Engagement: A Review of the Empirical Literature.', in: *Annual Review of Political Science* 7, pp. 315-44.

Devlin, N./Parkin D./Gold, M. (2003): 'WHO evaluates NICE', in: *British Medical Journal* 327, pp. 1061-62.

Döhler, M./Manow-Borgwaldt, P. (1992): 'Gesundheitspolitische Steuerung zwischen Hierarchie und Verwaltung', in: *Politische Vierteljahresschrift* 4, pp. 571-96.

Dolan, P./Shaw, R./Tsuchiya, A./Williams, A. (2005): 'QALY Maximisation and People's Preferences: A Methodological Review of the Literature', in: *Health Economics* 14/2, pp. 197-208.

Elster, J. (1995): 'Introduction: The Idea of Local Justice', in: Elster, J. (ed.) *Local Justice in America*, New York: Russell Sage Foundation, pp. 1-24.

Fleck, L.M. (1992): 'Just Health-Care Rationing – A Democratic Decision-Making Approach', in: *University of Pennsylvania Law Review* 140/5, pp. 1597-1636.

Fondacaro, M./Frogner, B./Moss, R. (2005): 'Justice in Health Care Decision-Making: Patients' Appraisals of Health Care Providers and Health Plan Representatives', in: *Social Justice Research* 18/1, pp. 63-81.

Garpenby, P. (2003a): *Prioriteringsprocessen – Del I: övergripande strategier*, Rapport 2003:3, Linköping: PrioriteringsCentrum, National Centre for Priority Setting in Health Care.

Garpenby, P. (2003b): *Prioriteringsprocessen – Del I: övergripande strategier*. Rapport 2003:3, Linköping: PrioriteringsCentrum, National Centre for Priority Setting in Health Care.

Garpenby, P. (2004): *Prioriteringsprocessen – Del II: det interna förtroendet*, Rapport 2004:6, Linköping: PrioriteringsCentrum, National Centre for Priority Setting in Health Care.
Garpenby, P./Carlsson, P. (2007): 'Organisationsförändringar och prioritering i svensk sjukvård' in: Blomqvist, P. (ed.) *Vem styr vården? – Organisation och politisk styrning inom svensk hälso- och sjukvård*, Stockholm: SNS Förlag, pp. 63-84.
Gibson, J. L./Martin, D.K./Singer, P.A. (2005): 'Priority Setting in Hospitals: Fairness, Inclusiveness, and the Problem of Institutional Power Differences', in: *Social Science & Medicine* 61/11, pp. 2355-62.
Goold, S.D. (1996): 'Allocating Health Care Resources: Cost-Utility Analysis, Informed Democratic Decision Making, or the Veil of Ignorance?', in: *Journal Of Health Politics Policy And Law* 21/1, pp. 69-98.
Greven, M.T. (1999): *Die politische Gesellschaft. Kontingenz und Dezision als Probleme des Regierens in der Demokratie*, Opladen: Leske + Budrich.
Grimes, M. (2005): *Democracy's Infrastructure: The Role of Procedural Fairness in Fostering Consent*, Göteborg: Dept. of Political Science Univ.
Gulland, A. (2002): 'NICE Proposals for Citizen Councils Condemned by Patients', in: *British Medical Journal* 325, p. 406.
Holm, S. (2000): 'Developments in the Nordic Countries – Goodbye to the Simple Solutions', in: Coulter, A./Ham, C. (eds) *The Global Challenge of Health Care Rationing*, Buckingham, Philadelphia: Open University Press, pp. 29-37.
Hunter, D.J. (1997): *Desperately Seeking Solutions. Rationing Health Care*, London: Longman.
Klein, R. (1997): 'Dimension of Rationing: Who Should Do What?', in: *British Medical Journal* 307, pp. 30-31.
Kostova, T./Zaheer, S. (1999): 'Organizational Legitimacy under Conditions of Complexity: The Case of the Multinational Enterprise', in: *The Academy of Management Review* 24/1, pp. 64-81.
Lind, A./Kulik, C.T./Ambrose, M./de Vera Park, M. (1993): 'Individual and Corporate Dispute Resolution: Using Procedural Fairness as a Decision Heuristic', in: *Administrative Science Quarterly* 38/2, pp. 224-51.
Lomas, J. (1997): 'Reluctant Rationers: Public Input to Health Care Priorities', in: *Journal of Health Service Research and Policy* 2/1, pp. 103-11.
McIver, S. (1998): *Healthy Debate? – An Independent Evaluation of Citizens' Juries in Health Settings*, London: Kings Fund Publishing.
Mechanic, D. (1997): 'Muddling through Elegantly: Finding the Proper Balance in Rationing', in: *Health Affairs* 16, pp. 86-92.
NICE (2003): *Report of the Citizens' Council on Age*, London: NICE.
NICE (2004): *Report of the Citizens' Council: Determining Clinical Need*, London: NICE.
PrioriteringsCentrum (2008): *Resolving Health Care's Difficult Choices – Survey of Priority Setting in Sweden and an Analysis of Principles and Guidelines on Priorities in Health Care*, Report 2008:2, Linköping: PrioriteringsCentrum, National Centre for Priority Setting in Health Care.
Rawlins, M.D. (2005): 'Pharmacopolitics and Deliberative Democracy', in: *Clinical Medicine* 5/5, pp. 471-75.

Rawlins, M./Dillon, A. (2005): 'NICE discrimination', in: *Journal of Medical Ethics* 31, pp. 683-84.

Scharpf, F.W. (1970): *Demokratietheorie zwischen Utopie und Anpassung*, Konstanz: Universitätsverlag.

Scharpf, F. W. (1997): *Games Real Actors Play. Actor-Centered Institutionalism in Policy Research*, Boulder, Colorado: Westview Press.

Singer, P./Martin, D.K./Giacomini, M./Purdy, L. (2006): 'Priority Setting for New Technologies in Medicine: Qualitative Case Study', in: *British Medical Journal* 321, pp. 1316-18.

Steffen, M./Lamping, W./Lehto, J. (2005): 'Introduction: The Europeanization of Health Policies', in: Steffen, M. (ed.) *Health Governance in Europe. Issues, Challenges, and Theories*, London, New York: Routledge, pp. 1-17.

Tyler, T.R. (1994): 'Governing amid Diversity: The Effect of Fair Decisionmaking Procedures on the Legitimacy of Government', in: *Law & Society Review* 28/4, pp. 809-31.

Urban, H.J. (2001): 'Wettbewerbskorporatistische Regulierung im Politikfeld Gesundheit. Der Bundesausschuss der Ärzte und Krankenkassen und die gesundheitspolitische Wende', publication series of the working group Public Health, Berlin: Wissenschaftszentrum Berlin für Sozialforschung.

Williams, A. (1999): 'Economics, Ethics and the Public in the Health Care Policy', in: *International Social Science Journal* 51, pp. 297-312.

On the Contributors to this volume

Timm Beichelt is Professor of Political Science at the Europe-University Viadrina in Frankfurt/Oder. Major recent publications include *Demokratische Konsolidierung im postsozialistischen Europa. Die Rolle der politischen Institutionen* (Leske + Budrich: 2001), *Die Europäische Union nach der Osterweiterung* (VS Verlag für Sozialwissenschaften: 2004), and *Deutschland und Europa. Die Europäisierung des politischen Systems* (VS Verlag für Sozialwissenschaften: 2008).

Joachim Blatter is Professor of Political Science at the University of Luzern. His most recent books are *Qualitative Politikanalyse. Eine Einführung in Methoden und Forschungsansätze* (with F. Janning and C. Wagemann, VS Verlag für Sozialwissenschaften: 2006) and *Governance – theoretische Formen und historische Transformationen. Politische Steuerungs- und Integrationsformen in Metropolregionen der USA* (Nomos: 2007).

Ingolfur Blühdorn is Associate Professor in Politics and Political Sociology at the University of Bath. His most recent book publications are *Post-Ecologist Politics. Social Theory and the Abdication of the Ecologist Paradigm* (Routledge: 2000), *Economic Efficiency – Democratic Empowerment. Contested Modernisation in Britain and Germany* (ed. with U. Jun, Rowman & Littlefield: 2007), and *The Politics of Unsustainability. Eco-Politics in the Post-Environmental Era* (ed. with I. Welsh, Routledge: 2008).

Peter Bursens is Associate Professor in Politics at the University of Antwerpen. He is author and editor of several books including *Jaarboek SBOV 2004: Vlaanderen in/en Europa: omgaan met de Unie en vergelijkend leren* (with G. Bouckaert, R. Janvier and F. de Rynck, Die Keure: 2005), *Zoon*

Politikon: tussen effectiviteit en legitimiteit (with P. Thijssen, Vandenbroele: 2006), and *Europa is geen buitenland: over de relatie tussen het federale België en de Europese Unie* (with J. Beyers, Acco: 2006).

Oliver Fritsch is Research Fellow at the University of Aarhus. His publications include 'Transformations in Environmental Governance and Participation' (with M.S. Andersen, D. Fisher, Dana) in: A. Mol, D. Sonnenfeld and G. Spaargaren (eds) *The Ecological Modernization Reader* (Routledge 2009), *Environmental Governance, Multi-Level – And Effective?,* (with J. Newig), *(Environmental Policy and Governance* 19/3, 2009), and 'Under Which Conditions Does Public Participation Really Advance Sustainability Goals? Findings of a Meta-Analysis of Stakeholder Involvement in Environmental Decision-making' (with J. Newig), in: E. Brousseau, T. Dedeurwaerdere and B. Siebenhüner, Bernd (eds.) *Reflexive Governance for Global Public Goods*, Cambridge, MA: MIT Press (forthcoming).

Karen Heard-Laureote is Senior Lecturer in European Politics at the University of Portsmouth. She is author of, for example, 'Transnational Networks: Informal Governance in the European Political Space' (in: W. Kaiser and P. Starie (eds), *Transnational European Union: Towards a Common Political Space?* Routledge: 2005), 'The Commission's Advisory Groups and Committees in the Field of Agricultural Policy' (*Journal of European Integration* 30/4, 2008, pp. 579-97), and *European Union Governance. Efficiency and Legitimacy in European Commission Advisory Committees* (Routledge: 2009).

Uwe Jun is Professor of Political Science at the University of Trier. His most recent book publications include *Der Wandel von Parteien in der Mediendemokratie* (Campus: 2004), *Kleine Parteien im Aufwind* (ed. with H. Kreikenbom and V. Neu, Campus: 2006), *Economic Efficiency – Democratic Empowerment. Contested Modernisation in Britain and Germany* (ed. with I. Blühdorn, Rowman & Littlefield: 2007), and *Zukunft der Mitgliederpartei* (ed. with O. Niedermayer and E. Wiesendahl, Budrich: 2009).

Alexandra Kelso is Lecturer in Politics at the University of Southampton. Her publications include, inter alia, 'The House of Commons Modernisation Committee: Who needs it?' (*British Journal of Politics and International Relations* 9/1, 2007, pp. 138-57), 'Parliament and Political Disengagement: Neither Waving nor Drowning' (*Political Quarterly* 78/3, 2007, pp. 364-73) and *Parliamentary Reform at Westminster* (Manchester University Press: 2009).

Soile Kuitunen is Director of Net Effect Ltd., Finland. Her academic publications include *Kansalaisesta aktiiviksi, aktiivista edustajaksi: Tutkimus vuoden 1995 eduskuntavaaleista ja niiden ehdokasasetteluista* (A study of the 1995 parliamentary elections and candidate selection, edited with V. Helander and L. Paltemaa, UNIPAPS: 1997), and *What is the role of the EU Structural Funds in promoting RTDI? Review of some empirical findings* (Research Evaluation, 2002).

Kaisa Lähteenmäki-Smith is Senior Researcher at Net Effect Ltd., Finland. Her publications include *Globalization and regionalization as concurrent phenomena in the European governance structure* (Turun Yliplisto: 1999), and *Restructuring the state-regional impacts: a comparative Nordic perspective* (with L.O. Persson, Nordregio Report 2002).

Claudia Landwehr is Schumpeter Fellow at the Goethe University in Frankfurt/Main. Recent publications include 'Verhandlung und Deliberation in der Rationierung von Gesundheitsgütern', in W. Thaa (ed.), *Inklusion durch Repräsentation* (Nomos: 2007, pp. 167-83), 'Woher wissen wir, was wir wollen? Präferenzbildung als Prozess rationaler Entscheidung', in J. Behnke, T. Bräuninger and S. Shikano (eds), *Jahrbuch Handlungs- und Entscheidungstheorie* (VS Verlag für Sozialwissenschaften: 2008, pp. 223-43) and *Political Conflict and Political Preferences. Communicative Interaction between Facts, Norms and Interests* (ECPR Press: 2009).

Pierre Lefébure is Associated Researcher at Sciences Po in Bordeaux. His major publications include *Quelle étrange lucarne? Autour de l'analyse des fonctions socio-politiques de la télévision* (Revue française de science politique, 2004), *Vilvorde: protestation et espace public européen* (Revue de la gendarmerie nationale, 2005) and *Dictionnaire des Questions Politiques. 60 enjeux de la France contemporaine* (with N. Haudegand, Editions de l'Atelier: 2007).

Martino Maggetti is Lecturer in Politics at the University of Lausanne. He is author of *Les négociations sur la fiscalité de l'épargne entre Suisse et Union Européenne: prélude d'une européanisation impossible ou la "convergence parallèle"* (Faculté des SSP: 2003), *Etudier l'indépendance informelle des autorités de régulation formellement indépendantes* (Faculté des SSP: 2005) and *Assessing the De Facto Independence of Regulatory Agencies. The Case of the Swiss Federal Banking Commission in the Years 1990* (Université de Lausanne: 2006).

Ann-Charlotte Nedlund is a Doctoral candidate in Political Science at the University of Linköping. The subject of her thesis is *Fair institutions within the Health Care System*.

Jens Newig is Assistant Professor in Environmental Systems Research at the University of Osnabrück and currently holds a temporary Associate Professorship on Participation and Sustainable Development at Leuphana University, Lüneburg (Germany). Recent publications include 'Symbolic Environmental Legislation and Societal Self-Deception' (*Environmental Politics* 16/2, 2007), *Governance for Sustainable Development: Steering in Contexts of Ambivalence, Uncertainty and Distributed Contel* (ed. with J.P. Voß and J. Monstadt, Routledge, 2008), and 'Environmental Governance: Participatory, Multi-Level – And Effective?' (with O. Fritsch), (*Environmental Policy and Governanace* 19/3, 2009).

In S[illegible]